Information and Influence Propagation in Social Networks

Synthesis Lectures on Data Management

Editor
M. Tamer Özsu, *University of Waterloo*

Synthesis Lectures on Data Management is edited by Tamer Özsu of the University of Waterloo. The series will publish 50- to 125 page publications on topics pertaining to data management. The scope will largely follow the purview of premier information and computer science conferences, such as ACM SIGMOD, VLDB, ICDE, PODS, ICDT, and ACM KDD. Potential topics include, but not are limited to: query languages, database system architectures, transaction management, data warehousing, XML and databases, data stream systems, wide scale data distribution, multimedia data management, data mining, and related subjects.

Query Processing over Uncertain Databases
Lei Chen and Xiang Lian
2012

Foundations of Data Quality Management
Wenfei Fan and Floris Geerts
2012

Incomplete Data and Data Dependencies in Relational Databases
Sergio Greco, Cristian Molinaro, and Francesca Spezzano
2012

Business Processes: A Database Perspective
Daniel Deutch and Tova Milo
2012

Data Protection from Insider Threats
Elisa Bertino
2012

Deep Web Query Interface Understanding and Integration
Eduard C. Dragut, Weiyi Meng, and Clement T. Yu
2012

P2P Techniques for Decentralized Applications
Esther Pacitti, Reza Akbarinia, and Manal El-Dick
2012

Query Answer Authentication
HweeHwa Pang and Kian-Lee Tan
2012

Declarative Networking
Boon Thau Loo and Wenchao Zhou
2012

Full-Text (Substring) Indexes in External Memory
Marina Barsky, Ulrike Stege, and Alex Thomo
2011

Spatial Data Management
Nikos Mamoulis
2011

Database Repairing and Consistent Query Answering
Leopoldo Bertossi
2011

Information and Influence Propagation in Social Networks

Wei Chen, Laks V.S. Lakshmanan, and Carlos Castillo

ISBN: 978-3-031-00722-4   paperback
ISBN: 978-3-031-01850-3   ebook

DOI 10.1007/978-3-031-01850-3

A Publication in the Springers series
SYNTHESIS LECTURES ON DATA MANAGEMENT

Lecture #37
Series Editor: M. Tamer Özsu, *University of Waterloo*
Series ISSN
Synthesis Lectures on Data Management
Print 2153-5418   Electronic 2153-5426

Information and Influence Propagation in Social Networks

Wei Chen
Microsoft Research Asia

Laks V.S. Lakshmanan
University of British Columbia

Carlos Castillo
Qatar Computing Research Institute

SYNTHESIS LECTURES ON DATA MANAGEMENT #37

ABSTRACT

Research on social networks has exploded over the last decade. To a large extent, this has been fueled by the spectacular growth of social media and online social networking sites, which continue growing at a very fast pace, as well as by the increasing availability of very large social network datasets for purposes of research. A rich body of this research has been devoted to the analysis of the propagation of information, influence, innovations, infections, practices and customs through networks. Can we build models to explain the way these propagations occur? How can we validate our models against any available real datasets consisting of a social network and propagation traces that occurred in the past? These are just some questions studied by researchers in this area. Information propagation models find applications in viral marketing, outbreak detection, finding key blog posts to read in order to catch important stories, finding leaders or trendsetters, information feed ranking, etc. A number of algorithmic problems arising in these applications have been abstracted and studied extensively by researchers under the garb of *influence maximization*.

This book starts with a detailed description of well-established diffusion models, including the independent cascade model and the linear threshold model, that have been successful at explaining propagation phenomena. We describe their properties as well as numerous extensions to them, introducing aspects such as competition, budget, and time-criticality, among many others. We delve deep into the key problem of influence maximization, which selects key individuals to activate in order to influence a large fraction of a network. Influence maximization in classic diffusion models including both the independent cascade and the linear threshold models is computationally intractable, more precisely #P-hard, and we describe several approximation algorithms and scalable heuristics that have been proposed in the literature. Finally, we also deal with key issues that need to be tackled in order to turn this research into practice, such as learning the strength with which individuals in a network influence each other, as well as the practical aspects of this research including the availability of datasets and software tools for facilitating research. We conclude with a discussion of various research problems that remain open, both from a technical perspective and from the viewpoint of transferring the results of research into industry strength applications.

KEYWORDS

social networks, social influence, information and influence diffusion, stochastic diffusion models, influence maximization, learning of propagation models, viral marketing, competitive influence diffusion, game theory, computational complexity, approximation algorithms, heuristic algorithms, scalability.

To our families

Jian, Joice Yitao, and Ellie Yiqing

Sarada, Sundaram, Sharada, and Kaavya

Fabiola and Felipe

Contents

Acknowledgments

The material presented here has been deeply influenced by the research we conducted with many wonderful colleagues, students, and post-doctoral fellows as well as the numerous stimulating discussions we have had with them. We would like to express our gratitude to our collaborators, including: Smriti Bhagat, Francesco Bonchi, Alex Collins, Rachel Cummings, Aristides Gionis, Amit Goyal, Xinran He, Dino Ienco, Qingye Jiang, Te Ke, Yanhua Li, Zhenming Liu, Wei Lu, Michael Mathioudakis, David Rincón, Guojie Song, Xiaorui Sun, Antti Ukkonen, Suresh Venkatasubramanian, Chi Wang, Yajun Wang, Wei Wei, Siyu Yang, Yifei Yuan, Li Zhang, and Zhi-Li Zhang. We are grateful to Lewis Tseng, Yajun Wang, and Cheng Yang for helpful discussions on some technical sections of the book, and to Tian Lin for running a few additional evaluation tests on top of what previously published papers had and for generating relevant plots. Thanks are due to Qiang Li, Tian Lin, Wei Lu, Lewis Tseng, Yajun Wang, and Cheng Yang for their careful reading of and excellent comments on the manuscript which greatly improved our presentation. We appreciate Diane Cerra and Tamer Ozsu for their assistance throughout the preparation of this manuscript and for their patience. Tamer's editorial comments were especially helpful in improving the readability. Last but not the least, we are indebted to our families whose patience and support throughout this project has been invaluable.

Wei Chen, Laks V.S. Lakshmanan, and Carlos Castillo
August 2013

CHAPTER 1

Introduction

In this chapter we motivate the study of influence and information propagation by providing numerous examples. In addition, we provide some basic definitions.

1.1 SOCIAL NETWORKS AND SOCIAL INFLUENCE

Social networks have been studied extensively by social scientists for decades (e.g., see [Barnes, 1954, Radcliffe-Brown, 1940, Wasserman and Faust, 1994]). Earlier studies have had to confine themselves to extremely small datasets. Enabled by the Internet and sparked by the recent advent of online social networking sites such as Facebook, LinkedIn, and Tumblr, research on social networks is witnessing an unprecedented growth due to the ready availability of large scale social network data. This has at once led to the development of many exciting applications of online social networks and to the formulation and the subsequent study of many research questions. A rich body of such studies has come to be classified as *the analysis of influence and information propagation in social networks*.

It is our aim in this book to outline some of the key concepts, developments, and achievements in this area, as well as studying the driving applications that underlie this research and highlight important challenges that remain open. For convenience and consistency of terminology, we will use the term *social influence analysis* or just *influence analysis* to indicate the analysis of the diffusion of information or influence through a social network.

1.1.1 EXAMPLES OF SOCIAL NETWORKS

By a social network,[1] we mean a possibly directed graph. A social network may be homogeneous, where all nodes are of the same type, or heterogeneous, in which case the nodes fall into more than one type.

Examples of homogeneous networks include the underlying graphs representing friendships in basically all of the social networking platforms (e.g., the list of "friends" in Facebook), as well as the graphs representing co-authorship or co-worker relationships in collaboration networks.

Examples of heterogeneous networks include rating networks consisting of people and objects such as songs, movies, books, etc. Such networks can be found in media appraisal and consumption platforms such as Last.fm and Flixster. Here, people may be connected to one another

---

[1]Not be confused with an *online social networking site*, which is a mobile or web-based software platform that allows users to interact with their social connections.

via friendship or acquaintance, whereas objects (songs, movies, etc.) may be linked with one another by means of similarity of their metadata. For example, two songs may be linked since both are in the same genre or by the same artist. Similarly, two movies may be directed by the same director. In addition, links may be present between people and objects owing to their rating relationship: e.g., user Sam rating a specific model of Nikon SLR Camera produces a link between the corresponding nodes. Another example of a heterogeneous network is a scientific collaboration network between authors, augmented with articles (that are the result of collaboration), and the venues they are published in. This network consists of three types of nodes—authors, articles, and venues—and links between nodes of the same type as well as between nodes of different types.

In the bulk of this book, our focus will be on information propagation in homogeneous networks. We briefly return to heterogeneous networks in Chapter 7.

1.1.2 EXAMPLES OF INFORMATION PROPAGATION

We begin with some concrete examples of propagations or *information cascades* in current online social networking sites. Consider Facebook, where a user Sally updates her status or writes on a friend's wall about a new show in town that she enjoyed. Information about this action is typically communicated to her friends. When some of Sally's friends comment on her update, that information is passed on to their friends and so on. In this way, information about the action taken by Sally has the potential to propagate transitively through the network. Sam posts ("tweets") in Twitter about a nifty camera he bought which he is happy about. Some of his followers on Twitter reply to his tweet while others retweet it. In a similar fashion, viewing of movies by users tends to propagate on Flixster and MovieLens, information about users joining groups or communities tends to spread through Flickr, adoption of songs and artists by listeners spreads through last.fm, and interest in research topics propagates through scientific collaboration networks.

Is there a pattern to these propagation phenomena? What can we learn from analyzing them and how can we benefit from the results of such analysis? In this chapter, we will address these questions.

1.2 SOCIAL INFLUENCE EXAMPLES

We begin with a brief overview of several real-life stories that motivate the study of information propagation in social networks.

In a famous study published in the *New England Journal of Medicine*, Christakis and Fowler [2007] analyzed the medical records of about 12,000 patients. They extracted a real *offline* (as opposed to online) social network from these records, based on the relationships between the patients, including friendship, sibling, spouse, immediate neighbor, etc. Their goal was to study the relationship between non-infectious health conditions, including obesity, and one's social neighbors and understand the correlation between having obese social network neighbors and being obese oneself. Among other things, they found that having an obese friend makes an individual 171% more likely to be obese compared to a randomly chosen person. In cases of obese spouse and obese sibling, the corresponding numbers were 37% and 40%, respectively. It is to be noted that their study did not focus on causation but instead on correlation. Still, their study shows having obese social contacts is a good predictor of obesity.

The same authors, in an influential book [Christakis and Fowler, 2011] "present compelling evidence for our profound influence on one another's tastes, health, wealth, happiness, beliefs, even weight, as they explain how social networks form and how they operate." As specific examples, they argue that back pain spread from West Germany to East Germany once the Berlin wall came down, that suicide spreads through communities, that specific sexual practices spread through friendship networks among teenagers, and political beliefs and convictions propagate through networks, the conviction being more intense the denser one's connections.

In the business area, a famous case demonstrating information propagation leading to commercial success, is the Hotmail phenomenon [Hugo and Garnsey, 2002]. In the early 1990s, Hotmail was a relatively unknown e-mail service provider. They had a simple idea, which was appending to the end of each mail message sent by their users the text "Join the world's largest e-mail service with MSN Hotmail. http://www.hotmail.com." This had the effect of building and boosting a brand. In a mere 18 months, Hotmail became the number one e-mail provider, with 8 million users [Hugo and Garnsey, 2002]. The underlying phenomenon was that a fraction of the recipients of Hotmail messages were inspired by the appended message to try it for themselves. When they sent mail to others, a fraction of them felt a similar temptation. This phenomenon propagated transitively and soon, adoption of Hotmail became viral.

Viral phenomena of the sort discussed above have sometimes changed lives, as in the rags-to-riches story of Ted Williams [Zafar, 2012]. He was a homeless person in Columbus, Ohio, USA, and had had many a brush with the law. He was found at a street corner in January 2011 when he was interviewed by a journalist. The interview was posted on YouTube, including details that Williams was a former voice-over artist. Within months, the video attracted 11 million views, and triggered numerous messages of support including job offers, changing his life for ever.

On November 16, 2011, a song from the soundtrack of a then upcoming Indian (Tamil) movie, called "*Why this kolaveri di?*" was released. By November 21, it was a top trend in Twitter. Within a week of its release, it had attracted 1.3 million views on YouTube and more than a million "shares" on Facebook, reaching and propagating through many non-Tamil speakers. It eventually went on to win the Gold Award from YouTube for most views (e.g., 58 million as of June 2012) and was featured in mainstream media such as Time, BBC, and CNN.

"*Gangnam Style,*" a South Korean song released in July 2012, became the first video to reach 1 billion views on YouTube as of December 21, 2012. Within one year of its first release, it has been viewed more than 1.745 billion times, even surpassing Justin Bieber's "Baby!"

The power of online information diffusion has also been utilized by citizens responding to natural or man-made disasters. When there was a coordinated terror attack in Mumbai in November 2008, as the events were unfolding, tweets were being sent via SMS at the rate of about 16 per second, including in them such information as eye witness accounts, pleas for blood donors, location of blood banks and hospitals, etc. A Wikipedia page was up in minutes, providing a staggering amount of detail and extremely fast "live" updates. A newswire service Metroblog was set up in short order, containing 112 Flickr photos by a journalist giving a firsthand account of the aftermath. A Google map with main buildings involved in the attacks, with links to background and news stories was immediately set up. In Vancouver, Canada, in the summer of 2011, there were riots following the Stanley Cup final. Rioters, many of them teens, looted and destroyed properties in downtown. Many of them were bragging about it in social media, e.g., posing with Gucci bags in front of burning cars. This triggered a widespread reaction of disgust and was leveraged in mobilizing a cleanup effort. The amount of data made available for forensics was staggering: contrasted with 100 h of VHS footage from 1994 riots, there now was 5000 h worth of 100 types of digital video available for forensic analysis. This along with cooperation from the public enabled the police to apprehend most of the rioters.

1.3 SOCIAL INFLUENCE ANALYSIS APPLICATIONS

The study of information and influence propagation has found applications in several fields, including viral marketing, social media analytics, the spread of rumors, stories, interest, trust, referrals, the adoption of innovations in organizations, the study of human and non-human animal epidemics, expert finding, behavioral targeting, feed ranking, "friends" recommendation, social search, etc.

Among these, *viral marketing* or *word of mouth marketing* as it is otherwise called, is a "poster" application of influence analysis. The vision behind this is to activate a small number of "influential" individuals in a social network through which a large number of other individuals can be influenced by a viral propagation. Formally, consider a social network represented as a directed graph $G = (V, E)$ with nodes V corresponding to individuals and links $E \subset V \times V$ representing social ties. Furthermore, suppose there is a function $p : E \to [0, 1]$ that associates a weight or probability $p(u, v)$ with every link (u, v), representing the influence exerted by user u on v. This informally captures the intuition that whenever u performs an action, then v also performs the action after u, with probability $p(u, v)$. The idea behind viral marketing is that by getting a small set of users in V (a *seed set*) to use a product, for instance by giving it to them for free or at a discounted price, we can reach a much larger set of users through transitive propagation of influence.

Interestingly, a family of applications in seemingly different domains and settings fall into a pattern similar to the one we describe for viral marketing. Consider the water distribution network of a large metropolitan city [Leskovec et al., 2007, Ostfeld and Salomons, 2004, Ostfeld et al., 2006]: accidental or deliberate interference can introduce viruses or other contaminants in the water being distributed. There are sensors capable of detecting any outbreak, but each sensor is expensive both in itself and in terms of its deployment and maintenance. A natural question is whether we can find a small set of crucial junctions in the water distribution network in which to place the sensors, so as to detect any outbreak as quickly as possible. Alternatively, we may wish to minimize the size of the population potentially affected by the undetected contamination.

Similar ideas can also be applied to study the adoption of innovation in organizations and the propagation of rumors and information in general through society. An important aspect of this is the propagation of information through social media, including the blogosphere and microblogging platforms. In social media, posts are linked to other posts allowing us to study the propagation of stories and to determine who is an expert or an influencer on a given topics.

A spate of startups has sprung up around the notion of social media influence and we describe a few examples here. Klout (`http://klout.com/`) claims to compute the overall influence of users online based on their behavior and their followers' behavior in Facebook, Twitter, and LinkedIn. The "klout" score is computed as a function of the true reach, amplification probability, and network influence. PeerIndex (`http://peerindex.com/`), on the other hand, identifies authorities and determines authority scores over the social web on a per topic basis. PeerIndex and Influencer50 (`http://influencer50.com/`) explicitly work with a viral marketing business model, calculating users' influence scores by analyzing the likes and retweets they receive online and recommending the influential people they found to brand name companies. Users are encouraged to try their best to be influential and in return receive rewards and offers from such companies.

1.4   THE FLIP SIDE

The key hypothesis of viral marketing, namely that a small number of influential users can be found and leveraged to reach a large audience through a social network, is wrought in practice with many challenges.

Firstly, when and how can we say that there is influence between users? There are at least two different phenomena surrounding users' behavior that are different from influence, but may appear to be as such. There is the possibility of *homophily*, often explained with the popular phrase "birds of a feather flock together." What it means is that the tastes of two users who are connected may be similar. For example, a person who smokes may be married to another smoker, which in turn may make both of them more propense to develop respiratory diseases. If we observe that one spouse develops asthma, followed by the other one, can we really claim that the health of the first influenced that of the second? The existence of a social tie does not necessarily cause a certain behavior to propagate: the observation may be explained using correlation as opposed to causation.

The problem of homophily vs. influence has been tackled by some researchers. Anagnostopoulos et al. [2008] describe a technique called shuffle test for distinguishing between influence and correlation. Aral et al. [2009] describe a statistical method for distinguishing between influence and homophily. By analyzing the day-by-day mobile service adoption behavior of over 27 million Yahoo! users in Yahoo! instant messaging network, they show that over 50% of what was previously perceived as behavioral contagion is explained by homophily.

Secondly, researchers have asked whether influence can really drive substantial viral cascades over real-world social networks. In a series of papers, Watts and Peretti [2007] and Goel et al. [2012] have challenged the conventional notions and intuitions about social influence causing large viral spread. On several datasets, they find that, empirically, most adoptions are not due to peer influence and do not propagate beyond a first step. They argue that social epidemics are not always responsible for dramatic, possibly sudden social change. While the existence of influence can be difficult to detect, they do not altogether dismiss the role played by influence. They suggest that instead of a small number of individuals driving epidemic-like viral cascades, it may be more realistic to target a relatively large critical mass of users who can then carry the viral campaign. They call this "big seed" marketing.

On the other hand, there have been other studies [Huang et al., 2012, Iyengar et al., 2011] revealing the genuine existence of social contagion and influence. Huang et al. [Huang et al., 2012] show that even after removing the effects of homophily, there is clear evidence of influence. For instance, they find that people rate items recommended by their friends higher than they otherwise would. Iyengar et al. [Iyengar et al., 2011] analyzed data from a pharmaceutical company on drug prescriptions for chronic illnesses by physicians in three major U.S. metropolitan areas. Unlike traditional products, prescription drugs for chronic illnesses involve various risks, e.g., of the patients developing resistance to the drug. In this case, they found that even after controlling for other mass media marketing efforts, and global network wide changes, there is genuine social contagion at work. Gruhl et al. [2004] analyzed the blogosphere data and showed, among other things, that there are indeed influential individuals who are highly effective at contributing to the spread of "infectious" topics in the blogosphere.

To summarize, the existence of influence and its effectiveness for applications such as viral marketing depend on the datasets. There is both evidence supporting and challenging it, found from different datasets by researchers. For a given situation, careful analysis of evidence in available datasets should first be undertaken before deciding whether to adopt a viral marketing approach.

1.5   OUTLINE OF THIS BOOK

Propagation of information and its study is the central theme of this book. The next chapter (Chapter 2) describes formally a general framework of *stochastic diffusion models* to understand and model these phenomena, introduces the most studied models of propagation in the literature (independent cascade and linear threshold), and discusses their relationship with some other models that describe similar phenomena.

Chapter 3 studies the problem of *influence maximization* to which we have alluded in the present chapter, specifically in Section 1.3: how to select a small set of seed users to reach virally a large population through a social network. The complexity analysis of this problem shows that it is #P-hard under the two main models of propagation. Starting with a greedy algorithm for influence maximization which has provable approximation guarantees, we introduce a series of improvements to obtain highly scalable influence maximization algorithms. Some new results and analyses, such as the #P-hardness of even selecting a single best seed (Corollary 3.3) and the running time analysis of the original greedy algorithm (Theorem 3.7), have not appeared before in the literature and are included in this chapter.

Chapter 4 deals with variants of the influence maximization problem. Instead of performing influence maximization on a model of the influence propagations (a model-based approach), we describe a data-based approach in which the influence of the seed set is estimated from data about past propagations containing those nodes. We also study influence maximization in a competitive setting, where two or more ideas or viruses propagate simultaneously and compete with each other, as well as other extensions of the main paradigm. We include in this chapter some new results on the submodularity of homogeneous competitive independent cascade models under various tie-breaking settings (Theorems 4.9 and 4.10) that has not appeared in the literature.

Chapter 5 studies how to learn the parameters of influence propagation models from past observations. Given a social network and a set of actions that have propagated through it, we would like to know who is influential over whom and to what extent. There are many aspects of this problem that can be studied, including the fact that influence weights can change over time.

Chapter 6 addresses a pressing practical issue of this research which is the need for appropriate datasets for experimentation. In addition to describing the types of data that have been used by research in this field, we overview a set of existing software tools that may be helpful to researchers.

The last chapter (Chapter 7) describes key challenges for researchers in this area, many of them related to transferring this research into actual technologies. We also outline a few algorithmic problems that remain open.

The content of this book is based on the tutorial titled "Information and Influence Spread in Social Networks," given by the authors at the 18th ACM SIGKDD International Conference on Knowledge Discovery and Data Mining (KDD) in August 2012, the slides being available online [Castillo et al., 2012]. The tutorial slides can serve as a companion to this book, while the book includes more comprehensive and in-depth coverage of various diffusion models, influence maximization algorithms and their analysis, and also contains some more recent developments in the area since the tutorial.

CHAPTER 2

Stochastic Diffusion Models

We model a social network as a directed graph $G = (V, E)$, where V is a finite set of vertices or nodes, and $E \subseteq V \times V$ is the set of arcs or directed edges connecting pairs of nodes.[1] A node represents an individual in the social network, while an arc from u to v represents the relationship between individuals u and v. The relationship is directed, since in this book we are primarily interested in the influence relationship, that is, whether an individual u is easy or hard to influence another individual v, and such influence relationships are often directed and non-symmetric. We also refer to $G = (V, E)$ as the *social graph*. We assume the readers' familiarity with basic graph-theoretic terminologies, such as a node u's *outgoing arc* $(u, v) \in E$ or *incoming arc* $(v, u) \in E$, or u's *out-neighbors* $N^{out}(u)$ or *in-neighbors* $N^{in}(u)$, and will provide their notations when necessary. We also list notational conventions in the appendix of this book.

The diffusion of information or influence proceeds in discrete time steps, with time $t = 0, 1, 2, \ldots$. Each node $v \in V$ has two possible states, *inactive* and *active*. Intuitively, we can view the active state of a node u as u adopts the new information, new idea, or new product being propagated through the network, while inactive state means that u has not adopted the new information, idea, or product. Let $S_t \subseteq V$ be the set of active nodes at time t, referred to as the *active set* at time t. We call S_0 the *seed set* and nodes in this set the *seeds* of influence diffusion. These seed nodes are the initial nodes selected to propagate the influence, for example, the initial users selected by a company's promotional campaign to receive free samples of the company's new product.

Definition 2.1 Stochastic diffusion model. A *stochastic diffusion model (with discrete time steps) for a social graph $G = (V, E)$* specifies the randomized process of generating active sets S_t for all $t \geq 1$ given the initial seed set S_0.

Note that set S_t is a random set with the distribution determined by the randomized process defined by the stochastic diffusion model. To help understand the behavior of a stochastic diffusion model, we often find an equivalent diffusion model that provides an alternative view of the model.

Definition 2.2 Model equivalence. We say that *two stochastic diffusion models for a social graph $G = (V, E)$ are equivalent* if for any given seed set $S_0 \subseteq V$, for any time step $t \geq 1$ and any subsets $A_1, \ldots, A_{t-1} \subseteq V$, the event $\{S_1 = A_1, \ldots, S_{t-1} = A_{t-1}\}$ has either zero probability in both

---

[1]Occasionally we may also refer to undirected graphs. As a convention, in this book we use *arcs* or *directed edges* for directed graphs and *edges* for undirected graphs.

models, or non-zero probability in both models, and in the latter case, the conditional distributions of active set S_t under seed set S_0 conditioned on the event $\{S_1 = A_1, \ldots, S_{t-1} = A_{t-1}\}$ are the same for the two models. By the above definition, when two models are equivalent, the joint probability distributions of all active sets $S_1, S_2, \ldots$ under any given seed set S_0 for the two models must be the same.

For a class of diffusion models, once a node becomes active (or is activated), it stays active, that is, for all $t \geq 1$, $S_{t-1} \subseteq S_t$, and we call these models *progressive* models. In contrast, models in which nodes may switch back and forth between active and inactive states are called *non-progressive* models. Progressive models are typically used to model the diffusion of the adoptions of new technologies, new products, etc., such as the adoption of a new smart phone, or watching a new movie, since these adoptions are typically associated with a purchase behavior and are not easily reversible. Non-progressive models, on the other hand, usually model the diffusion of ideas and opinions, such as the attitude towards a news event or the support of different political proposals, which may switch back and forth based on new information gathered from the network.

In Section 2.1, we introduce two progressive diffusion models, which are the main focus of this book, while in Section 2.2 we briefly introduce several other models used in the study of information and influence diffusion, including some non-progressive ones. Throughout this book, we use the terms diffusion and propagation interchangeably.

2.1   MAIN PROGRESSIVE MODELS

In progressive diffusion models, since active sets are monotonically non-decreasing and the full set V is finite, within a finite number of steps the active set no longer changes. We call the eventually stable active set *final active set* and denote it as $\Phi(S_0)$, where S_0 is the initial seed set. Set $\Phi(S_0)$ is a random set determined by the stochastic process of the diffusion model. One major problem studied in the literature as well as in this book is to maximize the *expected* size of the final active set, given some constraints on the initial set (e.g., a maximum initial size). Let $\mathbb{E}(X)$ denote the expected value of a random variable X. For the above purpose, we define $\sigma(S_0) = \mathbb{E}(|\Phi(S_0)|)$ and call it the *influence spread* of seed set S_0, where the expectation is taken among all random events leading to the final active set $\Phi(S_0)$.

In this section, we introduce two classic progressive models, namely the independent cascade model and the linear threshold model, both of which were originally studied in mathematical sociology. We discuss their properties, including the important submodularity property, and then provide generalizations of the models.

2.1.1   INDEPENDENT CASCADE MODEL

Independent cascade (or IC) model is first described in the current form by Kempe et al. [2003], based on models in interacting particle systems [Durrett, 1988, Liggett, 1985] and marketing research [Goldenberg et al., 2001a,b]. The IC model is also related to epidemic models [Anderson and May, 2002] (see Section 2.2.1). The key feature of the model is that diffusion events along every arc in the social graph are mutually independent.

In the independent cascade model, every arc $(u, v) \in E$ has an associated *influence probability* $p(u, v) \in [0, 1]$ (also denoted as p_{uv}), corresponding to the extent to which node u influences node v. In the follow definition (and some later definitions), we will refer to a set S_{t-2} for $t \geq 1$, and thus as a convention we set $S_{-1} = \emptyset$. Also, for all $(u, v) \notin E$, we assume $p(u, v) = 0$. The technical definition of the model is given below.

Definition 2.3   Independent cascade model.   The *independent cascade (IC) model* takes the social graph $G = (V, E)$, the influence probability $p(\cdot)$ on all arcs, and the initial seed set S_0 as the input, and generates the active sets S_t for all $t \geq 1$ by the following randomized operation rule. At every time step $t \geq 1$, first set S_t to be S_{t-1}; next for every inactive node $v \notin S_{t-1}$, for every node $u \in N^{in}(v) \cap (S_{t-1} \setminus S_{t-2})$, u executes an *activation attempt* by performing a Bernoulli trial (flipping an independent coin) with success probability $p(u, v)$; if successful we add v into S_t and say u *activates* v *at time* t. If multiple nodes activate v at time t, the end effect is the same — v is added to S_t.

Informally, after a node u is newly activated at time $t - 1$, in the immediate next step t, u has a single chance of activating each of its inactive out-neighbors v with probability $p(u, v)$, and this activation is independent of any other activations. If u does not activate v at time t, it will not try to activate v in later steps. Once a node is activated, it stays active. If at some time t, no new nodes are activated, that is $S_t = S_{t-1}$, then the set of active nodes will no longer change, and the diffusion ends with the final active set S_t. We will see shortly that if we are only interested in the final active set, certain aspects of the model including single chance of activation and immediate activation are not essential.

Example 2.4   Figure 2.1 shows an example of a diffusion process. Initially at $t = 0$, two seed nodes v_1 and v_2 are activated (Figure 2.1(a)). At step $t = 1$, v_1 successfully activates v_5 but fails to activate v_3, while v_2 successfully activates v_3 and v_4 but fails to activate v_6 (Figure 2.1(b)). At step $t = 2$, v_3 fails to activate v_6, while v_5 successfully activates v_6 but fails to activate v_9 (Figure 2.1(c)). At step $t = 3$, v_6 fails to activate v_7 (Figure 2.1(d)). At this point, the diffusion stops and nodes v_1 to v_6 are active nodes while nodes v_7, v_8 and v_9 are inactive nodes.   ■

Intuitively, the independent cascade model is suitable for modeling the diffusion of information or viruses, where exposure to one source may be enough for an individual to be activated (e.g., either getting the information or getting the virus). Such diffusion behavior is referred to as *simple contagion* by social scientists [Centola and Macy, 2007].

To help understand the independent cascade model, we provide an alternative model based on live-arc graphs. Given a graph $G = (V, E)$, we mark each arc of G as either *live* or *blocked* based

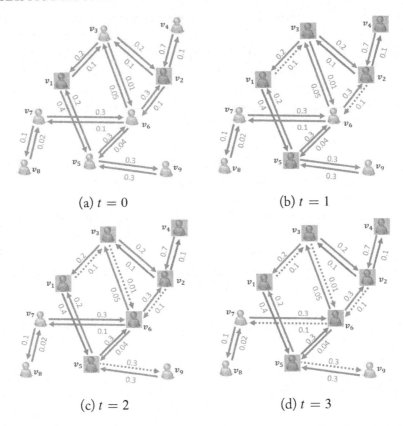

Figure 2.1: An example of the diffusion process of the independent cascade model. Orange nodes denote active nodes, and green nodes denote inactive nodes. Solid green arcs represent original arcs in the graph. Green numbers next to the arcs are influence probabilities of arcs. A solid red arc from a node u to a node v means that u successfully activates v through this arc. A dotted green arc from a node u to a node v means that u fails to activate v through this arc.

on certain randomized rule, and the random subgraph obtained from all nodes in V and all live arcs is called a *live-arc graph* (often referred to as live-edge graph in the literature). Let $d_G(S, v)$ denote the (geodesic) graph distance from node set S to a node v in graph G, which is the length of the shortest path among all paths from any node in S to node v in graph G (if no such path exists, we define $d_G(S, v) = \infty$, and if $v \in S$, $d_G(S, v) = 0$). For any $i = 0, 1, 2, \ldots$, let $R_G^i(S)$ denote the set of nodes that are reachable from S within i steps, i.e., $R_G^i(S) = \{v \in V \mid d_G(S, v) \quad i\}$. In particular, we have $R_G^0(S) = S$. We use $R_G(S)$ to represent the set of nodes in V that are reachable from S in graph G. Since the length of the shortest path from any node u to any node v is at most $n - 1$ unless u cannot reach v, we see that $R_G^{n-1}(S) = R_G(S)$, where $n = |V|$.

Definition 2.5   Live-arc graph model with independent arc selection.   Given a social graph $G = (V, E)$ and the influence probability $p(\cdot)$ on all arcs, we select a random live-arc graph G_L by selecting each arc $(u, v) \in E$ as a live arc independently with probability $p(u, v)$. Given seed set S_0, for any $t \geq 1$, the active set S_t is set to be $R_{G_L}^t(S_0)$.

Each live arc graph G_L can be seen as a possible world containing precisely those arcs of G present in G_L and none of the other arcs of G.

Theorem 2.6   *The independent cascade model (Definition 2.3) is equivalent to the live-arc graph model with independent arc selection (Definition 2.5).*

The above theorem provides an alternative view of the independent cascade model: before the diffusion process starts, for every arc $(u, v) \in E$ we flip a biased coin with probability $p(u, v)$ to decide whether the arc is live or blocked, and then starting from seed set S_0, the diffusion process simply follows the live arcs one step at a time to reach other nodes in the graph.

Proof (of Theorem 2.6).   Fix a seed set S_0. For any $t \geq 1$, consider any sequence of subsets $A_1, A_2, \ldots, A_t \subseteq V$ such that $A_1 \subseteq A_2 \subseteq \cdots \subseteq A_t$, and once two consecutive subsets are equal, all the subsequent subsets are also equal. If the sequence does not satisfy the above condition, it is obvious that both $\Pr(S_1 = A_1, \ldots, S_{t-1} = A_{t-1})$ and $\Pr(R_{G_L}^1(S_0) = A_1, \ldots, R_{G_L}^{t-1}(S_0) = A_{t-1})$ are zero, and thus we only need to focus on the sequences satisfying the above condition. By Definition 2.2, we want to show that for any such sequence, $\Pr(S_t = A_t \mid S_1 = A_1, \ldots, S_{t-1} = A_{t-1}) = \Pr(R_{G_L}^t(S_0) = A_t \mid R_{G_L}^1(S_0) = A_1, \ldots, R_{G_L}^{t-1}(S_0) = A_{t-1})$.

Under the independent cascade model (Definition 2.3), given $S_0, S_1 = A_1, \ldots, S_{t-1} = A_{t-1}$, active set S_t is A_t at time t if and only if each node $v \in A_t \setminus A_{t-1}$ is activated by at least one node in $A_{t-1} \setminus A_{t-2}$ and no node in $V \setminus A_t$ is activated by any node in $A_{t-1} \setminus A_{t-2}$ (recall that as a convention $A_{-1} = \emptyset$). Since all activation events are independent, we have

$$\Pr(S_t = A_t \mid S_1 = A_1, \ldots, S_{t-1} = A_{t-1}) =$$

$$\prod_{v \in A_t \setminus A_{t-1}} \left(1 - \prod_{u \in A_{t-1} \setminus A_{t-2}} (1 - p(u, v)) \right) \prod_{v \in V \setminus A_t} \prod_{u \in A_{t-1} \setminus A_{t-2}} (1 - p(u, v)). \tag{2.1}$$

Under the live-arc model with random arc selection (Definition 2.5), given $R_{G_L}^0(S_0), R_{G_L}^1(S_0) = A_1, \ldots, R_{G_L}^{t-1}(S_0) = A_{t-1}$, the t-step reachable set $R_{G_L}^t(S_0)$ is A_t if and only if each node $v \in A_t \setminus A_{t-1}$ is reached in one step by at least one node in $A_{t-1} \setminus A_{t-2}$, and no node in $V \setminus A_t$ is reached by any node in $A_{t-1} \setminus A_{t-2}$ in one step. Since in the live-arc graph, any node u reaches any node v in one step with probability $p(u, v)$ and every such event is independent of other events, we have

$$\Pr(R^t_{G_L}(S_0) = A_t \mid R^1_{G_L}(S_0) = A_1, \ldots, R^{t-1}_{G_L}(S_0) = A_{t-1}) =$$

$$\prod_{v \in A_t \setminus A_{t-1}} \left(1 - \prod_{u \in A_{t-1} \setminus A_{t-2}} (1 - p(u, v))\right) \prod_{v \in V \setminus A_t} \prod_{u \in A_{t-1} \setminus A_{t-2}} (1 - p(u, v)). \qquad (2.2)$$

Equations (2.1) and (2.2) are exactly the same, and thus for any subsets $A_1, A_2, \ldots, A_t \subseteq V$, $\Pr(S_t = A_t \mid S_1 = A_1, \ldots, S_{t-1} = A_{t-1}) = \Pr(R^t_{G_L}(S_0) = A_t \mid R^1_{G_L}(S_0) = A_1, \ldots, R^{t-1}_{G_L}(S_0) = A_{t-1})$. $\qquad \square$

In the independent cascade model, once $S_t = S_{t-1}$ for some $t \geq 1$, the active set no longer changes. As we mentioned before, often we are only interested in the final active set $\Phi(S_0)$. In such cases, Theorem 2.6 leads to further implications about the independent cascade model. Since the two models are equivalent, the marginal distributions of nodes on the final active set $\Phi(S_0)$ are also the same. For the live-arc graph model, the final active set is simply the reachable node set $R_{G_L}(S_0)$ from seed set S_0. With respect to the reachable node set $R_{G_L}(S_0)$, the live-arc graph model is a static model not involving time steps, while the independent cascade model describes a dynamic process involving time to reach the final node set. Thus, their equivalence implies that with respect to the final active set, the time aspect in the IC model is not essential. In particular, we could allow a newly activated node to delay its attempt to activate its inactive out-neighbors to a later step, or to different steps, or have a non-deterministic delay in its activation attempts, and the final active set $\Phi(S_0)$ would still have the same distribution. Moreover, we could even allow a node u to have multiple activation attempts to its out-neighbor v, each with a possibly different probability (e.g., a series of decaying probabilities). In this case, we can obtain the overall influence probability from u to v as $p(u, v) = 1 - \prod_i (1 - p_i(u, v))$, where $p_i(u, v)$ is the probability of u activating v in its i-th activation attempt. We then use this overall influence probability in the independent cascade model and the final active set distribution would be the same. This is summarized as the following corollary of Theorem 2.6.

Corollary 2.7   *In the independent cascade model, delaying the activation attempts of any node to any other node would not change the distribution of the final active set $\Phi(S_0)$. If we allow a node u to execute multiple independent activation attempts on a neighbor v with $p_i(u, v)$ denoting the success probability of the i-th attempt, then the distribution of the final active set $\Phi(S_0)$ would be the same as the independent cascade model where we use $p(u, v) = 1 - \prod_i (1 - p_i(u, v))$ as the influence probability on arc (u, v) and allow only one activation attempt from u to v.*

The above equivalence holds only when we are interested in the final active set $\Phi(S_0)$. In circumstances when we are interested in the size of the active set within a certain time period, the time and number of activation attempts become important. Interested readers are referred to the literature (e.g., [Chen et al., 2012, Goyal et al., 2012, Liu et al., 2012]) on model extensions for time-critical applications.

The equivalence given in Theorem 2.6 is essential in deriving some key properties of the independent cascade model, such as the submodularity property, which will be covered in Section 2.1.3.

2.1.2   LINEAR THRESHOLD MODEL

As described in the previous section, the independent cascade model is suitable to describe simple contagions where activations may be triggered from a single source, such as the adoption of information or viruses. However, there are many situations in which exposure to multiple independent sources are needed for an individual to change her behavior. For example, when adopting a new and unproven technology, or adopting a controversial idea, or adopting a costly new product, people may need positive reinforcement from many independent sources among their friends and acquaintances before they take an action.

Social scientists have proposed threshold behaviors to model such diffusions [Granovetter, 1978, Schelling, 1978]. When an aggregate function (e.g., count, or sum) of all of the positive signals received by a target exceeds a certain threshold, the target is activated. Centola and Macy [2007] refer to threshold behaviors in which an individual takes an action only after receiving influence from two or more sources as *complex contagion*.

The *linear threshold (or LT) model* is a stochastic diffusion model proposed by Kempe et al. [2003] to reflect this type of behavior. In the linear threshold model, every arc $(u, v) \in E$ is associated with an *influence weight* $w(u, v) \in [0, 1]$ (also denoted as w_{uv}), indicating the importance of u on influencing v. The weights are normalized such that for all v, the sum of weights of all incoming arcs of v is at most 1, i.e., $\sum_{u \in N^{in}(v)} w(u, v) \leq 1$ for all $v \in V$. For convenience, we set $w(u, v) = 0$ for all $(u, v) \notin E$. The formal definition is given below, followed by some intuitive explanations.

Definition 2.8   Linear threshold model.   The *linear threshold (LT) model* takes the social graph $G = (V, E)$, the influence weights $w(\cdot)$ on all arcs, and the seed set S_0 as the input, and generates the active sets S_t for all $t \geq 1$ by the following randomized operation rule. Initially, each node $v \in V$ independently selects a threshold θ_v uniformly at random in the range $[0, 1]$. At every time step $t \geq 1$, first set S_t to be S_{t-1}; then for any inactive node $v \in V \setminus S_{t-1}$, if the total weight of the arcs from its active in-neighbors is at least θ_v, i.e., $\sum_{u \in S_{t-1} \cap N^{in}(v)} w(u, v) \geq \theta_v$, then add v into S_t (i.e., v is activated at time t).[2]

Intuitively, the threshold θ_v is used to model the likelihood that v is influenced by its active neighbors: a large value of θ_v means that many active neighbors are required in order to activate

---

[2]With the convention that $w(u, v) = 0$ for all $(u, v) \notin E$, the inequality can be equivalently written as $\sum_{u \in S_{t-1}} w(u, v) \geq \theta_v$. The inequality in the main text provides more intuitive meaning, and we use these two type of expressions in the text interchangeably.

v while a small value of θ_v means that v is easily activated by a few active neighbors. The random selection of θ_v from 0 to 1 reflects our lack of knowledge of the individuals' internal thresholds. The only randomness is on the selection of thresholds. Once thresholds are determined, the remaining diffusion process is deterministic: in each time step, each node checks if it has enough in-neighbors that are already activated, where "enough" is measured by whether the total weight from these active in-neighbors reaches the threshold of the node. If so, the node is activated. From this process, it is clear that a higher influence weight on an arc (u, v) reflects higher influence power from u to v: v is more likely to be activated if the influence weight on (u, v) is higher and u is already activated. The model allows the total arc weight from all in-neighbors of a node to be less than 1, in which case if the random threshold θ_v is larger than the total arc weight, the node v will not be activated even if all of its in-neighbors are activated.

Example 2.9   Figure 2.2 shows an example of the diffusion process of the linear threshold model. Initially, the thresholds of all nodes are randomly chosen from $[0, 1]$ (the blue numbers shown under the node labels), and nodes v_1 and v_2 are selected as seeds (Figure 2.2(a)). At step $t = 1$ (Figure 2.2(b)), nodes v_1 and v_2 jointly activate node v_3, because their total weight toward v_3 is $0.1 + 0.5 = 0.6$, achieving the threshold of v_3. Node v_1 also activates v_5 and node v_2 activates v_4, because the corresponding arc weights exceed the thresholds of the target nodes. However, node v_6, although an out-neighbor of v_2, is not activated in this step because its threshold is 0.7 but the weight from its only active in-neighbor v_2 is 0.3. At step $t = 2$ (Figure 2.2(c)), three of v_6's in-neighbors, namely v_2, v_3, and v_5, are activated, and their total weight to v_6 is 0.7, achieving the threshold of v_3. Thus, v_6 is activated at this step. The diffusion stops at this point, since no other nodes can be activated by their active in-neighbors.   ∎

Note that due to the random selection of thresholds from the interval $[0, 1]$, it is still possible that one active in-neighbor of v may be enough to activate v, and thus strictly speaking we cannot say that linear threshold model is specifically for complex contagions, where at least two nodes are required to activate one node. Nevertheless, conceptually it is helpful to think about linear threshold model as closer to a model for complex contagions (e.g., adoptions of new technologies or controversial ideas) while independent cascade model as closer to a model for simple contagions (e.g., adoptions of information or viruses).

Similarly to the independent cascade model, the linear threshold model also has an equivalent live-arc graph model, defined below.

Definition 2.10   Live-arc graph model with proportional arc selection.   Given a social graph $G = (V, E)$ and the influence weights $w(\cdot)$ on all arcs, we select a random live-arc graph G_L such that for each node $v \in V$, at most one incoming arc of v is selected with probability proportional to the weight of the arc. More specifically, for each $v \in V$, among all incoming arcs of v, $(u, v) \in E$ is selected exclusively as the single live arc with probability $w(u, v)$, and no arc is selected as a live arc with probability $1 - \sum_{u \in N^{in}(v)} w(u, v)$. The selection of the incoming arc of v is independent

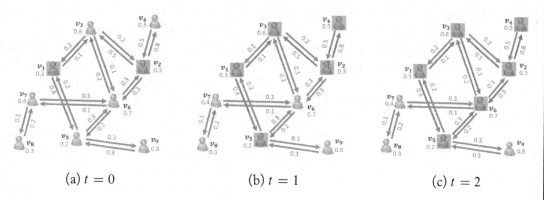

(a) $t = 0$ (b) $t = 1$ (c) $t = 2$

Figure 2.2: An example of the diffusion process of the linear threshold model. Orange nodes denote active nodes, and green nodes denote inactive nodes. Solid green arcs represent original arcs in the graph. Green numbers next to the arcs are the influence weights of the arcs. Blue numbers under the node labels are the randomly selected thresholds for the nodes. A set of red solid arcs pointing to the same node v means that the total weight of these arcs together causes the activation of v.

of the selection of incoming arcs of other nodes. Given a seed set S_0, for any $t \geq 1$, the active set S_t is set to be $R_{G_L}^t(S_0)$.

Theorem 2.11   *The linear threshold model (Definition 2.8) is equivalent to the live-arc graph model with proportional arc selection (Definition 2.10).*

The equivalence stated in the above theorem may not be as obvious as the equivalence between the independent cascade model and the live-arc graph model with random arc selection. The intuition of the equivalence is that, given a set A of active in-neighbors of v, set A activates v when the total weight of arcs from A to v is at least θ_v. Since θ_v is uniformly distributed from 0 to 1, the probability that A activates v is the same as the total weight of arcs from A to v. However, the total weight of arcs from A to v is also the probability that the live incoming arc of v is from some node in A. This builds the connection between live-arc graphs with proportional arc selection and the linear threshold model. We could view the single incoming arc (u, v) of v selected in the live-arc graph model as indicating the node u that adds the "final" weight causing v to be activated.

Note that the equivalence given in Theorem 2.11 is with respect to all active sets S_t's, while the original equivalence given by Kempe et al. [2003] (Claim 2.6) only refers to the final active set. The complete proof is given below, which is more detailed than the one by Kempe et al. [2003].

Proof (of Theorem 2.11). Fix a seed set S_0. For any $t \geq 1$, consider any sequence of subsets $A_1, A_2, \ldots, A_t \subseteq V$ such that $A_1 \subseteq A_2 \subseteq \cdots \subseteq A_t$, and once two consecutive subsets are equal, all the subsequent subsets are also equal. If the sequence does not satisfy the above condition, it is obvious that both $\Pr(S_1 = A_1, \ldots, S_{t-1} = A_{t-1})$ and $\Pr(R_{G_L}^1(S_0) = A_1, \ldots, R_{G_L}^{t-1}(S_0) = A_{t-1})$ are zero, and thus we only need to focus on the sequences satisfying the above condition. By Definition 2.2, we need to show that for any such sequence, we have that $\Pr(S_t = A_t \mid S_1 = A_1, \ldots, S_{t-1} = A_{t-1}) = \Pr(R_{G_L}^t(S_0) = A_t \mid R_{G_L}^1(S_0) = A_1, \ldots, R_{G_L}^{t-1}(S_0) = A_{t-1})$.

Under the linear threshold model (Definition 2.8), let $\mathcal{E}_1$ be the event $\{S_1 = A_1, \ldots, S_{t-1} = A_{t-1}\}$. Let $\mathcal{E}_2$ be the event that for every $v \in A_t \setminus A_{t-1}$, v is activated at time t and let $\mathcal{E}_3$ be the event that for every $v \in V \setminus A_t$, v is not activated by time t. Then we have $\Pr(S_t = A_t \mid S_1 = A_1, \ldots, S_{t-1} = A_{t-1}) = \Pr(\mathcal{E}_2 \wedge \mathcal{E}_3 \mid \mathcal{E}_1)$. Events $\mathcal{E}_2$ and $\mathcal{E}_3$ are independent conditioned on event $\mathcal{E}_1$, because they are determined by threshold values θ_v's, which are independently selected for each v, and by the states of nodes by time $t - 1$, which are determined in $\mathcal{E}_1$. Thus, $\Pr(\mathcal{E}_2 \wedge \mathcal{E}_3 \mid \mathcal{E}_1) = \Pr(\mathcal{E}_2 \mid \mathcal{E}_1) \cdot \Pr(\mathcal{E}_3 \mid \mathcal{E}_1)$. Hence, by Definition 2.8, and in particular using the fact that all thresholds are selected independently and uniformly at random from $[0, 1]$, we have

$$
\begin{aligned}
&\Pr(S_t = A_t \mid S_1 = A_1, \ldots, S_{t-1} = A_{t-1}) \\
&= \Pr(\mathcal{E}_2 \mid \mathcal{E}_1) \cdot \Pr(\mathcal{E}_3 \mid \mathcal{E}_1) \\
&= \prod_{v \in A_t \setminus A_{t-1}} \frac{\Pr(\sum_{u \in A_{t-2}} w(u, v) < \theta_v \le \sum_{u \in A_{t-1}} w(u, v))}{\Pr(\theta_v > \sum_{u \in A_{t-2}} w(u, v))} \cdot \prod_{v \in V \setminus A_t} \frac{\Pr(\theta_v > \sum_{u \in A_{t-1}} w(u, v))}{\Pr(\theta_v > \sum_{u \in A_{t-2}} w(u, v))} \\
&= \frac{\prod_{v \in A_t \setminus A_{t-1}} \sum_{u \in A_{t-1} \setminus A_{t-2}} w(u, v) \cdot \prod_{v \in V \setminus A_t} (1 - \sum_{u \in A_{t-1}} w(u, v))}{\prod_{v \in V \setminus A_{t-1}} (1 - \sum_{u \in A_{t-2}} w(u, v))}.
\end{aligned}
\tag{2.3}
$$

Under the live-arc graph model with proportional arc selection (Definition 2.10), let $\mathcal{E}_1'$ be the event $\{R_{G_L}^1(S_0) = A_1, \ldots, R_{G_L}^{t-1}(S_0) = A_{t-1}\}$. Let $\mathcal{E}_2'$ be the event that for every $v \in A_t \setminus A_{t-1}$, v is reached from S_0 in exactly t steps, and let $\mathcal{E}_3'$ be the event that for every $v \in V \setminus A_t$, v is not reached from S_0 in t steps. Thus, $\Pr(R_{G_L}^t(S_0) = A_t \mid R_{G_L}^1(S_0) = A_1, \ldots, R_{G_L}^{t-1}(S_0) = A_{t-1}) = \Pr(\mathcal{E}_2' \wedge \mathcal{E}_3' \mid \mathcal{E}_1')$. Events $\mathcal{E}_2'$ and $\mathcal{E}_3'$ are independent conditioned on event $\mathcal{E}_1'$, because they are determined by incoming live-arc selections of each node, which are independent, and by the reachability of nodes at step $t - 1$ or less, which are given in $\mathcal{E}_1'$. Therefore, we have $\Pr(\mathcal{E}_2' \wedge \mathcal{E}_3' \mid \mathcal{E}_1') = \Pr(\mathcal{E}_2' \mid \mathcal{E}_1') \cdot \Pr(\mathcal{E}_3' \mid \mathcal{E}_1')$. Thus, by Definition 2.10, we have

$$
\begin{aligned}
&\Pr(R_{G_L}^t(S_0) = A_t \mid R_{G_L}^1(S_0) = A_1, \ldots, R_{G_L}^{t-1}(S_0) = A_{t-1}) \\
&= \Pr(\mathcal{E}_2' \mid \mathcal{E}_1') \cdot \Pr(\mathcal{E}_3' \mid \mathcal{E}_1') \\
&= \prod_{v \in A_t \setminus A_{t-1}} \frac{\Pr(\exists u \in (A_{t-1} \setminus A_{t-2}), (u, v) \text{ is live})}{\Pr(\forall u \in A_{t-2}, (u, v) \text{ is not live})} \cdot \prod_{v \in V \setminus A_t} \frac{\Pr(\forall u \in A_{t-1}, (u, v) \text{ is not live})}{\Pr(\forall u \in A_{t-2}, (u, v) \text{ is not live})} \\
&= \frac{\prod_{v \in A_t \setminus A_{t-1}} \sum_{u \in A_{t-1} \setminus A_{t-2}} w(u, v) \cdot \prod_{v \in V \setminus A_t} (1 - \sum_{u \in A_{t-1}} w(u, v))}{\prod_{v \in V \setminus A_{t-1}} (1 - \sum_{u \in A_{t-2}} w(u, v))}.
\end{aligned}
\tag{2.4}
$$

Comparing Equation (2.4) with Equation (2.3), we have $\Pr(S_t = A_t \mid S_1 = A_1, \ldots, S_{t-1} = A_{t-1}) = \Pr(R_{G_L}^t(S_0) = A_t \mid R_{G_L}^1(S_0) = A_1, \ldots, R_{G_L}^{t-1}(S_0) = A_{t-1})$. $\square$

Similarly to our observation following for the independent cascade model (see Corollary 2.7), with respect to the final active set $\Phi(S_0)$, Theorem 2.11 implies that the weight of an active in-neighbor of v need not be applied immediately towards activating v. Instead, v's in-neighbor could delay the point at which it "throws" its weight toward activating u, to a later time.

Corollary 2.12   *In the linear threshold model, the distribution of the final active set $\Phi(S_0)$ would not change if we delay adding the weights of some outgoing arcs of a newly activated node u to a later time step.*

2.1.3   SUBMODULARITY AND MONOTONICITY OF INFLUENCE SPREAD FUNCTION

Both the independent cascade model and the linear threshold model share two important properties in terms of their influence spread function $\sigma(\cdot)$: submodularity and monotonicity.

Submodularity can be understood in this context as *diminishing marginal returns* when adding more nodes to the seed set. A set function $f : 2^V \to \mathbb{R}$ is *submodular* if for any subsets $S \subseteq T \subseteq V$ and any element $v \in V \setminus T$, the marginal contribution of element v when added to a set T can not exceed the marginal contribution of element v when added to a subset $S \subseteq T$. Formally,

$$f(S \cup \{v\}) - f(S) \geq f(T \cup \{v\}) - f(T) . \tag{2.5}$$

Another useful property is monotonicity, which in this context means that adding more elements to a seed set can not reduce the size of the final set. We say that a set function $f : 2^V \to \mathbb{R}$ is *monotone* if for any subsets $S \subseteq T \subseteq V$, $f(S) \leq f(T)$.

Theorem 2.13   *The influence spread function $\sigma(\cdot)$ in both the independent cascade model (IC) and the linear threshold model (LT) is monotone and submodular.*

Proof. We utilize the equivalent live-arc graph models to prove the theorem. Given a social graph $G = (V, E)$, let $\mathcal{G}$ denote the set of all possible live-arc graphs of G. Let G_L be a random live-arc graph, and let $\Pr(G_L)$ denote the probability that G_L is selected from among all live-arc graphs in $\mathcal{G}$. According to Theorems 2.6 and 2.11, the IC and LT models correspond to live-arc graphs with different probabilistic arc selections (Definitions 2.10 and 2.5), and thus $\Pr(G_L)$ is different for the IC and LT models. However, by Theorems 2.6 and 2.11, for both models we have

$$\sigma(S_0) = \sum_{G_L \in \mathcal{G}} \Pr(G_L) |R_{G_L}(S_0)|.$$

It is well known that the linear combination of monotone (resp. submodular) functions with non-negative coefficients is also monotone (resp. submodular). Therefore, to prove that $\sigma(\cdot)$ is monotone (resp. submodular), it is sufficient to show that for any live-arc graph $G_L \in \mathcal{G}$, $|R_{G_L}(\cdot)|$ is monotone (resp. submodular).

The monotonicity of $|R_{G_L}(\cdot)|$ is straightforward, so we focus on proving its submodularity. By the definition of submodularity, it is sufficient to show that for any two subsets $S \subseteq T \subseteq V$ and a node $v \in V \setminus T$, $R_{G_L}(T \cup \{v\}) \setminus R_{G_L}(T) \subseteq R_{G_L}(S \cup \{v\}) \setminus R_{G_L}(S)$. For any $u \in R_{G_L}(T \cup \{v\}) \setminus R_{G_L}(T)$, u is reachable from $T \cup \{v\}$ but not reachable from T in G_L. This implies that u is reachable from v. Since $S \subseteq T$, it must be the case that u is not reachable from S but is reachable from $S \cup \{v\}$, and thus $u \in R_{G_L}(S \cup \{v\}) \setminus R_{G_L}(S)$. Thus, function $|R_{G_L}(\cdot)|$ is submodular for all G_L's, which means $\sigma(\cdot)$ is submodular. □

One remark on the monotonicity of $\sigma(S_0)$ is that it relies on the definition $\sigma(S_0)$ to count nodes in S_0 in the influence spread. If one excludes the size of the seed set S_0 from the definition of influence spread function $\sigma(S_0)$, then monotonicity no longer holds, since using this definition the influence spread of the full set V is 0 — there are no nodes to be influenced when all nodes are seeds!

Submodularity and monotonicity together lead to an important algorithm design choice for the problem of influence maximization, which will be discussed in Chapter 3.

2.1.4 GENERAL THRESHOLD MODEL AND GENERAL CASCADE MODEL

Even though both the independent cascade and the linear threshold models correspond to certain live-arc graph models, and they both have the submodularity and monotonicity properties, they are not equivalent. Given a social graph G with IC model parameters, we cannot always find a suitable set of LT model parameters to make them behave equivalently as per Definition 2.2. This is shown by the following example.

Example 2.14   Figure 2.3 shows a graph such that no parameters can make the IC and LT models equivalent in this graph. Graph G contains three nodes $\{x, y, z\}$ and two arcs from x and y to z. The IC model for G has two parameters $p(x, z)$ and $p(y, z)$, while the LT model has two parameters $w(x, z)$ and $w(y, z)$. If the two models are equivalent, then when we set seed set S_0 to be $\{x\}$, we must have $w(x, z) = p(x, z)$ since this is the only way to make the probability of $z \in S_1$ the same in both models. Similarly, when we set S_0 to $\{y\}$, we conclude that $w(y, z) = p(y, z)$. However, when we set S_0 to $\{x, y\}$, in the IC model, z is activated in step 1 with probability $1 - (1 - p(x, z))(1 - p(y, z))$, while in the LT model, z is activated in step 1 with probability $w(x, z) + w(y, z)$. Since $w(x, z) = p(x, z)$ and $w(y, z) = p(y, z)$, we know that in general $1 - (1 - p(x, z))(1 - p(y, z))$ is different from $w(x, z) + w(y, z)$ (unless one of $w(x, z)$ and $w(y, z)$ is zero), and thus no parameter settings can make the two models equivalent. ∎

However, as defined by Kempe et al. [2003], the independent cascade model can be generalized to the general cascade model, the linear threshold model can be generalized to the general threshold model, and these two *generalized* models are indeed equivalent. These generalized

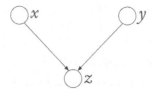

Figure 2.3: A simple graph for showing that the IC and LT models are not equivalent.

models are helpful in understanding the difference and relationship between the basic IC and LT models, and thus we provide their definition here.

Definition 2.15 General cascade model. In the *general cascade model*, for a social graph $G = (V, E)$, every node $v \in V$ has an *activation function* $p_v : N^{in}(v) \times 2^{N^{in}(v)} \to [0, 1]$ such that $p_v(u, S) \in [0, 1]$, for $S \subset N^{in}(v)$ and $u \in N^{in}(v) \setminus S$. Given seed set S_0, at every time step $t \geq 1$, first set S_t to be S_{t-1}; next for every inactive node $v \notin S_{t-1}$, order v's just activated in-neighbors, i.e., set $N^{in}(v) \cap (S_{t-1} \setminus S_{t-2})$ in an order $u_1, u_2, \ldots, u_\ell$; follow this order to try to activate v: if $u_1, \ldots, u_{i-1}$ have failed to activate v, then the set of in-neighbors of v that have failed to activate v is $S = (N^{in}(v) \cap S_{t-2}) \cup \{u_1, \ldots, u_{i-1}\}$; for u_i to activate v, we flip an independent coin with success probability $p_v(u_i, S)$ and if successful, add v into S_t and refer to it as u_i *activates* v *at time* t. We require that function $p_v(u, S)$ to be *order-independent*, that is, if in-neighbors $u_1, u_2, \ldots, u_\ell$ try to activate v, the probability that v is activated at the end of these ℓ attempts is the same no matter in which order these ℓ activation attempts are made.

According to this definition, the independent cascade model is a special case of the general cascade model when activation function $p_v(u, S)$ is a constant $p(u, v)$ independent of set S.

Definition 2.16 General threshold model. In the *general threshold model*, for a social graph $G = (V, E)$, every node $v \in V$ has a *threshold function* $f_v : 2^{N^{in}(v)} \to [0, 1]$. We require that function $f_v(\cdot)$ be monotone and $f_v(\emptyset) = 0$. Initially, each node $v \in V$ selects a threshold θ_v uniformly at random in the range $[0, 1]$, and this selection is independent of all other threshold selections. Starting from a given seed set S_0, at every time step $t \geq 1$, first set S_t to be S_{t-1}; then for any inactive node $v \in V \setminus S_{t-1}$, if $f_v(S_{t-1} \cap N^{in}(v)) \geq \theta_v$, add v into S_t (i.e., v is activated at time t).

According to this definition, the linear threshold model is a special case of the general threshold model, since we can set $f_v(S) = \sum_{u \in S} w(u, v)$ where $w(u, v)$ is the influence weight on arc (u, v) in the linear threshold model.

Although the general cascade model and the general threshold model have different randomized processes for diffusion, they are equivalent in the sense that for any general cascade model with activation functions $p_v(u, S)$ for each $v \in V$, there exist corresponding threshold functions $f_v(S)$ for each $v \in V$, such that the two models under these sets of functions are equivalent according to Definition 2.2, and conversely. We now provide an informal derivation of the relationship between $p_v(u, S)$'s and $f_v(S)$'s.

Suppose that we have a general cascade model with activation functions $p_v(u, S)$ for all $v \in V$. Let $S = \{u_1, u_2, \ldots, u_\ell\}$ be a set of in-neighbors of v. Let $A_i = \{u_1, u_2, \ldots, u_i\}$ for all $i = 1, 2, \ldots, \ell$, and $A_0 = \emptyset$. The probability that one of nodes in S successfully activates v, given that nodes in S are already active, is $1 - \prod_{i=1}^{\ell}(1 - p_v(u_i, A_{i-1}))$. In the general threshold model, since the threshold θ_v is selected uniformly at random from $[0, 1]$, to achieve the above success probability we just need to set the threshold function to be

$$f_v(S) = 1 - \prod_{i=1}^{\ell}(1 - p_v(u_i, A_{i-1})). \tag{2.6}$$

Note that $p_v(u, S)$ is order-independent, thus Equation (2.6) always provides the same value of $f_v(S)$ no matter how we choose the order of nodes in S. Moreover, $f_v(S)$ defined above is monotone with $f_v(\emptyset) = 0$, so it is a valid threshold function.

For the converse direction, suppose that we have a general threshold model with threshold functions $f_v(S)$ for all $v \in V$. Given an in-neighbor set S of v and an in-neighbor $u \in N^{in}(v) \setminus S$, $p_v(u, S)$ represents the conditional probability that u activates v conditioned on that none of nodes in S activates v. In the general threshold model, we know that the probability that none of the nodes in S activates v is $1 - f_v(S)$, since threshold θ_v is uniformly distributed on $[0, 1]$. When $f_v(S) < 1$, we can see that u activates v if and only if threshold θ_v is between $f_v(S)$ and $f_v(S \cup \{u\})$, which means that we can set $p_v(u, S)$ as follows if $f_v(S) < 1$:

$$p_v(u, S) = \frac{f_v(S \cup \{u\}) - f_v(S)}{1 - f_v(S)}. \tag{2.7}$$

When $f_v(S) = 1$, there is no need to define $p_v(u, S)$ since nodes in S are guaranteed to activate v. It is easy to verify that $p_v(u, S)$ defined by Equation (2.7) satisfies order-independent property. Note that we need the monotonicity of $f_v(S)$ to guarantee that $p_v(u, S)$ defined by Equation (2.7) is non-negative. As for the requirement that $f_v(\emptyset) = 0$, if $f_v(\emptyset) > 0$, v is a special node that can be activated without any active in-neighbors with probability $f_v(\emptyset)$ in step 1. This cannot be directly modeled by the general cascade model on the same graph G. However, we can add a special node s to graph G, such that s is always selected as a seed, and s has an arc to v with weight $f_v(\emptyset)$, and v's threshold function is changed to f_v' with $f_v'(\emptyset) = 0$ and $f_v'(S) = f_v(S \setminus \{s\})$ for all $S \neq \emptyset$ and $s \in S$. For all $S \neq \emptyset$ and $s \notin S$, there is no need to define $f_v'(S)$ since s is always the seed and $f_v'(S)$ is never used. The new graph has the same activation behavior as the old graph, and it has an equivalent counterpart in the general cascade model. Formally, we have the following theorem.

Theorem 2.17 *For any general cascade model with activation functions $p_v(u, S)$ for all $v \in V$, the corresponding general threshold model with $f_v(S)$ defined according to Equation (2.6) is equivalent to* *the general cascade model with $p_v(u, S)$. Conversely, for any general threshold model with threshold functions $f_v(S)$ for all $v \in V$, the corresponding general cascade model with $p_v(u, S)$ defined according to Equation (2.7) for all $f_v(S) < 1$ is equivalent to the general threshold model with $f_v(S)$.*

We leave the full proof of the theorem as an exercise to the interested reader.

Theorem 2.17 establishes the equivalence of the two general models. By this theorem, we can see that the independent cascade model with parameters $p(u, v)$ has an equivalent representation in the general threshold model as $f_v(S) = 1 - \prod_{u \in S}(1 - p(u, v))$, while the linear threshold model with parameters $w(u, v)$ has an equivalent representation in the general cascade model as $p_v(u, S) = \frac{w(u,v)}{1 - \sum_{x \in S} w(x,v)}$.

General threshold models or general cascade models "embed" a large class of models with wide range of possible diffusion behaviors, yet they satisfy the basic property of monotonicity.

Theorem 2.18   *The influence spread function $\sigma(\cdot)$ for any general cascade model or general threshold model is monotone.*

Proof (sketch). We consider the general threshold model and fix the threshold θ_v for all nodes $v \in V$. It is easy to verify that when the seed set S_0 grows, the final active set also grows under these fixed thresholds, due to the monotonicity of the threshold functions $f_v(S)$. Then $\sigma(S_0)$ is simply the integration of the size of all final active sets among all possible threshold values θ_v's, and thus is monotone. A similar argument shows the monotonicity of $\sigma(S_0)$ for the general cascade model. □

However, these general models may not satisfy the important submodularity property. As an example, consider the following fixed threshold model, which also appears in the literature on modeling influence diffusions [Ben-Zwi et al., 2009, Chen, 2008, Kempe et al., 2003].

Definition 2.19   Fixed threshold model.   A *fixed threshold model* on a social graph G has the same threshold functions $f_v(S)$ as the general threshold model. The only difference is that each node v has a fixed threshold $\theta_v \in [0, 1]$ as the input instead of being uniformly sampled from $[0, 1]$. The dynamic process starting from seed set S_0 is exactly the same as the general threshold model after the thresholds are given.

A fixed threshold model is a special case of the general threshold model by the following transformation: for any $f_v(S)$ and θ_v, define $f_v'(S) = 1$ if $f_v(S) \geq \theta_v$ and $f_v'(S) = 0$ if $f_v(S) < \theta_v$. The general threshold model with threshold functions $f_v'(S)$ is exactly the fixed threshold model with parameters $f_v(S)$ and θ_v.

Consider a very simple form of the fixed threshold model where $f_v(S) = |S|/|N^{in}(v)|$ for all $S \subseteq N^{in}(v)$, which means each in-neighbor of v contributes equal weight in activating v. Even such a simple fixed threshold model is not submodular. For example, consider the same simple graph G shown in Figure 2.3. Node z has a threshold $\theta_z = 0.6$. Then we have $\sigma(\emptyset) = 0$,

$\sigma(\{x\}) = \sigma(\{y\}) = 1$ and $\sigma(\{x, y\}) = 3$. Therefore, if we set $S = \emptyset$ and $T = \{x\}$, we have $\sigma(S \cup \{y\}) - \sigma(S) = 1 < 2 = \sigma(T \cup \{y\}) - \sigma(T)$, which means $\sigma(\cdot)$ is not submodular. Essentially, this is because the last seed added into the seed set, which causes the total weight of active in-neighbors of some node to exceed its threshold, provides more marginal contribution than adding the seed earlier into the seed set.

Even though general threshold or cascade models may not satisfy submodularity, we can add restrictions to the models so that submodularity is satisfied. The following theorem was conjectured by Kempe et al. [2003] and later proven by Mossel and Roch [2007], and it shows that it is enough to require the threshold functions $f_v(\cdot)$ to be submodular to guarantee the submodularity of the influence spread function $\sigma(\cdot)$.

Theorem 2.20   *In the general threshold model with threshold functions $f_v(\cdot)$ for all $v \in V$, if $f_v(\cdot)$ is submodular for all $v \in V$, then the influence spread function $\sigma(\cdot)$ of the model is also submodular.*

The theorem nicely builds connections between the behavior of local diffusion and global diffusion. If local diffusion behaviors as specified by $f_v(\cdot)$ are all submodular, then the global diffusion behavior as specified by the influence spread function $\sigma(\cdot)$ is also submodular. This directly impacts the feasibility of the influence maximization problem, to be discussed in the next chapter.

Mossel and Roch [2007] actually provide a more general result than Theorem 2.20. They allows a more general influence spread function $\sigma'(S) = \mathbb{E}(\omega(\Phi(S_0)))$, where S_0 is the seed set, $\Phi(S_0)$ is the final active set, and $\omega(\cdot)$ is a set function about the weight of the final active set. They generalize Theorem 2.20 such that if $\omega(\cdot)$ is submodular and individual threshold function $f_v(\cdot)$'s are submodular, then $\sigma'(S)$ is submodular. Set function $\omega(\cdot)$ allows us to assign different weights on the nodes, e.g., we can maximize the influence to a subset of nodes instead to all nodes, and the corresponding objective function is still submodular.

Before we conclude this section, we address one more question that may arise when understanding the linear threshold or general threshold models. How crucial is it to require the threshold θ_v to be uniformly distributed on the interval $[0, 1]$? Is it possible to use other distributions? The general answer is yes, other distributions can be used. Let $F_v(\cdot)$ be the cumulative distribution function of threshold θ_v, for all $v \in V$. The following theorem shows that extending the general threshold model with an arbitrary threshold distribution is equivalent to a general threshold model with a different threshold function, where the threshold is sampled uniformly at random.

Theorem 2.21   *If we extend the general threshold model with threshold functions $f_v(S)$ such that for any $v \in V$, threshold θ_v is selected randomly according to a distribution $F_v(\cdot)$, then it is the same as a general threshold model with threshold functions $f_v'(S)$ where $f_v'(S) = F_v(f_v(S))$, and thresholds are chosen uniformly at random from $[0, 1]$.*

Proof. First, $F_v(\cdot)$ as a cumulative distribution must be non-decreasing, and since θ_v only takes values in $[0, 1]$, $F_v(0) = 0$. Thus, we know that f'_v must be monotone and $f'_v(\emptyset) = 0$. Second, when threshold θ_v is selected according to distribution $F_v(\cdot)$, we have $\Pr(f_v(S) \geq \theta_v) = 1 - F_v(f_v(S)) = 1 - f'_v(S)$. However, this is exactly the probability of $f'_v(S) \geq \theta_v$ when θ_v is uniformly distributed on $[0, 1]$. Therefore, the randomized process of the general threshold model with threshold functions $f'_v(S)$ and uniform distribution for threshold selection is exactly the same as the randomized process if we use threshold functions $f_v(S)$ and distribution function $F_v(\cdot)$ for threshold θ_v.   □

With the above equivalence, it is easy to see that to maintain submodularity, it is sufficient to require that the distribution function $F_v(\cdot)$ be concave in $[0, 1]$. Recall that a real-valued function f is *concave* in an interval $[a, b]$ if for any $x_1, x_2 \in [a, b]$, and any value $\alpha \in [0, 1]$, we have $f(\alpha x_1 + (1 - \alpha)x_2) \geq \alpha f(x_1) + (1 - \alpha)f(x_2)$.

Corollary 2.22   *If we extend the general threshold model such that for any $v \in V$, the threshold θ_v is selected randomly according to distribution $F_v(\cdot)$, then the influence spread function $\sigma(\cdot)$ is monotone and submodular if all $F_v(\cdot)$ are concave in the interval $[0, 1]$ and all threshold functions $f_v(S)$ are submodular.*

Proof (sketch). One just needs to verify a general result that if a set function $f(S)$ is monotone and submodular with range $[a, b]$, and a real-valued function $g(\cdot)$ is concave in $[a, b]$, then the set function $g \circ f(S)$ is also submodular. We leave the verification of the above result to the reader.

With the above general result verified, the corollary is immediate from Theorems 2.20 and 2.21, and the facts that the threshold function f_v is submodular and the cumulative distribution function F_v is concave on $[0, 1]$.   □

2.2   OTHER RELATED MODELS

In this section, we briefly describe several other models that have been considered in the study of information and influence diffusion. Our intention is not to provide a comprehensive introduction to all these models, but to help the understanding of the relationships and differences between these models compared to the main diffusion models introduced in Section 2.1. A mathematical treatment of the models discussed in this section as well as other related models such as percolation models can be found in [Grimmett, 2010] and the references therein.

2.2.1   EPIDEMIC MODELS

Epidemic models are used originally to study the spread of diseases among biological populations, including humans. Various epidemic models have been proposed and extensively studied over many years, starting from the early 20th century. Recently, researchers have also applied epidemic models to the diffusion of information and influence in social networks. In this section, we only cover the most basic concepts of epidemic models and make a connection with the independent cascade model. The interested reader is referred to this book by Newman [2010, Ch. 17] and references therein for a more comprehensive coverage of epidemic models.

The classic epidemic models are *fully mixed* models, in that they assume that every individual may have direct contact with every other individual to potentially transfer a disease in a time unit. In other words, they do not consider an explicit network of contacts, or equivalently they assume the contact network is a complete graph. These models are often treated as continuous-time models, and differential equations are applied to obtain analytical or numerical results on the epidemic dynamics in the population.

Each individual (or node) transitions between several possible states, which typically include state S (for *susceptible*), state I (for *infected*), and state R (for *recovered or removed*). A node in state S does not have the disease but is susceptible to getting the disease upon contact with an infected node. A node in state I has the disease and can transmit the disease to susceptible nodes upon contact, with infection rate β, which is interpreted as the probability of successful transmission of the disease from an infected node to a susceptible node in a time unit.

The simplest model allows only two states S and I and one transition from S to I on each node according to the above transition rule, which is referred to as the *SI model*. Let s and i be variables for the fractions of susceptible and infected nodes over time, respectively, and let n be the total number of nodes in the system. Then in a small time unit dt, each infected node contacts all other nodes, among which $s \cdot n$ of them are susceptible nodes. Upon contact with a susceptible node, with probability β, the susceptible node get infected, and β is also referred to as the *infection rate*. Since there are $i \cdot n$ infected nodes in total, after dt time unit, the reduction to the fraction of suspected node is $i \cdot n \cdot s \cdot n \cdot \beta / n = \beta \cdot s \cdot i \cdot n$. Therefore, we have the following differential equation:

$$\frac{ds}{dt} = -\beta \cdot s \cdot i \cdot n. \tag{2.8}$$

On noting $s + i = 1$, one can solve the differential equation with the following closed-form solution for the fraction of infected nodes $i(t)$ at time t:

$$i(t) = \frac{i(0)e^{\beta nt}}{1 - i(0) + i(0)e^{\beta nt}}. \tag{2.9}$$

The above solution corresponds the classic logistic growth curve (or S-shaped curve) as illustrated in Figure 2.4. The figure shows that initially the infection in the population is slow, and after the initial period, there is a fast growth period in which a large fraction of population gets infected in a short time period, followed by a remaining long period before all nodes are infected.

One may also include state R (for recovered) on each node, and allow a node in state I to transition to state R but not to transition from R to any other state, meaning that an infected node is recovered from the disease and becomes immune to further infection (some researchers have interpreted R as the infected node becoming dead and thus being removed from the system). This model is referred to as the *SIR model*, and intuitively it could model diseases such as measles and

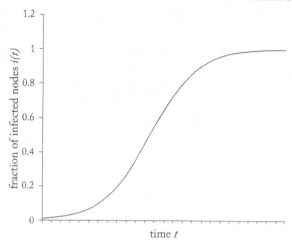

Figure 2.4: Logistic growth curve (S-shaped curve) for the SI model.

mumps that, except for very rare cases, generate life-time immunity after getting infected once. Transition from I to R follows the *recovery rate* γ, which is the probability that an infected node becomes recovered in a time unit. Let r be the fraction of recovered nodes in the system. Then we know that in a time unit dt, the reduction to the fraction of infected nodes due to recovery is $\gamma \cdot i$. Therefore, we can easily write the following system of differential equations:

$$\frac{ds}{dt} = -\beta \cdot s \cdot i \cdot n, \tag{2.10}$$

$$\frac{di}{dt} = \beta \cdot s \cdot i \cdot n - \gamma \cdot i, \tag{2.11}$$

$$\frac{dr}{dt} = \gamma \cdot i, \tag{2.12}$$

$$s + i + r = 1. \tag{2.13}$$

Numerical solutions on the fraction of nodes in each category at every point in time can be obtained using the above differential equation system. The fraction r in the end (when time goes to infinity) reflects the *epidemic size*, the fraction of nodes in the population that has ever been infected through the history of the disease diffusion. An important metric of the SIR model and other epidemic models is the *basic reproduction number* R_0, which is the average number of susceptible nodes an infected node can infect in the early stage of the diffusion before the node is recovered from the disease. For the SIR model, we have $R_0 = \beta n / \gamma$, because in one unit of time on average βn susceptible nodes are infected by an infected node and the infected node remains infectious on average for $1/\gamma$ time units. An important result for the SIR model is that when $R_0 = \beta n / \gamma > 1$, a significant portion of nodes are infected, but when $R_0 < 1$, only a small fraction of nodes are infected and the disease dies out exponentially fast. Intuitively, when $R_0 < 1$, the spread of disease is not as fast as the rate of recovery, so the disease cannot reach a large fraction of the population, while when $R_0 > 1$, before an infected node recovers, it can transmit the disease to more than one person and so the number of infected nodes multiplies quickly, faster than the speed of recovery. The threshold of $R_0 = \beta n/\gamma = 1$ is referred to as the *epidemic threshold* of the model.

Another frequently used model is the *SIS model*, where an infected node may transition back to state S with probability γ in every time unit, so that the node becomes susceptible to disease again (e.g., repeated infection by flu). Similar differential equations can be derived for the SIS model. In the steady state of the SIS model (when time goes to infinity) a fixed fraction of nodes are infected (with the possibility that no nodes are infected). Similar to the SIR model, the basic reproduction number $R_0 = \beta n/\gamma$, and the epidemic threshold is $R_0 = \beta n/\gamma = 1$: if $R_0 > 1$, a non-zero fraction of nodes are infected in the steady state, while if $R_0 < 1$, the disease dies out exponentially fast and no node is infected in the steady state.

Other more sophisticated models are available, such as the *SIRS* model (see [Newman, 2010]), but we omit the introduction of these models in this book.

Epidemic models *on a contact network* assume that a node can only transmit a disease to its neighbors, as in the independent cascad and linear threshold models introduced in Section 2.1. More specifically, at each time unit an infected node contacts all its neighbors in the network and with independent probability β it infects each susceptible neighbor. For SIR or SIS models, each node also has a probability of γ to become recovered or susceptible, respectively.

The SIR model on a network is closely related to the independent cascade model in the following way. Given an SIR model on a social graph $G = (V, E)$ with parameters β and γ, we can regard that on every arc $(u, v) \in E$, an infected u has $1/\gamma$ chances to infect v, with success probability β in each attempt. Therefore, the overall success probability is $1 - (1 - \beta)^{1/\gamma}$, which is approximately β/γ if the value is small. This means that we can use an independent cascade model with influence probability $p(u, v) = 1 - (1 - \beta)^{1/\gamma} \approx \beta/\gamma$ to represent the SIR model, such that the distribution on the final active set of nodes is the same. In the reverse direction, given an IC model on a social graph $G = (V, E)$ with influence probabilities $p(u, v)$ for all $(u, v) \in E$, we can use $\gamma = 1$, and an arc specific infection rate $\beta(u, v) = p(u, v)$, and ensure in the model that before a node recovers, it always has one chance to infect its neighbors. This will give us an SIR model on G that has the same effect as the IC model.

Existing studies of epidemic models on networks typically focus on deriving the epidemic thresholds under various network conditions (e.g., [Chakrabarti et al., 2008, Ganesh et al., 2005, Newman, 2002, 2005, Prakash et al., 2011]), or investigating immunization strategies under various models (e.g., [Briesemeister et al., 2003, Cohen et al., 2003, Madar et al., 2004]). For example, recent studies [Chakrabarti et al., 2008, Ganesh et al., 2005, Prakash et al., 2011] show that the epidemic threshold of SIS or SIR or related models in an undirected graph is closely connected with the first eigenvalue of the adjacency matrix of the graph. The immunization studies in [Briesemeister et al., 2003, Cohen et al., 2003, Madar et al., 2004] focus on analytical or empirical evaluations of certain simple immunization strategies on specific graph classes such as power-law graphs. On the other hand, the focus of this book and its related studies are on the algorithmic aspects of social influence diffusion, in particular, influence maximization under independent cascade, linear threshold, and other related diffusion models. Therefore, the main theme of this book can be viewed as complimentary to the studies in mathematical epidemiology, and it may provide further insights and lend algorithmic tools to mathematical epidemiology.

2.2.2   VOTER MODEL

The voter model is a classic stochastic model for interacting particle systems, originally described by Clifford and Sudbury [1973]. In the most basic form of the model, we are given an undirected graph $G = (V, E)$, and each node in the graph has two states 0 and 1. In each time step, a node v randomly selects one of its neighbors u and mimics the state that u had in the previous step. Since the state of each node may change back and forth between 0 and 1, the voter model is a non-progressive model. The voter model can be used to model the interactions and diffusions of conflicting opinions (e.g., opinions on political candidates) in the network, where people's opinion may change due to the interaction with their friends, and it has been adopted as the basis for influence diffusion in several studies ([Even-Dar and Shapira, 2007, Li et al., 2013, Pathak et al., 2010]).

The advantage of the voter model is its simple representation in matrix form, and its connection with random walks on graphs. Let $\mathbf{x}_t$ be the column vector where the i-th component $x_t(i)$ is the probability that node i is in state 1 at time step t, while $\mathbf{x}_0$ is the initial state of all nodes. Let M be the stochastic transition matrix, with $M(i, j) = 1/d_i$, where d_i is the degree of node i in graph G. Then the dynamic of the voter model in the basic form can be represented as:

$$\mathbf{x}_t = M\mathbf{x}_{t-1}. \tag{2.14}$$

This is because, in the scalar form, $x_t(i) = \sum_j M(i, j)x_{t-1}(j)$, which means that node i has probability $M(i, j) = 1/d_i$ to take the state of node j in step $t - 1$, which is 1 with probability $x_{t-1}(j)$. Thus, matrix algebra can help deriving the states of nodes at any step and at the steady state when $t \to \infty$.

The voter model can be interpreted as random walks in the following way. At time t, according to the voter model, node i randomly selects its neighbor j with probability $M(i, j)$, and adopts j's state in time $t - 1$. This can be viewed as saying a random walker starts at node i at time t, randomly chooses neighbor j with probability $M(i, j)$ and walks to j, but it walks "back in time" so that it arrives j at time $t - 1$, and picks up the state of j at time $t - 1$ as the state of i at time t. If the random walker continues its random walk on the graph as described above, and each walk step causes the time to go back one time slot, then after t steps, the walker arrives at a node j_0 at time 0, and picks up the state of j_0 at time 0 as the state of i at time t. In other words, the state of node i at time t can be obtained by conducting a random walk from i on the graph for t steps to reach a node j_0 and taking the initial state of j_0 as the state of i at time t. Since any two random walks starting from any two nodes eventually meet in a connected and aperiodic graph, we know that eventually all nodes have the same state in such graphs (see [Even-Dar and Shapira, 2007] for more discussions on the relationship between the voter model and the random walks on graphs).

The voter model is also related to the non-progressive version of the linear threshold model. To make the LT model non-progressive, we allow each node v to randomly choose its threshold θ_v^t for every time step $t \geq 1$, and v is active at step t when the sum of weights of its active in-neighbors in step $t - 1$ exceeds threshold θ_v^t. To connect the non-progressive LT model with the voter model, we first extend the voter model to directed graphs with arc weights, and let node v randomly pick one of its in-neighbors proportional to the in-arc weight and adopt the state of the selected in-neighbor. It is straightforward to verify that when the stochastic transition matrix M is defined on the weighted directed graph, Equation (2.14) still holds for the voter model dynamic. The voter model extended in this way is equivalent to the non-progressive LT model, in that the probability of a node v being active at time t in the non-progressive LT model is exactly the probability of v in state 1 at time t in the voter model, if we set the states of all seed nodes in the non-progressive LT model to be in state 1 in the voter model.

Even-Dar and Shapira [2007] investigate the influence diffusion based on the voter model, and show some results related to influence maximization. In particular, they show that selecting k nodes with the largest degrees and setting them to state 1 is the best strategy in this model to maximize the probability of nodes in state 1 in the steady state, which maps to high-degree heuristics often used in practice. Pathak et al. [2010] propose a generalized model allowing multiple cascades and a background state at every node. Li et al. [2013] extend the voter model to signed networks representing both friend and foe relationships among individuals, and derive analytical results on short-term and long-term dynamics of the model, and show how to apply them to influence maximization. Interested readers can look into these and other related studies for more details on the application of voter model to influence diffusion dynamics.

2.2.3   MARKOV RANDOM FIELD MODEL

A *Markov Random Field (MRF)* is a set of random variables the dependency of which is described by an undirected graph [Kindermann and Snell, 1980]. In a Markov random field, each random variable X_v corresponds to a node v in the undirected graph G (and thus we use random variables and nodes interchangeably in this context). If two subsets of random variables A and B are separated by another set of random variables S in graph G, then A and B are conditionally independent given set S. Domingos and Richardson were the first to apply Markov random fields to model social influence and study the influence maximization problem in their models [Domingos and Richardson, 2001, Richardson and Domingos, 2002]. Strictly speaking, a Markov random field model describes the correlation among activation events of the neighbors and does not explicitly model the dynamic of influence diffusion in a network. We still include a brief introduction of this model, since [Domingos and Richardson, 2001, Richardson and Domingos, 2002]) use the Markov random field model to introduce the important influence maximization problem, which is the focus of Chapter 3.

Let $G = (V, E)$ be an undirected social graph. Each node v in the graph has an associated binary variable X_v, with value 1 indicating that v buys a product, or in general, is activated, and value 0 indicating otherwise. Let $N(v)$ denote the set of neighbors of v in the undirected graph G. Let $\mathbf{N}_v = \{X_u \mid u \in N(v)\}$. Based on the property of Markov random fields, X_v depends on $\mathbf{N}_v$ but is conditionally independent of non-neighbors' variables conditioned on $\mathbf{N}_v$. Let S_0 be the seed set, which means for all $v \in S_0$, $X_v = 1$ with probability 1. For every non-seed $v \in V \setminus S_0$, we need to compute its probability of activation $\Pr(X_v = 1 \mid \{X_v = 1\}_{v \in S_0})$, in short $\Pr(X_v \mid S_0)$.[3] Let $\bar{\mathbf{N}}_v = \mathbf{N}_v \setminus \{X_u \mid u \in S_0\}$. let $C(\bar{\mathbf{N}}_v)$ be all possible configurations of states of nodes in $\bar{\mathbf{N}}_v$, and $\tilde{\mathbf{N}}_v \in C(\bar{\mathbf{N}}_v)$ be one of the possible configurations. Then we have

$$
\begin{aligned}
\Pr(X_v \mid S_0) &= \sum_{\tilde{\mathbf{N}}_v \in C(\bar{\mathbf{N}}_v)} \Pr(X_v, \tilde{\mathbf{N}}_v \mid S_0) \\
&= \sum_{\tilde{\mathbf{N}}_v \in C(\bar{\mathbf{N}}_v)} \Pr(X_v \mid \tilde{\mathbf{N}}_v, S_0) \Pr(\tilde{\mathbf{N}}_v \mid S_0).
\end{aligned}
\tag{2.15}
$$

As suggested by Domingos and Richardson [2001], we approximate $\Pr(\tilde{\mathbf{N}}_v \mid S_0)$ by its maximum entropy estimate given the marginals $\Pr(X_u \mid S_0)$ for $u \in N(v) \setminus S_0$. Then Equation (2.15) is approximated by

$$
\Pr(X_v \mid S_0) = \sum_{\tilde{\mathbf{N}}_v \in C(\bar{\mathbf{N}}_v)} \Pr(X_v \mid \tilde{\mathbf{N}}_v, S_0) \prod_{u \in N(v) \setminus S_0} \Pr(X_u \mid S_0).
\tag{2.16}
$$

Equation (2.16) expresses the activation probability of node v, $\Pr(X_v \mid S_0)$, in terms of the activation probabilities of non-seed neighbors of v, $\Pr(X_u \mid S_0)$ for $u \in N(v) \setminus S_0$. Therefore, iterative computation can be applied using Equation (2.16) with appropriate chosen initial assignment. The summation in Equation (2.16) has number of terms exponential in the size of non-seed neighbors of v. Domingos and Richardson [2001] propose to use some standard method such as Gibbs sampling [German and German, 1984] to reduce the computation cost, for general coefficients $\Pr(X_v \mid \tilde{\mathbf{N}}_v, S_0)$.

The coefficient $\Pr(X_v \mid \tilde{\mathbf{N}}_v, S_0)$ is the activation probability of v when the states of v's neighbors are all fixed. This can be determined depending on the model of choice. For example, Richardson and Domingos [2002] uses a simple linear function $\Pr(X_v \mid \tilde{\mathbf{N}}_v, S_0) = \sum_{u \in N(v), \tilde{\mathbf{N}}_v(u)=1 \text{ or } u \in S_0} w(u, v)$, where $w(u, v)$ is a numerical weight with $w(u, v) \geq 0$ and $\sum_{u \in N(v)} w(u, v) = 1$. One can see that this matches with the linear threshold model in terms of the local activation probability. With this linear function, one can easily verify that summing

---

[3]For simplicity of exposition, we simplify the set of marketing action variables $\mathbf{M}$ in [Domingos and Richardson, 2001, Richardson and Domingos, 2002] to the deterministic activation of seed set S_0, and ignore the set of product feature variables $\mathbf{Y}$.

through all possible configurations is not necessary, and Equation (2.16) can be simplified to

$$\Pr(X_v \mid S_0) = \sum_{u \in N(v)} w(u, v) \Pr(X_u \mid S_0). \tag{2.17}$$

We may also try another function $\Pr(X_v \mid \tilde{N}_v, S_0) = 1 - \prod_{u \in N(v), \tilde{N}_v(u)=1 \text{ or } u \in S_0} (1 - p(u, v))$, where $p(u, v)$'s are parameters in the range $[0, 1]$, which matches to the independent cascade model. Again, with the above function, Equation (2.16) can be simplified to

$$\Pr(X_v \mid S_0) = 1 - \prod_{u \in N(v)} (1 - p(u, v) \Pr(X_u \mid S_0)). \tag{2.18}$$

Note that even if the formulation of $\Pr(X_v \mid \tilde{N}_v, S_0)$ may be very close to the linear threshold or independent cascade models as discussed above, the main recursive formulation in Equations (2.17) and (2.18) depart from the LT and IC models. Intuitively, the formulation of Equations (2.17) and (2.18) allow two neighbors u and v to mutually contribute to each other's activation probabilities when iteratively computing them, but this is not allowed in IC or LT model: either u activates v or v activates u, and their activation probabilities cannot be recursively depending on each other.

2.2.4   PERCOLATION THEORY

Percolation theory studies graphs (directed or undirected, including infinite graphs) where (directed) edges or nodes can be independently open or closed with certain probabilities [Bollobás and Riordan, 2006]. In the percolation context, edges or arcs are also referred to as bonds and nodes are referred as sites, and thus *bond percolation* studies graphs with edges or arcs being either open or closed independently while *site percolation* studies graphs with nodes being either open or closed independently. Typically, the questions that percolation theory addresses include (a) in a d-dimensional grid with n nodes on each side and each edge being open with probability p, what is the probability that an open path exists between two opposite faces of the grid? or (b) in an infinite d-dimensional grid where each edge is open with probability p, what is the critical probability p such that with non-zero probability an infinite number of nodes are connected with a given node by open paths?

Bond percolation is related to the independent cascade model, in particular, the equivalent live-arc graph model with independent arc selection. A live (resp. blocked) arc in the live-arc graph corresponds to an open (resp. closed) arc in bond percolation. Thus influence diffusion from the seed set can be viewed as bond percolation from the seed set. However, the questions we would like to answer in influence diffusion are often different from the questions studied in percolation theory. For example, in the influence diffusion context, we would like to ask what is the expected number of active nodes given a seed set, or what is the best seed set of some size k that generates the largest influence spread in the network. These questions are of computation nature, and is not the central concern in percolation theory. Nevertheless, techniques and results in percolation theory may be useful to study certain aspects of the live-arc graph model and thus the IC model.

CHAPTER 3

Influence Maximization

One strong motivation for studying information and influence diffusion models and mechanisms is *viral marketing*, as introduced in Chapter 1. That is, a company may want to promote a new product or innovation through word-of-mouth effects in social networks. A cost-effective way to do it could be to target influencers in the network, investing resources in getting them to adopt the product, for instance by giving them product samples for free or at a deeply discounted price. The hope is that these influencers will be able to drive other people in the network to adopt the product, generating a potentially large cascade in the network.

To achieve the goal of a viral marketing campaign, it is thus important to accomplish two tasks well: (a) to model in detail the influence diffusion process in the network, including learning the models' parameters; and (b) to design an efficient way of identifying which nodes to target in the network under the learned diffusion models. In this chapter, we focus on the second task, and defer the discussion of the first task to Chapter 5.

Influence maximization as an algorithmic technique for viral marketing was first proposed by Domingos and Richardson [2001], within a probabilistic framework based on Markov random fields (see Section 2.2.3). Kempe et al. [2003] were the first to formulate influence maximization as a discrete stochastic optimization problem; the content of this chapter follows their approach.

As discussed in Chapter 1, while viral marketing is an important application of influence maximization, we would like to remark that other applications, such as expert finding, trendy topic monitoring, disease outbreak detection, etc., may also benefit from the study of influence maximization.

We can now formally define the influence maximization problem as follows:

Problem 3.1 Influence maximization *Influence maximization* is the following stochastic optimization problem: Given a social graph $G = (V, E)$, a stochastic diffusion model on G, and a budget k, find a seed set $S_0 \subseteq V$ with $|S_0| \leq k$, such that the influence spread of S_0, $\sigma(S_0)$, under the given diffusion model is maximized. That is, compute $S^* \subseteq V$ such that[1]

$$S^* = \underset{S_0 \subseteq V, |S_0| = k}{\operatorname{argmax}} \quad \sigma(S_0).$$

---

[1]Rigorously speaking, argmax returns a set of optimal seed sets, and S^* computed is one of them. We ignore this level of detail when it is obvious from the context.

One remark on the above problem definition is identifying a *set* of k nodes with the largests influence is not the same as identifying the top k nodes with the largest individual influence *each*. Intuitively, if two top influencers both have strong influence on the same set of people, both of them may be identified as top influencers, but for influence maximization, only one of them may be selected as a seed.

The above definition provides the basic formulation of the influence maximization problem, and will be the main focus of this chapter. One may easily extend it to many variants of the optimization problem, such as expressing the budget as a sum of individual costs instead of a number of nodes, or maximizing the active set within a certain time constraint instead of maximizing the size of final active set, or minimizing the seed set size while guaranteeing certain coverage of the influence spread, etc. Many of these variants have been studied in the literature, and we will discuss them in Chapter 4.

3.1 COMPLEXITY OF INFLUENCE MAXIMIZATION

For influence maximization, we focus on the two basic diffusion models introduced in Chapter 2, namely the independent cascade (IC) model and the linear threshold (LT) model.

Given an influence diffusion model such as the IC or LT model, there are two computational tasks. The first task, called *influence computation*, is to compute the influence spread $\sigma(S_0)$ given a seed set S_0, and the second is to find the seed set that maximizes influence spread as defined in Problem 3.1. Both problems are computationally hard.

The following theorem shows that the first task, namely influence computation, is #P-hard for both IC and LT models. The class of #P problems are counting problems associated with decision problems in NP: a problem in NP needs to answer if a problem instance has a solution (e.g., if a conjunctive-normal-form (CNF) formula has a satisfying assignment) while a #P problem needs to provide the number of solutions to the problem instance (e.g., the number of satisfying assignments to a CNF formula). A problem is #P-complete if it is in class #P and every problem in #P can be reduced to it by a polynomial time reduction. A computation problem is #P-hard if it can be reduced in polynomial time from a #P-complete problem. Note that #P-hardness is at least as hard as NP-hardness, since counting the number of solutions directly answers whether a solution exists.

Theorem 3.2 (Theorem 1 of [Wang et al., 2012] and Theorem 1 of [Chen et al., 2010]). *Computing the influence spread $\sigma(S_0)$ in a social graph $G = (V, E)$ with seed set S_0 is #P-hard under both IC and LT models, even when S_0 is a singleton set.*

Proof (sketch). The #P-hardness under the IC model is by a reduction from the #P-complete s-t connectedness counting problem in a directed graph [Valiant, 1979], while the #P-hardness under the LT model is by a reduction from the #P-complete simple path counting problem [Valiant, 1979]. See [Wang et al., 2012] and [Chen et al., 2010] for a complete reduction. □

The above theorem shows the hardness of influence computation due to the particular model aspects in the IC and LT models. It also implies the #P-hardness of the influence maximization problem.

Corollary 3.3   *The influence maximization problem is #P-hard under both IC and LT models, even for $k = 1$.*

Proof. We reduce the influence computation task to the influence maximization task. Given a social graph $G = (V, E)$ with $|V| = n$, suppose we want to compute the influence spread of a node $s \in V$, and we can use an influence maximization oracle to solve this problem. From graph G, we construct a new graph G'' in the following way (see Figure 3.1). First, we construct a graph G' by adding a node s' together with $n - 1$ other nodes, such that there is an arc from s' to s and each of the other $n - 1$ newly added nodes. The arc weights of these n added arcs are such that s' will influence s and the other $n - 1$ nodes with probability one: in the IC model, this means that the influence probability of each such arc is 1, and in LT model, this means that the influence weight of each such arc is 1. The result of this construction is that in G', the influence spread of s' is at least $n + 1$ (s' itself, s, and the other $n - 1$ new nodes) while the influence spread of any other node is at most n. Therefore, s' is the node with the largest influence spread in G'. Moreover, the influence spread of s' in G' is exactly the influence spread of s in G plus n.

To compute the influence spread of s' in G', we add a simple stand-alone subgraph H, which is a star graph with a center node u connecting to $2n - 1$ other nodes in the graph. The influence spread of u in the star graph is simply the sum of arc weights plus 1 (for both IC and LT models), and thus it could range from 1 to $2n$, based on the arc weights to be determined shortly. When putting both G' and H together, we obtain a combined graph G''. The property of G'' is that the node with the maximum influence spread in G'' must be either s' or u, and the influence spread of s' is between $n + 1$ and $2n$.

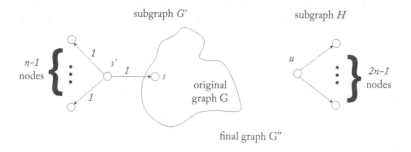

Figure 3.1: Illustration of the #P-hardness graph construction, from the original graph G to the constructed graph G''.

We then feed the graph G'' to the influence maximization oracle with $k = 1$. The oracle would return either s' or u, from which we know which of s' or u has larger influence spread. Then we can use the method of binary search: by adjusting the arc weights of star subgraph H, we can gradually obtain more and more accurate estimate of influence spread of s' in G'', and thus the influence spread of s in G. Suppose the influence weights on arcs of G takes at most ℓ bits, then it is easy to see that the influence spread granularity is at most $1/2^{n\ell}$. Thus, there are at most $n2^{n\ell}$ possibilities for the influence spread of s in G, and we need $O(n\ell)$ binary searches to find the exact value of the influence spread, which is polynomial to the input size. This means that given an influence maximization oracle for $k = 1$, we can solve the influence computation task for one seed, but since by Theorem 3.2 the latter problem is #P-hard, we know that influence maximization problem with $k = 1$ is also #P-hard. □

The hardness of influence maximization given in Corollary 3.3 relies on the hardness of influence computation. In fact, due to the combinatorial nature of finding a set of k seeds when k is an input instead of being a constant, influence maximization under IC or LT models also contains NP-complete problems as special cases, making it NP-hard without relying on the counting hardness of influence computation, as shown below.

Theorem 3.4 (Theorems 2.4 and 2.7 in [Kempe et al., 2003]). *Influence maximization problems under both IC and LT models contain NP-complete problems as special cases, and thus are NP-hard. Moreover, influence maximization under the IC model is NP-hard even if the influence computation can be done in polynomial time.*

Proof (sketch). Influence maximization under the IC model contains the NP-complete set cover problem as a special case, while influence maximization under the LT model contains the NP-complete vertex cover problem as a special case, therefore both are NP-hard (see the proofs of Theorem 2.4 and 2.7 of [Kempe et al., 2003]). Moreover, for influence maximization under the IC model, its set cover special case is a bipartite graph with arcs from one partition to the other partition, with influence probabilities as 1 on all arcs. In such special cases, influence computation given any seed set is trivial by computing the size of the reachable set of nodes from the seed set, so influence computation can be done in polynomial time. □

3.2 GREEDY APPROACH TO INFLUENCE MAXIMIZATION

The previous section shows that influence maximization problem is hard, and the hardness comes from two sources. One is the combinatorial nature of the problem, and the other is the hardness of influence computation even for one seed node. In this section, we introduce a greedy approach to partly overcome the combinatorial source of hardness, and use Monte Carlo simulations to overcome the influence computation source of hardness.

Algorithm 1 Greedy(k, f): general greedy algorithm.

Input: k: size of returned set; f: monotone and submodular set function
Output: selected subset

1: initialize $S \leftarrow \emptyset$
2: **for** $i = 1$ to k **do**
3:      $u \leftarrow \text{argmax}_{w \in V \setminus S}(f(S \cup \{w\}) - f(S))$
4:      $S \leftarrow S \cup \{u\}$
5: **end for**
6: **return** S

3.2.1   GREEDY ALGORITHM FOR INFLUENCE MAXIMIZATION

The greedy approach relies on the important properties of the influence spread function $\sigma(\cdot)$ we described on Section 2.1.3, namely its submodularity and monotonicity, as given by Theorem 2.13. Note that the greedy approach actually works for any diffusion models in which the influence spread function satisfies submodularity and monotonicity, such as the general threshold model with submodular threshold functions (Theorems 2.18 and 2.20). For simplicity, we focus our attention on the greedy approach for IC and LT models.

The greedy algorithm, as depicted in Algorithm 1, is a natural approach for set selection for any set function f. In each round i, one element u is added into the candidate set S, such that u provides the largest marginal contribution to function f with respect to set S (line 3). This selection process is repeated until k elements are selected into the candidate set.[2]

The greedy algorithm may not perform well in general, but when set function f is monotone and submodular, it provides an approximation guarantee, as shown by the following classic theorem. Since this is a crucial theorem for our algorithm design, we reproduce the proof below.

Theorem 3.5   [Nemhauser et al., 1978].   *Let $S^* = \text{argmax}_{|S| \leq k} f(S)$ be the set maximizing $f(S)$ among all sets with size at most k. If set function f is monotone and submodular and $f(\emptyset) = 0$, then for the set S^g computed by* Greedy(k, f) *of Algorithm 1, we have*

$$f(S^g) \geq \left(1 - \frac{1}{e}\right) f(S^*),$$

where e is the base of natural logarithm.

Proof. Let $S^* = \{s_1^*, s_2^*, \ldots, s_k^*\}$. Let the algorithm Greedy(k, f) select elements $s_1, s_2, \ldots, s_k$ in this order, such that $S^g = \{s_1, s_2, \ldots, s_k\}$. Let $S_i^* = \{s_1^*, \ldots, s_i^*\}$ and $S_i^g = \{s_1, \ldots, s_i\}$ for

---

[2]Technically, if the largest marginal gain determined in line 3 is zero, then we can simply stop and do not need to complete k iterations. We ignore this detail in later greedy-based algorithms.

$i = 1, \ldots, k$, and $S_0^* = S_0^g = \emptyset$. Then for every $i = 0, 1, \ldots, k - 1$, we have

$$
\begin{aligned}
f(S^*) &\le f(S_i^g \cup S^*) && \{\text{by the monotonicity of } f\} \\
&= f(S_i^g \cup S_{k-1}^* \cup \{s_k^*\}) \\
&\le f(S_i^g \cup \{s_k^*\}) - f(S_i^g) + f(S_i^g \cup S_{k-1}^*) && \{\text{by the submodularity of } f\} \\
&\le f(S_{i+1}^g) - f(S_i^g) + f(S_i^g \cup S_{k-1}^*) && \{\text{by line 3 of Algorithm 1}\} && (3.1) \\
&\le k(f(S_{i+1}^g) - f(S_i^g)) + f(S_i^g). && \{\text{by repeating the above steps } k \text{ times}\}
\end{aligned}
$$

Rearranging the inequality, we have

$$
f(S_{i+1}^g) \ge \left(1 - \frac{1}{k}\right) f(S_i^g) + \frac{f(S^*)}{k}. \tag{3.2}
$$

Multiplying by $(1 - 1/k)^{k-i-1}$ on both sides of Inequality (3.2) and then adding up all inequalities for $i = 0, 1, \ldots, k - 1$, we obtain

$$
\begin{aligned}
f(S^g) &= f(S_k^g) \\
&\ge \sum_{i=0}^{k-1} \left(1 - \frac{1}{k}\right)^{k-i-1} \cdot \frac{f(S^*)}{k} \\
&= \left(1 - \left(1 - \frac{1}{k}\right)^k\right) f(S^*) \\
&\ge \left(1 - \frac{1}{e}\right) f(S^*).
\end{aligned}
$$

The theorem follows. □

We remark that the greedy algorithm can be extended to the case where the costs of selected element are is non-uniform and the total cost of selected elements cannot exceed a given budget. The adapted greedy algorithm can achieve an approximation ratio of $(1 - 1/\sqrt{e})$ [Krause and Guestrin, 2005], while a more involved and less efficient algorithm can achieve an approximation ratio of $1 - 1/e$ [Khuller et al., 1999, Krause and Guestrin, 2005, Sviridenko, 2004].

Applying Theorem 3.5 to the influence maximization context, since the influence spread function for both IC and LT models is monotone and submodular (Theorem 2.13), we know that using the greedy algorithm as given in Algorithm 1 with σ replacing f leads to a greedy approximation algorithm that guarantees an approximation ratio of $1 - 1/e$. However, algorithm Greedy(k, σ) requires repeated evaluations of $\sigma(S)$ (line 3), which as shown in Theorem 3.2, is #P-hard. Therefore, we need to get around the hardness of influence computation.

As proposed originally by Kempe et al. [2003], we can use Monte Carlo simulations of the diffusion process to estimate the influence spread $\sigma(S)$. Given seed set S, we can simulate the randomized diffusion process with seed set S for R times. Each time we count the number of active nodes after the diffusion ends, and then take the average of these counts over the R times.

Algorithm 2 MC-Greedy(G, k): Monte Carlo greedy algorithm for influence maximization.

Input: G: social graph including arc weights for IC or LT model; k: size of seed set
Output: selected seed set
1: initialize $S \leftarrow \emptyset$
2: **for** $i = 1$ to k **do**
3:     $u \leftarrow \text{argmax}_{w \in V \setminus S} \text{MC-Estimate}(S \cup \{w\}, G)$
4:     $S \leftarrow S \cup \{u\}$
5: **end for**
6: **return** S
7: **function** MC-Estimate(S, G)
8:     $count \leftarrow 0$
9:     **for** $j = 1$ to R **do**
10:         simulate diffusion process on graph G with seed set S
11:         $n_a \leftarrow$ the number of activate nodes after the diffusion ends
12:         $count \leftarrow count + n_a$
13:     **end for**
14:     **return** $count / R$
15: **end function**

We can increase R to get arbitrarily high accuracy in our estimate of $\sigma(S)$. Algorithm 2 presents the Monte Carlo based greedy algorithm MC-Greedy(G, k) for the influence maximization problem. The main structure of the algorithm is the same as Algorithm 1. The new addition is the function MC-Estimate(S, G), which uses Monte Carlo simulations to estimate influence spread of S in graph G.

For a value $\gamma > 0$, we say that an estimate $\hat{v}$ is a *(multiplicative) γ-error estimate of true value* v if $|\hat{v} - v| \leq \gamma v$; a set function estimate $\hat{f}$ is a *(multiplicative) γ-error estimate of set function* f if for any subset S, $\hat{f}(S)$ is a multiplicative γ-error estimate of value $f(S)$. Since Monte Carlo simulations only return an estimate of $\sigma(S)$, not the exact value, we cannot directly apply Theorem 3.5 to claim that algorithm MC-Greedy(G, k) achieves $(1 - 1/e)$-approximation of the optimal solution. However, an adjustment to Theorem 3.5 allows us to claim $(1 - 1/e - \varepsilon)$-approximation for any $\varepsilon > 0$, as shown below.

Theorem 3.6   *Let* $S^* = \text{argmax}_{|S| \leq k} f(S)$ *be the set maximizing* $f(S)$ *among all sets with size at most k, where f is monotone and submodular, and $f(\emptyset) = 0$. For any $\varepsilon > 0$, for any γ with $0 < \gamma \leq \frac{\varepsilon/k}{2 + \varepsilon/k}$, for any set function estimate $\hat{f}$ that is a multiplicative γ-error estimate of set function f, the output S^g of* Greedy($k, \hat{f}$) *guarantees*

$$f(S^g) \geq \left(1 - \frac{1}{e} - \varepsilon\right) f(S^*).$$

Proof. The proof follows the same proof structure as the proof of Theorem 3.5. The main change is at Inequality (3.1), where we can no longer claim $f(S_i^g \cup \{s_k^*\}) \leq f(S_{i+1}^g)$, because the element s_{i+1} found by algorithm Greedy$(k, \hat{f})$ may not be the optimal element with respect to f. Suppose $\bar{s}_{i+1} = \text{argmax}_{w \in V \setminus S_i^g}(f(S_i^g \cup \{w\}) - f(S_i^g)) = \text{argmax}_{w \in V \setminus S_i^g} f(S_i^g \cup \{w\})$. Then we have

$$f(S_i^g \cup \{s_k^*\}) \leq f(S_i^g \cup \{\bar{s}_{i+1}\})$$

$$\leq \frac{1}{1-\gamma} \hat{f}(S_i^g \cup \{\bar{s}_{i+1}\}) \qquad \{\text{by } \gamma\text{-error estimate of } \hat{f}\}$$

$$\leq \frac{1}{1-\gamma} \hat{f}(S_i^g \cup \{s_{i+1}\}) \qquad \{\text{by algorithm Greedy}(k, \hat{f})\}$$

$$\leq \frac{1+\gamma}{1-\gamma} f(S_i^g \cup \{s_{i+1}\}). \qquad \{\text{by } \gamma\text{-error estimate of } \hat{f}\} \qquad (3.3)$$

Plugging Inequality (3.3) into Inequality (3.1), we have $f(S^*) \leq k(\frac{1+\gamma}{1-\gamma} f(S_{i+1}^g) - f(S_i^g)) + f(S_i^g)$. Rearranging it, we have

$$f(S_{i+1}^g) \geq \frac{1-\gamma}{1+\gamma}\left(\left(1 - \frac{1}{k}\right) f(S_i^g) + \frac{f(S^*)}{k}\right). \qquad (3.4)$$

Multiplying by $((1 - 1/k)(1 - \gamma)/(1 + \gamma))^{k-i-1}$ on both sides of the above inequality and then adding up all inequalities for $i = 0, 1, \ldots, k - 1$, we have

$$f(S) = f(S_k^g)$$

$$\geq \sum_{i=0}^{k-1}\left(\frac{(1 - 1/k)(1 - \gamma)}{1 + \gamma}\right)^{k-i-1} \cdot \frac{1-\gamma}{(1+\gamma)k} \cdot f(S^*)$$

$$= \frac{1 - \left(\frac{1-\gamma}{1+\gamma}\right)^k \left(1 - \frac{1}{k}\right)^k}{(1+\gamma)k/(1-\gamma) - k + 1} f(S^*)$$

$$\geq \frac{1 - \left(\frac{1-\gamma}{1+\gamma}\right)^k \cdot \frac{1}{e}}{(1+\gamma)k/(1-\gamma) - k + 1} f(S^*)$$

$$\geq \frac{1 - \frac{1}{e}}{(1+\gamma)k/(1-\gamma) - k + 1} f(S^*)$$

$$\geq \left(1 - \frac{1}{e}\right)\left(1 - \frac{(1+\gamma)k}{1-\gamma} + k\right) f(S^*) \qquad \{\text{since } \frac{1}{1+x} \geq 1 - x, \forall x \geq 0\}$$

$$\geq \left(1 - \frac{1}{e} - \left(\frac{(1+\gamma)k}{1-\gamma} - k\right)\right) f(S^*)$$

$$\geq \left(1 - \frac{1}{e} - \varepsilon\right) f(S^*). \qquad \{\text{since } \gamma \leq \frac{\varepsilon/k}{2 + \varepsilon/k}\}$$

The theorem follows. □

Note that, when ε is small, $\frac{\varepsilon/k}{2+\varepsilon/k} \approx \frac{\varepsilon}{2k}$. Intuitively, it means that the greedy algorithm has k rounds, and in each round the estimate $\hat{f}$ may either under-estimate the marginal contribution of the true seed candidate ($\bar{s}_i$ in the proof) or over-estimate the marginal contribution of another node, and thus to control the error of overall influence spread estimate within ε, the error of each individual estimate of $\hat{f}$ should be controlled within $\frac{\varepsilon}{2k}$.

Theorem 3.6 shows that we can use approximations of influence spread function to achieve influence maximization with approximation ratio arbitrarily close to $1 - 1/e$. Monte Carlo simulation as given in Algorithm 2 provides such an estimation, and we can use a large value of R in the algorithm to provide accurate estimate of influence spread.

The time complexity of the algorithm is given as $O(knRm)$ with $n = |V|$ and $m = |E|$, since the algorithm has k iterations, in each iteration we need to go through all nodes $w \in V \setminus S$ to find the one with the maximum marginal influence spread, and for each node w we need to run R simulations, and each simulation may need a traversal of all graph arcs. Theoretically, we can also provide a bound on R so that with high probability MC-Greedy(G, p, k) can achieve $(1 - 1/e - \varepsilon)$ approximation ratio, as shown below.

Theorem 3.7 *With probability $1 - 1/n$, algorithm MC-Greedy(G, k) achieves $(1 - 1/e - \varepsilon)$ approximation ratio in time $O(\varepsilon^{-2}k^3n^2m \log n)$, for both IC and LT models.*

Proof (sketch). By Theorem 3.6, to achieve $(1 - 1/e - \varepsilon)$ approximation ratio, we need to guarantee the influence spread estimate error $\gamma \leq \frac{\varepsilon/k}{2+\varepsilon/k}$. For all valid ε, it is sufficient to use $\gamma \leq \frac{\varepsilon}{3k}$. We then use the Chernoff bound to bound R. Let $X_1, X_2, \ldots, X_R$ be R independent random variables and with X_i having range $[0, 1]$. Let $\bar{X} = \sum_{i=1}^{R} X_i / R$. The Chernoff bound [Mitzenmacher and Upfal, 2005] states that, for any $0 < t < 1$:

$$\Pr(|\bar{X} - \mathbb{E}(\bar{X})| \geq t\mathbb{E}(\bar{X})) \leq 2 \exp\left(-\frac{Rt^2\mathbb{E}(\bar{X})}{3}\right). \tag{3.5}$$

For the case of Monte Carlo simulation, X_i is the number of active nodes in the i-th simulation for some seed set S divided by n, $\bar{X}$ is the return value of the Monte Carlo estimate after R simulations divided by n, $\mathbb{E}(\bar{X})$ is the true influence spread $\sigma(S)$ divided by n, and t is $\frac{\varepsilon}{3k}$.[3] When $t = \frac{\varepsilon}{3k}$, event $\{|\bar{X} - \mathbb{E}(\bar{X})| \leq t\mathbb{E}(\bar{X})\}$ implies that $n\bar{X}$ is a $\frac{\varepsilon}{3k}$-error estimate of $n\mathbb{E}(\bar{X}) = \sigma(S)$. Thus, if event $\{|\bar{X} - \mathbb{E}(\bar{X})| \leq t\mathbb{E}(\bar{X})\}$ is true for all seed sets S, then we have a $\frac{\varepsilon}{3k}$-error estimate of influence spread function $\sigma(\cdot)$, and as argued above, by Theorem 3.6 the greedy algorithm achieves $(1 - 1/e - \varepsilon)$ approximation ratio. Finally, in the greedy algorithm, we estimate influence spread for totally nk seed sets. Thus, we want the probability of exceeding the multiplicative $\frac{\varepsilon}{3k}$ error for each seed set to be at most $\frac{1}{n^2k}$, so that by union bound we can have probability of at most $1/n$ that some estimate exceeds the $\frac{\varepsilon}{3k}$ error bound. Putting all these into Inequality (3.5), we need

---

[3]Technically, X_i and $\bar{X}$ depend on S, and thus expressions $X_i(S)$ and $\bar{X}(S)$ would be more accurate.

to have R to be at the level of $\Theta(\varepsilon^{-2}k^2 n \log(n^2 k))$, which means that the algorithm would run in time $O(\varepsilon^{-2}k^3 n^2 m \log n)$.   □

The time complexity given in Theorem 3.7 shows that MC-Greedy(G, k) is a polynomial time randomized algorithm, but it could be rather slow. In fact, empirical evaluations demonstrate its inefficiency. Improving the efficiency of the greedy approach and making it scalable is the subject matter of Section 3.3.

One more remark on the approximation ratio of the greedy algorithm is that the ratio $1 - 1/e$ cannot be further improved, at least for the IC model. This is due to the fact that influence maximization in the IC model encodes max k-cover as a special case, which has been shown to be not approximable within ratio $1 - 1/e + \varepsilon$ unless P = NP (Theorem 5.3 of [Feige, 1998]).

3.2.2   EMPIRICAL EVALUATION OF MC-Greedy(G, k)

In this section, we provide a brief evaluation of the effectiveness of the Monte Carlo greedy algorithm, and compare it with a number of baseline algorithms. More comprehensive evaluations can be found in [Kempe et al., 2003] and many other papers studying scalable influence maximization, such as [Chen et al., 2009, 2010, Goyal et al., 2009, Wang et al., 2012].

In the evaluation, we use a dataset called NetHEPT, which has been used in the aforementioned papers. The location of this and several other datasets is included in Chapter 6.

NetHEPT contains the undirected collaboration network extracted from the e-print arXiv (http://www.arxiv.org/), the section on "High Energy Physics - Theory," in the time period from 1991–2003. Each node in the network represents an author, and each edge connecting two nodes indicates that the two authors have co-authored a paper. The network is an undirected network with duplicated edges connecting two nodes. The number of edges connecting two authors indicates the number of papers they have co-authored. For working with our algorithms, we remove the duplicated edges (and also re-weight edges as discussed shortly) to obtain a simple graph with no duplicate edges. Table 3.1 reports the basic statistics of the NetHEPT network.

Table 3.1: Statistics of NetHEPT dataset. Except for the row on "Number of edges with duplicated edges," all other statistics are on the graph after removing the duplicate edges

Number of nodes	15233
Number of edges with duplicated edges	58891
Number of edges	31398
Average degree	4.12
Maximal degree	64
number of connected components	1781
Largest component size	6794
Average component size	8.55

To work with the IC and LT models, we turn the undirected graph into a directed graph where each edge is replaced with two arcs pointing in the opposite directions. Then for each arc, we assign its IC or LT model weight with the following simple synthetic settings, which are used by Kempe et al. [2003] and other follow-up studies.

- IC-UP[0.01]: IC model with uniform arc influence probabilities $p = 0.01$, that is, all arcs have the same influence probability of 0.01. Note that, this is for the graph with duplicated arcs. If two nodes u and v have $c(u, v)$ number of duplicated edges between them in the undirected graph, then the arc influence probability $p(u, v) = p(v, u) = 1 - (1 - p)^{c(u,v)}$ in the graph after removing duplicated arcs.

- IC-WC: IC model with weighted cascade probabilities, that is, each in-coming arc of v has probability $1/d(v)$, where $d(v)$ is the in-degree of v before removing duplicated arcs. Again, if there are $c(u, v)$ arcs from u to v, we have $p(u, v) = 1 - (1 - 1/d(v))^{c(u,v)}$ in the graph with duplicated arcs removed. Note that with this setting, for any edge (u, v) in the undirected graph, $p(u, v) \neq p(v, u)$ whenever $d(u) \neq d(v)$, making the graph asymmetric in terms of arc influence probabilities.

- LT-UW: LT model with uniform arc weights, that is, each (duplicated) in-coming arc of v has weight $1/d(v)$, where $d(v)$ is the in-degree of v before removing duplicated arcs. This means each arc has equal contribution in activating v and the total weight of all incoming arcs is 1. If there are $c(u, v)$ arcs from u to v, we have $w(u, v) = c(u, v)/d(v)$ in the graph with duplicated arcs removed. Similar to the IC-WC setting, the graph is asymmetric in terms of arc influence weights with the LT-UW setting.

We compare the influence spread of the Monte Carlo greedy algorithm with two baseline heuristics. The following is the list of the algorithms we tested. Other baseline algorithms have been extensively tested in the literature ([Chen et al., 2009, 2010, Goyal et al., 2009, Kempe et al., 2003, Wang et al., 2012]).

- MC-Greedy[R]: The Monte Carlo greedy algorithm with R simulations for each estimate of the influence spread. We test the cases of $R = 200, 2{,}000, 20{,}000$ to see the effect of the number of simulations on the final influence spread of the selected seed set.

- Degree: The high-degree heuristic, in which the top k nodes with the highest degree in the graph with duplicated edges removed is returned.

- Random: The baseline algorithm of randomly select k nodes as seeds.

Given a seed set selected by any algorithm above, we run 20,000 Monte Carlo simulations of the diffusion process to obtain an accurate estimate of the influence spread of the seed set.

We use the C++ implementation provided by Chen et al. [2010], Wang et al. [2012]. The test is on a server with the Intel Xeon CPU E5530 (2.4GHz, 2 processors, 16 cores), 48GB memory, and 64-bit Windows Server 2008 R2.

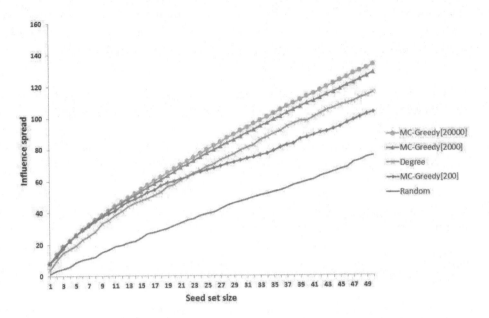

Figure 3.2: Influence spread of tested algorithms on NetHEPT with the IC-UP[0.01] model.

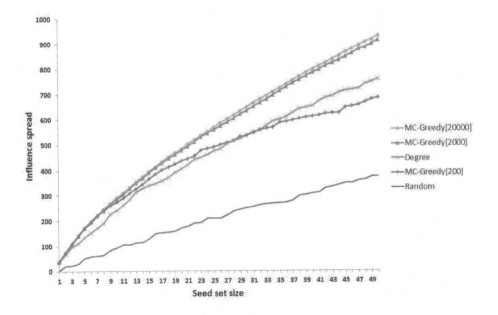

Figure 3.3: Influence spread of tested algorithms on NetHEPT with the IC-WC model.

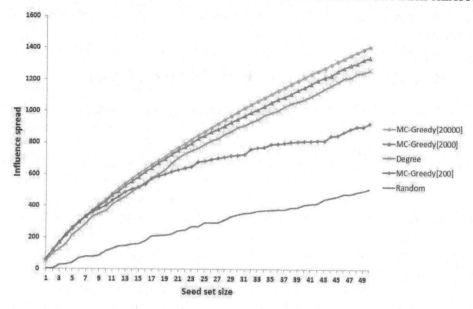

Figure 3.4: Influence spread of tested algorithms on NetHEPT with the LT-UW model.

Figures 3.2–3.4 show the results of our tests. In all figures, the x-axis is the size of the seed set ranging from 1–50, while the y-axis is the influence spread result. For ease of reading, the legends for the algorithms are ranked in the same order as the corresponding influence spread with 50 seed nodes. We obtain the following observations from these results, which are consistent across all different tests.

- MC-Greedy[20000] is always the best algorithm, consistently beating all other algorithms, with significant margins in most cases comparing against the baseline heuristics Degree and Random.

- When we reduce the number of simulations of the greedy algorithm, the influence spread drops, and when we use $R = 200$, the influence spread drops significantly and becomes worse than the high-degree heuristic. This means that accurate estimations of influence spread is crucial for maintaining the effectiveness of the greedy algorithm, and we have to maintain a large number of simulations (e.g., $R = 20,000$) to obtain accurate estimates of influence spread.

The test results above, together with extensive empirical results reported in the literature, demonstrate that the greedy algorithm with a large number of Monte Carlo simulations achieves the best influence coverage among different algorithms. In fact, no other algorithm that could out-perform the greedy algorithm significantly in terms of the influence spread has been reported in the literature.

3.3   SCALABLE INFLUENCE MAXIMIZATION

One serious drawback of the naive Monte Carlo greedy algorithm MC-Greedy(G, k) is its inefficiency. For example, we have tested the greedy algorithm without any optimization on NetHEPT using the unsatisfactory parameters of $R = 200$ and 2,000, and it takes 6.6 h and 73.6 h, respectively for the algorithm to find 50 seeds on our test server for the fastest test case of IC-UP[0.01]. This essentially makes it infeasible to run the greedy algorithm without optimization even for graphs with a moderate size of tens of thousands of nodes and arcs. Fortunately, there are a number of optimizations available to speed up the greedy algorithm and achieve scalable influence maximization, as to be discussed in this section. In fact, the results in Figures 3.2–3.4 are obtained by running the greedy algorithm with the lazy evaluation optimization to be explained in Section 3.3.1.

Taking a closer look at the algorithm MC-Greedy(G, k), we see mainly two sources of inefficiency. First, the number of influence spread evaluations is large. The algorithm takes k rounds, and in each round it needs to estimate $\sigma(S \cup \{w\})$ for every $w \in V \setminus S$, and thus totally it needs $O(nk)$ evaluations of influence spread. Second, each influence spread evaluation relies on slow Monte Carlo simulations. For each evaluation of influence spread done by function MC-Estimate(S, G), it needs R independent simulations of the diffusion process, and our test results show that R has to be a large value to maintain the effectiveness of the greedy algorithm.

Extensive research has been done to address both issues and develop more scalable greedy-based influence maximization algorithms. In this section, we describe a few key optimization techniques and briefly survey others that have appeared in the literature.

3.3.1   REDUCING THE NUMBER OF INFLUENCE SPREAD EVALUATIONS

Lazy Evaluation
For general submodular set functions, a well-known optimization technique called *lazy evaluations* can be applied to significantly reduce the number of evaluations without changing the output of the greedy algorithm. The technique was first proposed by Minoux [1978], who called it *accelerated greedy algorithm*. Leskovec et al. [2007] show empirically that lazy evaluations provide up to 700 times of speed-up for network optimization problems related to influence maximization.

As the name suggests, the idea of lazy evaluations is to avoid evaluations when they are not necessary. Given a general monotone and submodular function f, let $f(u \mid S)$ denote the marginal gain of element u given set S, that is, $f(u \mid S) = f(S \cup \{u\}) - f(S)$. Suppose in the i-th iteration of the greedy algorithm Greedy(k, f), the current selected set is S and the algorithm has evaluated $f(w \mid S)$ for some $w \in V \setminus S$. If in an earlier iteration when the set is $S' \subset S$, the algorithm has evaluated $f(x \mid S')$ for some $x \in V \setminus S$ and $f(x \mid S') \leq f(w \mid S)$, then by submod-

Algorithm 3 LazyGreedy(k, f): general greedy algorithm with lazy evaluations.

Input: k: size of returned set; f: monotone and submodular set function

Output: selected subset

1: initialize $S \leftarrow \emptyset$; priority queue $Q \leftarrow \emptyset$; *iteration* $\leftarrow 1$
2: **for** $i = 1$ to n **do**
3:     $u.mg \leftarrow f(u \mid \emptyset)$; $u.i \leftarrow 1$
4:     insert element u into Q with $u.mg$ as the key
5: **end for**
6: **while** *iteration* $\leq k$ **do**
7:     extract top (max) element u of Q
8:     **if** $u.i = iteration$ **then**
9:         $S \leftarrow S \cup \{u\}$; *iteration* $\leftarrow$ *iteration* $+ 1$;
10:    **else**
11:        $u.mg \leftarrow f(u \mid S)$; $u.i \leftarrow iteration$
12:        re-insert u into Q
13:    **end if**
14: **end while**
15: **return** S

ularity we have $f(x \mid S) \leq f(x \mid S') \leq f(w \mid S)$. This means that in the i-th iteration, x cannot be selected into the set and there is no need to evaluate $f(x \mid S)$ in this iteration.

The above idea can be implemented using a priority queue, as shown in Algorithm 3. For each element u we maintain two fields ($u.mg, u.i$): $u.mg$ is the latest computed marginal gain of u, and $u.i$ is the iteration in which this marginal gain is last updated. In the first iteration, the marginal gain of every element u, $f(u \mid \emptyset)$ is computed and stored in the priority queue with the marginal gain as the key. Then a top entry v in the priority queue (one with the largest marginal gain) is taken out of the queue. If $v.i$ is the current iteration number, meaning that its marginal gain $v.mg$ is up to date and is indeed the largest, then v is selected as the next seed. If $v.i$ is an earlier iteration, then update its marginal gain to $f(v \mid S)$ with S being the current seed set and its $v.i$ to the current iteration, and re-insert it into the priority queue.

Figure 3.5 shows the running times (top) and the numbers of influence spread evaluations (bottom) of LazyGreedy[R] to find 50 seeds, with R simulations for each influence spread evaluation under the three different diffusion settings, where R is set to 200, 2,000, and 20,000. First, we see that the number of influence spread evaluations are all significantly lower than the number without lazy evaluation, which would be around $k \times n = 50 \times 15{,}233 \approx 750K$, where $n = 15{,}233$ is the number of nodes in NetHEPT graph. This means that lazy evaluations are very effective in reducing the number of influence spread evaluations. Second, it is interesting to see that in all test cases LazyGreedy[200] actually runs slower than LazyGreedy[2000]. This is because the less accurate estimates on influence spread in LazyGreedy[200], the less effective the lazy evaluations

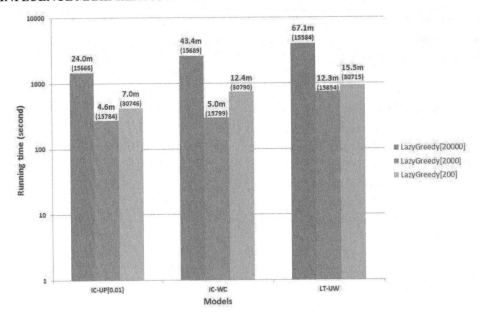

Figure 3.5: Running times and the number of influence spread evaluations of the greedy algorithms to find 50 seeds, with lazy evaluations on NetHEPT with three different diffusion settings. The upper number shows the running time in hours (h) or minutes (m). The lower number in parenthesis shows the numbers of influence spread evaluations.

which in turn causes more influence spread evaluations, and these extra evaluations also occur when the seed set size gets larger, and thus it takes much more time to complete these extra simulations. Hence, it demonstrates that reducing the number of simulations R not only hurts the performance of influence spread, but also fails to achieve savings on running time. Overall, the greedy algorithm with lazy optimizations takes dozens of minutes to find 50 seeds even on our moderate-sized test network of 15K nodes. While it is a significant improvement over the naive greedy algorithm, it is still not scalable to larger graphs or diffusion models with large cascade sizes, as reported by Chen et al. [2009, 2010], Wang et al. [2012] (see Section 3.3.2 for more discussions).

Lazy evaluation is a general technique that works for all monotone and submodular functions. Recently, Goyal et al. [2009] propose a CELF++ algorithm to further enhance the lazy evaluation technique for the influence maximization problem under IC and LT models [Goyal et al., 2009]. The idea of CELF++ is when updating the marginal gain $u.mg$ of node u for the current seed set S, it further computes and stores the marginal gain of u for set $S \cup \{prev\_best\}$, where $prev\_best$ is the best candidate seen so far in the current iteration. This will save the evaluation of the marginal gain of u in the next iteration if $prev\_best$ is indeed selected as the next seed.

The saving works because for the IC and LT models, Monte Carlo simulations for computing $\sigma(u \mid S)$ and $\sigma(u \mid S \cup \{prev\_best\})$ can be done together using one set of simulations. CELF++ gains 17% to 61% improvement in running time over lazy evaluations. Interested readers are invited to check out their study in more detail [Goyal et al., 2009].

Batch Estimate of Influence Spread

Another way to improve the efficiency of influence spread evaluations is to avoid independent Monte Carlo simulations when estimating marginal influence spread of all nodes in one iteration of the greedy algorithm. This approach relies on the equivalence between IC (or LT) model and the live-arc graph model, as shown by Theorems 2.6 and 2.11, and has been explored by Kimura et al. [2007] and Chen et al. [2009].

The idea is that in one iteration of the greedy algorithm, one could generate R live-arc graphs used for evaluations of marginal influence spread of all nodes. Due to the equivalence result shown by Theorems 2.6 and 2.11, the influence spread of a candidate node u together with the current seed set S is estimated as the average size of the reachable set from $S \cup \{u\}$. Naive computation of this average size for all $u \in V \setminus S$ still takes $O(nRm)$ time. However, more efficient batch computation of size of reachable sets are available. In particular, for the IC model, Chen et al. [2009] propose to use an efficient randomized algorithm by Cohen [1997] to estimate the size of reachable sets of all nodes in T sample runs, where T is a much smaller number than n. This reduces the influence spread computation in each iteration from $O(nRm)$ to (TRm), and thus the total time from $O(knRm)$ to $O(kTRm)$ with T a small constant much smaller than n. For the LT model, since the equivalent live-arc graph has the property that every node has in-degree at most one, the live-arc graph is a simple collection of one-directional chains and rings, and thus computing the average size of reachable sets in this case is easy and only takes $O(Rn)$ time.

However, the above batch estimate approach is incompatible with the lazy evaluation approach in general, since the latter is trying to avoid influence spread evaluations for all nodes in each iteration, while the former estimates all influence spread in a batch. It turns out, as investigated in [Chen et al., 2009], the first iteration of lazy evaluations has to go through all nodes (lines 2–5 of Algorithm 3), and it becomes a good candidate to be optimized by batch estimate approach. Chen et al. report that this mixed approach improves running time of the lazy evaluations for influence maximization in the IC models from 15% to 34% in various tests [Chen et al., 2009].

3.3.2 SPEEDING UP INFLUENCE COMPUTATION

Even with the lazy evaluations and batch estimates that provide hundreds of times of improvement to the original greedy algorithm, the resulting algorithm is still not practical for graphs having hundred of thousands of nodes [Chen et al., 2010, Wang et al., 2012] (e.g., Chen et al. [2010] reported that on a directed graph with $76K$ nodes and $509K$ arcs, it took 62 h to find

50 seeds). The main problem is due to the slow Monte Carlo simulations to estimate individual influence spread of seed sets. As shown in Figures 3.2–3.5, simply reducing the number of Monte Carlo simulations for each influence spread evaluation not only significantly reduces influence spread, but also fails to significantly reduce the running time. To deal with this problem, a number of heuristic schemes have been proposed [Chen et al., 2009, 2010, Goyal et al., 2011b, Jung et al., 2012, Wang et al., 2012]. A common theme behind these schemes is that they avoid Monte Carlo simulations by exploiting specific aspects of the graph structure and the diffusion model to significantly speed up the influence computations. We take the MIA/PMIA algorithm for the IC model [Wang et al., 2012] and the SimPath algorithm for the LT model [Goyal et al., 2011b] as two representatives to illustrate their main optimization ideas.

Maximum Influence Arborescence (MIA) Algorithm for the IC Model

As shown by Theorem 3.2, computing influence spread in the IC model for general graphs is #P-hard. However, certain type of graph structures, such as trees, allow efficient influence spread computation. The *Maximum Influence Arborescence (MIA)* algorithm [Wang et al., 2012] is built on the idea of using an easy-to-compute graph skeleton, such as a tree, to represent influence diffusion and avoid Monte Carlo simulations.[4] To implement this idea, the MIA algorithm first restricts the graph to a tree representation in a local influence region surrounding each node v. This serves two purposes: (a) influence diffusion decays very fast, so there is no need to include remote nodes when considering the influence to or from a node v, which significantly saves computation time; and (b) it is hard to approximate global influence diffusion using a global tree structure, but locally it is relatively easy to approximate local influence diffusion of some node v through a tree structure rooted at v. MIA efficiently constructs a local tree structure and conducts efficient influence computation on local trees. Moreover, between iterations of the greedy algorithm, MIA also finds an efficient way to update marginal influence spread of every node on a tree in time linear in the size of the tree. These techniques together make the MIA algorithm very efficient. We now provide a brief explanation of the MIA algorithm, and refer the readers to the full paper [Wang et al., 2012] for more details.

Given a social graph $G = (V, E)$ with influence probabilities $p(u, v)$ on all arcs $(u, v) \in E$, the influence probability of a path P from u to v, denoted by $p(P)$ is the product of influence probabilities of all arcs in the path. The *maximum influence path MIP(u, v)* is the path with the maximum influence probability among all paths from u to v. When multiple such paths exist, the tie is broken in a predetermined and consistent way such that any sub-path in $MIP(u, v)$ from x to y is also $MIP(x, y)$. We use a threshold $\lambda \in [0, 1]$ to ignore paths with too small probabilities. A *maximum influence in-arborescence* of a node v given threshold λ, $MIIA(v, \lambda)$, is the in-arborescence built from all maximum influence paths from nodes to v that exceed the λ threshold,

---

[4]*Arborescence* is a graph-theoretic term for a tree in a directed graph where all arcs either point towards the root (in-arborescence) or away from the root (out-arborescence).

Algorithm 4 $ap(u, S, T)$: Recursive computation of activation probabilities.

Input: u: node in T; S: seed set; T: an in-arborescence
Output: activation probability of u in in-arborescence T with seed set S
1: **if** $u \in S$ **then**
2:     $ap(u) \leftarrow 1$ ▷ $ap(u)$ is a short-hand for $ap(u, S, T)$
3: **else**
4:     $ap(u) \leftarrow 1 - \prod_{w \in N^{in}(u)} (1 - ap(w) \cdot p(w, u))$
5: **end if**

---

namely [5]

$$MIIA(v, \lambda) = \cup_{u \in V, p(MIP(u,v)) \geq \lambda} MIP(u, v).$$ (3.6)

Note that if we convert $p(u, v)$ to a distance weight $\log(1/p(u, v))$ for every arc $(u, v) \in E$, then $MIP(u, v)$ is simply the shortest path from u to v under this distance weight. Therefore, for any $v \in V$, computing $MIIA(v, \lambda)$ can be done using Dijkstra's single-source shortest path algorithm with the above converted distance weights on arcs, and stopping when the distance from a node u to v is larger than $\log(1/\lambda)$.

Given any in-arborescence T and a seed set S, the *activation probability* of any node u is the probability that u is activated after the diffusion process from the seed set S, and is denoted as $ap(u, S, T)$, or $ap(u)$ when the context is clear. Computing $ap(u)$ in T can be done recursively as shown in Algorithm 4. The key recursive step in line 4 is based on the feature of the IC model: an in-neighbor w of u activates u with probability $ap(w)p(w, u)$ because w needs to be active and the activation attempt from w to u needs to be successful, and thus $\prod_{w \in N^{in}(u)} (1 - ap(w) \cdot p(w, u))$ is the probability that none of the in-neighbors of u activates u, due to the independence of these activation attempts. The computation of $ap(u)$ for all u in T using Algorithm 4 can be done by a single traversal of T starting from the leaves of T.

The in-arborescence $MIIA(v, \lambda)$ forms the *local influence region* of v. That is, we approximate the influence diffusion from a seed set S to v in the original graph G by assuming influence only diffuses through tree branches of $MIIA(v, \lambda)$ to reach v. This is a heuristic that does not provide theoretical guarantee, but by choosing maximum influence paths, it tries to approximate the influence diffusion in G, and extensive empirical evaluations in [Wang et al., 2012] and other related studies have shown this heuristic to be very effective.

Based on this heuristic, the influence spread $\sigma(S)$ is approximated by $\sum_{v \in V} ap(v, S, MIIA(v, \lambda))$. It turns out that when applying it to the greedy algorithm, we never need to compute such explicit summation over all nodes in the graph. This is due to the sequential seed addition in the greedy algorithm, as explained next. Let $InfSet(u)$ denote the

---

[5]Equation (3.6) is a simplified representation meaning that the set of vertices of $MIIA(v, \lambda)$ is the union of the sets of vertices in qualified $MIP(u, v)$'s and the set of arcs of $MIIA(v, \lambda)$ is the union of the sets of arcs in qualified $MIP(u, v)$'s.

Algorithm 5 Update(S, u): Update marginal influence spread of nodes after u is added into the seed set S.

Input: S: current seed set; u: new seed added to the seed set.

Output: updated values of $IncInf(w)$'s and $IncInf(w, v)$'s, for all $v \in InfSet(u) \setminus S$ and $w \in MIIA(v, \lambda) \setminus (S \cup \{u\})$.

1: **for** $v \in InfSet(u) \setminus S$, $w \in MIIA(v, \lambda) \setminus S$ **do**
2:     $IncInf(w) \leftarrow IncInf(w) - IncInf(w, v)$ ▷ subtract current marginal influence
3: **end for**
4: **for** $v \in InfSet(u) \setminus (S \cup \{u\})$, $w \in MIIA(v, \lambda) \setminus (S \cup \{u\})$ **do**
5:     $IncInf(w, v) \leftarrow ap(v, S \cup \{u, w\}, MIIA(v, \lambda)) - ap(v, S \cup \{u\}, MIIA(v, \lambda))$
6:     $IncInf(w) \leftarrow IncInf(w) + IncInf(w, v)$ ▷ add new marginal influence
7: **end for**

---

set of nodes whose in-arborescences contain u, i.e. $InfSet(u) = \{v \mid u \in MIIA(v, \lambda)\}$.[6] Let S be the current seed set. Suppose that the marginal influence spread $\sigma(w \mid S)$ for all $w \in V \setminus S$ has been computed and stored. When the next seed u is selected and added into S, only nodes in $InfSet(u)$ change their activation probabilities, and thus only those nodes $w \in MIIA(v, \lambda)$ with $v \in InfSet(u)$, i.e., those nodes sharing at least one in-arborescence with u need to update their marginal influence spread. This greatly reduces the number of updates in each iteration of the greedy algorithm.

Algorithm 5 shows the procedure to update marginal influence spread of nodes after a new seed u is added into the current seed set S. Let $IncInf(w)$ be the variable storing the marginal influence spread of w, and $IncInf(w, v)$ be the variable storing the marginal contribution of w towards v's activation probability. The procedure first subtracts the current marginal influence of w on v (before adding u as the seed) from the marginal influence of w, for all $v \in InfSet(u) \setminus S$, and all $w \in MIIA(v, \lambda) \setminus S$ (lines 1–3). Then, for each of such v and w, we recompute the new marginal influence from w to v by Algorithm 4 (line 5) and add it back to $IncInf(w)$. The reason we break the subtractions and additions into two separate for-loops is for convenience when we introduce our last optimization shortly after. Algorithm 5 shows that updates are limited to nodes sharing in-arborescences with the new seed, and the update computation (line 5) is efficient, which provides significant gain in efficiency of the greedy algorithm.

With the update procedure, the main structure of the MIA algorithm is given in Algorithm 6. In lines 2–8 $MIIA(v, \lambda)$'s for all $v \in V$ are constructed via the Dijkstra's shortest path algorithm, and during the construction variables $IncInf(w, v)$'s and $IncInf(w)$ are also properly initialized. Then in the main loop (lines 9–13) the node u with the largest marginal influence

---

[6]Notation $u \in MIIA(v, \lambda)$ is a short-hand for $u \in V(MIIA(v, \lambda))$, where $V(G)$ is the set of vertices of graph G. In [Wang et al., 2012], the out-arborescence rooted at v, $MIOA(v, \lambda)$ is used instead of $InfSet(u)$, which contains all $MIP(v, u)$'s with probability at least λ. We remark that the tree structure of $MIOA(v, \lambda)$ is not essential, and only the set $InfSet(u) = V(MIOA(v, \lambda))$ is needed for the MIA algorithm.

Algorithm 6 MIA(G, k, λ): Main structure of the MIA algorithm.

Input: G: social graph with influence probabilities on arcs; k: size of seed set.

Output: selected seed set

1: Initialize $S \leftarrow \emptyset$; $IncInf(w) \leftarrow 0$ for all $w \in V$
2: **for** $v \in V$ **do**
3:     compute $MIIA(v, \lambda)$ and $InfSet(v)$;   ▷ via Dijkstra's shortest path algorithm
4:     **for** $w \in MIIA(v, \lambda)$ **do**   ▷ this for-loop is done during $MIIA(v, \lambda)$ computation
5:         $IncInf(w, v) \leftarrow p(MIP(w, v))$ ▷ since w is the only seed
6:         $IncInf(w) \leftarrow IncInf(w) + IncInf(w, v)$
7:     **end for**
8: **end for**
9: **for** $i = 1$ to k **do**
10:     $u \leftarrow \text{argmax}_{v \in V \setminus S} IncInf(v)$
11:     Update(S, u)
12:     $S \leftarrow S \cup \{u\}$
13: **end for**
14: **return** S

spread is selected in each iteration, marginal influence spread of nodes are updated by the update procedure Update(S, u), and u is added into seed set S, as in the standard greedy algorithm.

The MIA algorithm described so far is already efficient, but it still allows a further optimization. In the second for-loop of Update(S, u) in Algorithm 5, for each in-arborescence $MIIA(v, \lambda)$, the current algorithm needs to go through all nodes w in this in-arborescence, and for each w the computation of $IncInf(w, v)$ (line 5) needs a couple of traversals of $MIIA(v, \lambda)$ again, and thus it takes $O(|MIIA(v, \lambda)|^2)$ time to complete the update in $MIIA(v, \lambda)$, where $|MIIA(v, \lambda)|$ is the number of arcs in $MIIA(v, \lambda)$. This update can be improved to linear time $O(|MIIA(v, \lambda)|)$ by exploiting a linear relationship between activation probabilities, as described below.

From line 4 of Algorithm 4, it is not difficult to derive a linear relationship between $ap(w)$ and $ap(v)$, the activation probabilities of w and v respectively, as $ap(v) = \alpha(v, w)ap(w) + \beta(v, w)$, when activating probabilities of other nodes are fixed. The important feature is that linear coefficients $\alpha(v, w)$'s for all $w \in MIIA(v, \lambda)$ can be computed recursively, as shown in Algorithm 7. It is easy to see that the recursive computation in Algorithm 7 can be implemented by one traversal of $MIIA(v, \lambda)$ starting from the root v, so that all $\alpha(v, w)$'s are computed.

Once the $\alpha(v, w)$ is computed, the incremental influence of w on v, $IncInf(w, v)$, can be computed as $\alpha(v, w)(1 - ap(w))$, where $ap(w)$ is the current activation probability of w. Hence, the update procedure in Algorithm 5 can be improved to a new procedure as given in Algorithm 8. Therefore, the update of marginal influence spread for all nodes in $MIIA(v, \lambda)$ can be done by one traversal of $MIIA(v, \lambda)$ to compute $ap(w)$'s, another traversal of $MIIA(v, \lambda)$ to compute $\alpha(w, v)$'s,

---

Algorithm 7 Compute $\alpha(v, w)$.

Input: $MIIA(v, \lambda)$: in-arborescence rooted at v; S: seed set; $ap(w, S, MIIA(v, \lambda))$: activation probability of w, for all w in $MIIA(v, \lambda)$

Output: $\alpha(v, w)$: linear coefficient, for all w in $MIIA(v, \lambda)$

1: **if** $w = v$ **then**
2:      $\alpha(v, w) \leftarrow 1$
3: **else**
4:      set x to be the out-neighbor of w in $MIIA(v, \lambda)$
5:      **if** $x \in S$ **then**
6:          $\alpha(v, w) \leftarrow 0$ ▷ w's influence to v is blocked by seed x
7:      **else**
8:          $\alpha(v, w) \leftarrow \alpha(v, x) \cdot p(w, x) \cdot \Pi_{u' \in N^{in}(x) \setminus \{w\}}(1 - ap(u') \cdot p(u', x))$
9:      **end if**
10: **end if**

Algorithm 8 Update$'(S, u)$: New update procedure for updating the marginal influence spread of nodes after u is added into the seed set S.

Input: S: current seed set; u: new seed added to the seed set.

Output: updated values of $IncInf(w)$'s and $IncInf(w, v)$'s, for all $v \in InfSet(u) \setminus S$ and $w \in MIIA(v, \lambda) \setminus (S \cup \{u\})$.

1: **for** $v \in InfSet(u) \setminus S, w \in MIIA(v, \lambda) \setminus S$ **do**
2:      $IncInf(w) \leftarrow IncInf(w) - IncInf(w, v)$ ▷ subtract current marginal influence
3: **end for**
4: **for** $v \in InfSet(u) \setminus (S \cup \{u\})$ **do**
5:      compute $ap(w, S \cup \{u\}, MIIA(v, \lambda))$ for all $w \in MIIA(v, \lambda)$ ▷ via Algorithm 4
6:      compute $\alpha(v, w)$ with seed set $S \cup \{u\}$, for all $w \in MIIA(v, \lambda)$ ▷ via Algorithm 7
7:      **for** $w \in MIIA(v, \lambda) \setminus (S \cup \{u\})$ **do**
8:          $IncInf(w, v) \leftarrow \alpha(v, w)(1 - ap(w, S \cup \{u\}, MIIA(v, \lambda)))$
9:          $IncInf(w) \leftarrow IncInf(w) + IncInf(w, v)$ ▷ add new marginal influence
10:      **end for**
11: **end for**

---

and then apply formula $\alpha(w, v)(1 - ap(w))$, making the entire updates for nodes in $MIIA(v, \lambda)$ in time $O(|MIIA(v, \lambda)|)$.

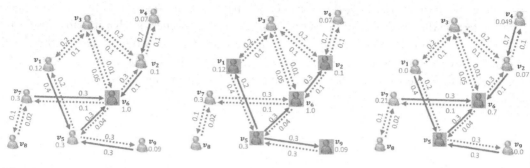

(a) $MIIA(v_6, 0.05)$, and $IncInf(w, v_6)$ for all $w \in MIIA(v_6, 0.05)$.

(b) The set of gray nodes is $InfSet(v_5) \setminus \{v_5\}$.

(c) Updated $IncInf(w, v_6)$ for all $w \in MIIA(v_6, 0.05)$, after v_5 is selected as a seed.

Figure 3.6: An example of computation of MIA algorithm. The blue number under a node w is $IncInf(w, v_6)$.

The main MIA computation structure of Algorithm 6 together with the new update procedure of Algorithm 8 gives the complete MIA algorithm, originally given by Wang et al. [2012]. We now provide a brief example illustrating the key steps in the MIA algorithm.

Example 3.8 Figure 3.6 shows an example of several key steps in the MIA algorithm. The network is the same example network as in Example 2.4. In this example, we choose the MIA threshold $\phi = 0.05$. Figure 3.6(a) shows the in-arborescence $MIIA(v_6, 0.05)$ rooted at node v_6 as the collection of the gray arcs in the graph. For every node w in this in-arborescence, we show its marginal influence to v_6, $IncInf(w, v_6)$, as the blue number under the node label, when there is no seed selected yet. For example, $IncInf(v_2, v_6) = 0.1$ because $p(v_2, v_6) = 0.1$ and thus if v_2 is a seed, the activation probability of v_6 is 0.1. Figure 3.6(b) shows the set $InfSet(v_5) \setminus \{v_5\}$ as those gray nodes. The in-arborescences of these nodes contain node v_5, and thus when v_5 becomes the seed, all nodes in these in-arborescences need to update their marginal influences. The collection of the red arcs in the figure actually shows the out-arborescence $MIOA(v_5, 0.05)$ rooted at v_5. Figure 3.6(c) shows that, after v_5 is selected as the first seed, we need to update the marginal influence $IncInf(w, v_6)$ for all $w \in MIIA(v_6, 0.05)$ since $v_6 \in InfSet(v_5)$ (updates in other $MIIA(v, 0.05)$ for $v \in InfSet(v_5)$ are not shown). The updated marginal influence are shown as the blue numbers under node labels. For example, $IncInf(v_2, v_6)$ is changed to 0.07, because v_2 can influence v_6 only when v_5 fails to activate v_6, and thus v_6 is activated due to v_2 with probability $(1 - 0.3) \cdot 0.1 = 0.07$. The marginal influence of v_1 and v_9 to v_6 becomes 0 because v_5 blocks their influence path to v_6 in $MIIA(v_6, 0.05)$.

Wang et al. [2012] further improve MIA to obtain a prefix-excluding MIA (PMIA) algorithm. One issue in the MIA algorithm is that one seed u may block the influence of another seed

u' in the in-arborescence $MIIA(v, \lambda)$ if u is on the path from u' to root v in the in-arborescence. It is preferable that seeds do not block one another in arborescences so that it maps closer to diffusions in the original graph. To keep the in-arborescence structure while addressing the blocking issue, PMIA recomputes the in-arborescence after adding a seed so that existing seeds are not on paths from future seeds to the root (see [Wang et al., 2012] for more details).

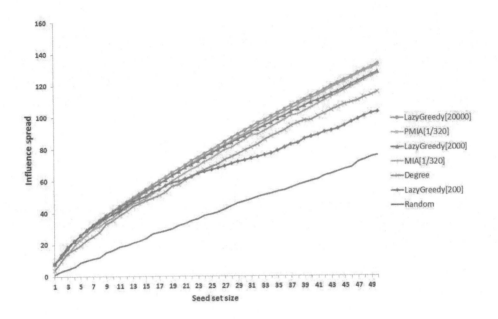

Figure 3.7: Influence spread of MIA/PMIA and other algorithms on NetHEPT with the IC-UP[0.01] model.

Figures 3.7–3.9 show test results on NetHEPT with MIA/PMIA algorithms in the two IC model diffusion settings IC-UP[0.01] and IC-WC. For MIA and PMIA, we set the threshold λ to 1/320 as suggested by Wang et al. [2012]. The influence spread results (Figures 3.7 and 3.8) show that PMIA algorithm almost matches LazyGreedy[20000] algorithm in influence spread, and it performs slightly better than MIA algorithm. Comparing the running time results (Figure 3.9), we see that both MIA and PMIA finish selecting 50 seeds in less than a second, with MIA being slightly faster than PMIA. Their running time is close to four orders of magnitude faster than LazyGreedy[20,000] and three orders of magnitude faster than LazyGreedy[2000], the fastest greedy variant in our test. Wang et al. [2012] include much more empirical results on various networks with various diffusion settings, and all results consistently show that MIA/PMIA algorithms provide three orders of magnitude improvement in running time comparing to the optimized greedy algorithm while maintaining influence spread almost the same as the greedy algorithm. For the largest dataset they tested with $655K$ nodes and 2 million edges, PMIA algorithm finishes

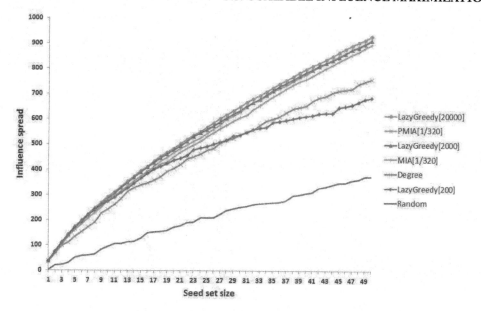

Figure 3.8: Influence spread of MIA/PMIA and other algorithms on NetHEPT with the IC-WC model.

selecting 50 seeds in 3 min in the IC-WC diffusion setting. Therefore, empirical evidence strongly supports MIA/PMIA to be a scalable heuristic algorithm for the IC model, with influence spread competitive to the greedy algorithm while running time three orders of magnitude smaller than the optimized greedy algorithm.

The idea of using local computable graph structure to approximate influence diffusion in the MIA algorithm has been applied to other settings. In particular, Chen et al. use the same approach to design the LDAG algorithm for the linear threshold model [Chen et al., 2010]. LDAG restricts influence diffusion to node v on a local directed acyclic graph (LDAG) of v, since influence spread can be accurately computed in directed acyclic graphs in the LT model. Other techniques, such as linear update of marginal influence spread for an LDAG structure, are similar to the MIA algorithm. They also show that LDAG algorithm improves running time for three orders of magnitude while almost matching the influence spread of the greedy algorithm in the LT model. Later, these ideas and techniques have also been applied to influence maximization with negative opinions [Chen et al., 2011], influence-blocking maximization [He et al., 2012], time-critical influence maximization [Chen et al., 2012], etc. In lieu of the LDAG algorithm, in the next section, we describe the SimPath algorithm, which is the state of the art heuristic for influence maximization under the LT model.

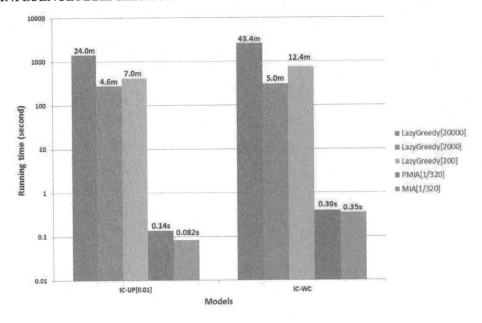

Figure 3.9: Running time of MIA/PMIA and greedy algorithms in selecting 50 seeds.

SimPath Algorithm for the LT Model

SimPath [Goyal et al., 2011b] is a scalable algorithm for influence maximization under the LT propagation model. As with IC model, influence maximization under the LT model suffers from two orthogonal levels of hardness. Finding the optimal seed set is NP-hard and computing the influence spread of a given seed set is #P-hard. SimPath is a recently developed heuristic to address this problem at scale. Specifically, it replaces expensive Monte Carlo simulations that are conventionally used for estimating the influence spread by enumerating simple paths proceeding from the given seed set and adding up their contributions to the influence spread. Since enumerating *all* simple paths is #P-hard [Valiant, 1979], one restricts attention to simple paths within a small neighborhood of the seed nodes, exploiting the fact that the probabilities of paths rapidly diminish as the path length increases. We can control the size of the neighborhood we are willing to explore and trade accuracy for performance. A second source of overhead in the traditional greedy approach to influence maximization is the number of calls to the influence spread estimation procedure. This is addressed by algorithms such as CELF [Leskovec et al., 2007] and CELF++ [Goyal et al., 2009]. However, those algorithms do not pay attention to the number of calls made in the *first iteration*. Furthermore, as the seed set size grows through iterations, the influence spread estimation procedure slows down considerably. All these issues are addressed in the SimPath algorithm. We begin our discussion with a fundamental result.

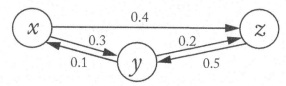

Figure 3.10: Example network used for illustration of SimPath.

As defined in Definition 2.8, in the LT model we have a directed social graph $G = (V, E)$ with arc weight $w(u, v)$ for every arc $(u, v) \in E$, and the sum of weights of all arcs pointing to a node is at most 1. For a subset $U \subseteq V$, the *induced subgraph* of G w.r.t. U is the graph $G' = (U, E')$, where $E' = \{(u, v) \in E \mid u, v \in U\}$. Given a set of seed nodes $S \subseteq U$, we let $\sigma(S)$ denote the influence spread of S in the whole graph (under the LT model) and let $\sigma^U(S)$ denote the influence spread of S in the subgraph of G induced by U. For simplicity, we denote the set difference $V \setminus S$ as $V - S$ and the set union $S \cup \{u\}$ involving a singleton set as $S + u$. Thus, $V - S + u$ denotes $(V \setminus S) \cup \{u\}$ and $\sigma^{V-S+u}(S)$ denotes the influence spread of S in the subgraph of G induced by the subset of nodes $(V \setminus S) \cup \{u\}$. Figure 3.10, taken from Goyal et al. [2011b], shows an example network with three nodes. Let $S = \{x, y\}$, then the subgraph induced by $V - S + y$ consists of nodes y and z and the two arcs between them along with their weights.

By exploiting the equivalence between the LT model and live-arc graph model, we can show that $\sigma(S)$ can be computed as the sum of the probabilities of each node in V being active given the seed set S. More precisely, let $\Upsilon_{S,v}$ denote the probability that node v will be active given the seed set S.[7] We refer to this as the *activation probability of v given seed set S*. Then we can show that

$$\sigma(S) = \sum_{v \in V} \Upsilon_{S,v}. \tag{3.7}$$

As a special case, $\Upsilon_{u,v}$ denotes the probability that v will be active if we seed a single node u, i.e., the activation probability of v given seed u. How can we compute this? Let $\mathcal{P}(u, v)$ denote the set of all simple directed paths from u to v.[8] The probability of a path $\mathsf{P} \in \mathcal{P}$, $\Pr(\mathsf{P})$, is defined as the product of weights of the arcs on the path. Each such path is an influence path from u to v. It can be shown by exploiting the connection between the LT model and live-arc graph model that the product of the arc weights on a path P is indeed the probability of all those arcs being live in the live-arc graph model and hence is the probability that the destination node is active given that the source node is chosen as a seed.

---

[7]Conceptually, $\Upsilon_{S,v}$ is similar to the activation probability $ap(v, S, T)$ defined in the previous section. However, since they are for two different diffusion models, two different algorithms, and have different input parameters, we use separate notations for them.

[8]A path is simple if and only if no nodes on the path are repeated.

Then we have

$$\Upsilon_{u,v} = \sum_{P \in \mathcal{P}(u,v)} \Pr(\mathsf{P}). \tag{3.8}$$

For example, in Figure 3.10, $\Upsilon_{x,z} = 0.3 \times 0.2 + 0.4 = 0.46$. Next, to calculate $\Upsilon_{S,v}$, we can consider the contributions to this quantity from each of the terms $\Upsilon_{u,v}$, for $u \in S$. Intuitively, we would like to sum these quantities in order to calculate $\Upsilon_{S,v}$. Unfortunately, this would be incorrect. E.g., let $S = \{x, y\}$. Let's calculate $\Upsilon_{\{x,y\},z}$, the probability of activating z, given the seed set $\{x, y\}$. This is simply $0.4 + 0.2 = 0.6$. On the other hand, $\Upsilon_{x,z} = 0.4 + 0.3 \times 0.2 = 0.46$ and $\Upsilon_{y,z} = 0.2 + 0.1 \times 0.4 = 0.24$ and $\Upsilon_{x,z} + \Upsilon_{y,z} \neq \Upsilon_{\{x,y\},z}$. The issue is that some of the influence paths from a seed node to z may pass through other seed nodes! It is incorrect to account such paths since the seed nodes through which these paths pass, may in turn influence z themselves. This can be fixed by considering only influence paths from each seed node that do not pass through any other seed nodes. In Figure 3.10, we can compute $\Upsilon_{\{x,y\},z}$ by taking the sum of $\Upsilon_{x,z}^{V-S+x}$ and $\Upsilon_{y,z}^{V-S+y}$, where $\Upsilon_{x,z}^{V-S+x}$ is the activation probability of z given seed x in the subgraph induced by $V - S + x$. Specifically, we ensure that we only consider influence paths from each seed node that do not pass through other seed nodes. Returning to our example, we have $\Upsilon_{x,z}^{V-S+x} = 0.4$ and $\Upsilon_{y,z}^{V-S+y} = 0.2$, and adding them up yields 0.6, which is exactly the value of $\Upsilon_{\{x,y\},z}$. More generally, we can show the following.

Theorem 3.9 *In the LT model, the influence spread of a seed set S is the sum of the influence spread of each node $u \in S$ on subgraphs induced by $V - S + u$. That is, $\sigma(S) = \sum_{u \in S} \sigma^{V-S+u}(u)$.*

Proof. It suffices to prove $\Upsilon_{S,v} = \sum_{u \in S} \Upsilon_{u,v}^{V-S+u}$. The theorem then follows from Equation (3.7). We prove this claim by induction on the length of influence paths. Note, $\Upsilon_{S,v} = \sum_t \Upsilon_{S,v}(t)$ where $\Upsilon_{S,v}(t)$ is the activation probability of v given seed set S, restricted to paths of length t. We next show $\Upsilon_{S,v}(t) = \sum_{u \in S} \Upsilon_{u,v}^{V-S+u}(t)$, $\forall t$.

Base Case: The path length $t = 0$. Suppose $v \notin S$. Then $\Upsilon_{S,v}(0) = 0 = \Upsilon_{u,v}^{V-S+u}(0)$, $\forall u \in S$. Suppose $v \in S$. Then $\Upsilon_{S,v}(0) = 1$ and $\Upsilon_{v,v}^{V-S+v}(0) = 1$, and $\Upsilon_{u,v}^{V-S+u}(0) = 0$, $\forall u \neq v$. The claim holds.

Induction: Assume the claim for paths of length t and consider paths of length $t + 1$ from any node in S to v. Every such path must contain a path segment of length t that ends in some in-neighbor x of v. Since these paths are simple, the path segment cannot itself pass through v. Thus, we have

$$\Upsilon_{S,v}(t + 1) = \sum_{x \in N^{in}(v)} \Upsilon_{S,x}^{V-v}(t) \times w(x, v), \tag{3.9}$$

where $N^{in}(v)$ denotes the set of in-neighbors of v. By induction hypothesis, this yields

Algorithm 9 Simpath-Spread: compute influence spread estimate using simple path enumeration.

Input: seed set S, cut-off threshold δ
Output: influence spread estimate.
1: $\sigma(S) = 0$
2: **for** each $u \in S$ **do**
3:     $\sigma(S) \leftarrow \sigma(S) + \text{BackTrack}(u, \delta, V - S + u)$
4: **end for**
5: **return** $\sigma(S)$

Algorithm 10 BackTrack: compute influence spread over simple paths starting at a node.

Input: node u, threshold δ, set of nodes W
Output: sum of influence spreads over simple paths starting at u with probability above δ.
1: $Q \leftarrow \{u\}; spd \leftarrow 1; pp \leftarrow 1; D \leftarrow null$
2: **while** $Q \neq \emptyset$ **do**
3:     $[Q, D, spd, pp] \leftarrow \text{Forward}(Q, D, spd, pp, \delta, W)$.
4:     $u \leftarrow Q.last(); Q \leftarrow Q - u; delete\ D[u]; v \leftarrow Q.last()$
5:     $pp \leftarrow pp/b_{v,u}$
6: **end while**
7: **return** spd

$$\Upsilon_{S,v}(t+1) = \sum_{x \in N^{in}(v)} \sum_{u \in S} \Upsilon_{u,x}^{V-v-S+u}(t) \times w(x,v). \tag{3.10}$$

By switching the summations, we get $\Upsilon_{S,v}(t+1) = \sum_{u \in S} \sum_{x \in N^{in}(v)} \Upsilon_{u,x}^{V-v-S+u}(t) \times w(x,v) = \sum_{u \in S} \Upsilon_{u,v}^{V-S+u}(t+1)$, which was to be shown. $\square$

The overall SimPath approach is to calculate the influence spread $\sigma(S)$ by summing up the influence spread of each of the nodes $u \in S$ in the subgraph induced by $V - S + u$, making use of the above theorem. We calculate the influence spread of a node u by enumerating simple paths from u whose probabilities are above a threshold δ. Algorithm BackTrack given in Algorithm 10 shows how this is done.

This algorithm repeatedly invokes Algorithm Forward to enumerate the next unexplored path from u that has a probability above the threshold δ and adds up the influence spread contribution from each such path, returned by Algorithm Forward, to calculate the influence spread contribution of u. Here, $D[u]$ maintains the out-neighbors of u that have not been explored so far and u is the top node of the stack Q. Once a path's contribution is added, it removes the top node u from Q as well as the set $D[u]$ and backtracks and invokes Algorithm Forward again. The algorithm is self-explanatory: obvious checks are made to ensure that the path enumerated is simple ($y \notin Q$) and is present in the subgraph being considered ($y \in W$) and follows an out-neighbor of the last node x of the path that is not yet considered ($y \notin D[x]$). Once explored, y is added to the set of explored out-neighbors of x, $D[x]$.

Algorithm 11 Forward: find next simple path with probability above threshold.

Input: queue Q, out-neighbors D, current influence spread spd, path probability pp, threshold δ, node sets W, U

Output: next simple path with probability $> \delta$.

1: $x \leftarrow Q.last()$
2: **while** $\exists y \in N^{out}(x): y \notin Q, y \notin D[x], y \in W$ **do**
3:     **if** $pp \cdot b_{x,y} < \delta$ **then**
4:         $D[x].insert(y)$
5:     **else**
6:         $Q.add(y)$
7:         $pp \leftarrow pp \cdot b_{x,y}; spd \leftarrow spd + pp$
8:         $D[x].insert(y); x \leftarrow Q.last()$
9:     **end if**
10: **end while**
11: **return** $[Q, D, spd, pp]$

So far, we have an efficient heuristic algorithm for estimating the influence spread of a given set of seed nodes. In the greedy algorithm for seed selection, optimized using lazy evaluations (Section 3.3.1), we can replace the expensive Monte Carlo simulations with Algorithm Simpath-Spread and obtain an efficient algorithm for influence maximization. We can optimize this even further.

Optimizing the first iteration.   While the greedy algorithm with lazy evaluations optimizes the number of calls made for the influence spread estimation procedure, it does nothing to the calls made in the very first iteration. In that iteration, we need to compute or estimate the influence spread of every single node in the graph, resulting in $|V|$ calls to the influence spread estimation procedure. We can optimize this by exploiting the property of the LT model, where influence spread of a node can be expressed as a linear combination of the influence spread of its out-neighbors in suitable subgraphs. More precisely, we can show the following.

Theorem 3.10   *In the LT model, the influence spread of a node linearly depends on the influence spread of its out-neighbors as follows.*

$$\sigma(v) = 1 + \sum_{u \in N^{out}(v)} w(v, u) \cdot \sigma^{V-v}(u).$$

Rather than giving the proof, for which we refer the reader to [Goyal et al., 2011b], we illustrate the intuition with an example. Consider the influence spread of node v in the graph shown in Figure 3.11. The intuition is that the influence spread of node v can be computed as the sum of influence spread of its out-neighbors x, y, z, but in computing the latter influence spreads, we should not count node v.

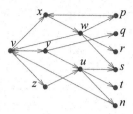

Figure 3.11: Illustrating Theorem 3.10.

How can this result help us? Consider the underlying undirected graph of G, obtained by ignoring direction of arcs and deleting duplicate edges. Let C be any vertex cover of this graph. For each node in $u \in C$, we simultaneously calculate $\sigma(u)$ and $\sigma^{V-v}(u)$, for each in-neighbor v of u in $V - C$. Then, we can compute the influence spread $\sigma(v)$ for each node in $V - C$ simply by summing up the relevant influence spreads of its out-neighbors a la Theorem 3.10. The smaller the cover C, the greater the savings. Finding the minimum vertex cover is NP-complete. We can use any of the well-known efficient approximation algorithms [Garey and Johnson, 1990, Karakostas, 2009]. However, it is important to make sure the overhead of finding a vertex cover does not overshadow the savings effected by using one. It may be practically more prudent to use an extremely fast heuristic in place of an approximation algorithm when we take all factors into account [Goyal et al., 2011b].

Optimizing subsequent iterations.   As iterations go by, the seed set size grows, up to the given budget. As a result, later iterations incur a greater number of influence spread estimation calls. More precisely, let S_i^g be the current seed set in iteration i. Then finding the next seed requires $(i + 1)$ calls to BackTrack in order to estimate the marginal gain $\sigma(S_i^g + x) - \sigma(S_i^g)$. This is repeated once for every candidate seed that is tried, until the lazy evaluation optimization succeeds in finding the next seed, say after j attempts. Thus, we rack up a total of $j(i + 1)$ influence spread estimation calls. We can optimize this by keeping a list of ℓ promising candidate seeds U from the LazyGreedy queue (Algorithm 3) and computing the marginal gain w.r.t. each of them effectively in batch. The idea is the following. We have

$$\sigma(S_i^g + x) = \sum_{u \in S_i^g + x} \sigma^{V-S_i^g-x+u}(u) \qquad (3.11)$$

$$= \sigma^{V-S_i^g}(x) + \sum_{u \in S_i^g} \sigma^{V-S_i^g-x+u}(u) \qquad (3.12)$$

$$= \sigma^{V-S_i^g}(x) + \sigma^{V-x}(S_i^g) . \qquad (3.13)$$

Notice that we can calculate $\sigma^{V-S_i^g}(x)$, $\forall x \in U$ in one shot, at the beginning of iteration $i + 1$. We can compute $\sigma^{V-x}(S_i^g)$ for each $x \in U$, by invoking BackTrack. Then we can maintain

ℓ promising seed candidates U from an iteration and update their influence spread during an invocation of Forward. All we need to do is that when computing the influence spread contribution of the current path Q, we also update the influence spread w.r.t. $V - v$, for every $v \in U - Q$. We refer the reader to [Goyal et al., 2011b] for details, where the authors show that the SimPath algorithm with all discussed optimizations incorporated, registers a significant performance improvement over LDAG [Chen et al., 2010], the previous state-of-the-art algorithm for efficient influence maximization under the LT model. In particular, based on experiments conducted on NetHEPT, last.fm, Flixster, and DBLP, they showed that SimPath achieves 1.7–8.9% improvement in the accuracy of influence spread estimation; 21.7–67.2% savings in running time; and 62.9–87.5% improvement in memory consumption, over LDAG. Here, accuracy is w.r.t. influence spread estimated using Monte Carlo simulations.

3.3.3   OTHER SCALABLE INFLUENCE MAXIMIZATION SCHEMES

Scalable influence maximization has received a lot of attention in the research community in recent years, and many other schemes have been proposed to address this problem. Wang et al. [2010] apply community detection to help influence maximization, such that influence maximization can be done mainly at local community level to speed up the computation. Jiang et al. [2011] demonstrate the effectiveness of using simulated annealing meta-heuristic to influence maximization. These approaches can be combined together with fast influence computation heuristics such as MIA, LDAG, and SimPath to achieve combined improvement effect. Jung et al. [2012] improve MIA algorithm in both time and space usage by applying belief propagation approach to enable fast global ranking of marginal influence spread, and restricting expensive influence spread computation only for the current seed set.

In a very recent paper, Borgs et al. [2012] proposes an interesting idea of reversing the influence diffusion direction and conducting reverse Monte Carlo sampling to significantly improve the theoretical running time bound on influence maximization. They prove that their algorithm only takes $O(\varepsilon^{-3}(m + n)k \log n)$ time to achieve the approximation ratio of $1 - 1/e - \varepsilon$ for influence maximization in the IC model. This bound significantly improves the theoretical running time of the simple greedy algorithm as given in Theorem 3.7, and is shown to be close to the theoretical lower bound. However, it is still pending empirical evaluation to assess its practical significance comparing to other state-of-the-art scalable algorithms for influence maximization.

CHAPTER 4

Extensions to Diffusion Modeling and Influence Maximization

In Chapter 3, we introduced the influence maximization problem and presented greedy-based algorithms for influence maximization. Extensive research has been done to study various extensions to the influence diffusion models and to the influence maximization problem. In this chapter, we explain several of such extensions in detail, while briefly surveying other extensions that have appeared in the literature.

4.1 A DATA-BASED APPROACH TO INFLUENCE MAXIMIZATION

The methodology for influence maximization that is adopted in the literature for the most part is two-fold: (i) given a social network and past action propagation traces, use one of the algorithms we will describe in Chapter 5 (e.g., [Goyal et al., 2010, Saito et al., 2008]) to learn influence probabilities associated with arcs under an *assumed* propagation model such as IC or LT; and (ii) then *simulate* possible propagations by sampling from the set of possible worlds using Monte Carlo simulations, in order to estimate the influence spread of a given seed set; using this as a basic routine, make use of the greedy algorithm for selecting a good set of seed nodes.

We notice that there may be some information loss when following this procedure, as the action propagation traces that are part of the input are *actual* diffusions that really happened. A natural question is whether one can avoid the intermediate learning and simulation phase, which is expensive, and build a model to directly predict the influence spread of any seed set based on the actual diffusions that occurred. Figure 4.1, taken from Goyal et al. [2011a], illustrates the vision behind this question.

Goyal et al. [2011a] develop a *data-based approach* (as opposed to a model-based approach) to influence maximization based on a *credit distribution* (CD) model. The intuition is that each actual propagation corresponds to an action and an influenced node distributes influence credits to its predecessors and ancestors in the action trace, i.e., those nodes that performed that action

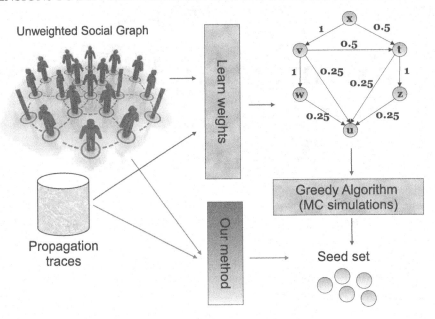

Figure 4.1: The standard influence maximization process under a model-based approach (in light blue), and a data-based approach (in magenta).

before it did.[1] The logic of credit distribution can be parameterized and configured depending on the data set.

The influence spread under any propagation model m can be couched in terms of possible worlds, which are deterministic graphs obtained from the given probabilistic graph G by making a set of probabilistic choices. For the IC model, a possible world corresponds to a live-arc graph with independent arc selection (Definition 2.5), which is decided by a set of coin tosses associated with the arcs. Each toss decides whether an arc is present or absent. The set of nodes that are reachable from the seeds are the nodes that are active in that possible world. For the LT model, we can consider the equivalent live-arc graph model with proportional arc selection (Definition 2.10): each random live-arc graph G_L selected by proportional arc selection, where every node selects at most one of its predecessors with a probability proportional to the arc weight, is a possible world. The nodes reachable from the seeds are said to be active in the possible world. Thus, for a propagation model m,

$$\sigma_m(S) = \sum_{X \in \mathbb{G}} \Pr(X) \cdot \sigma_m^X(S), \tag{4.1}$$

---

[1]We use the terms in-neighbor and predecessor interchangeably and the term ancestor to mean the transitive closure of in-neighbor.

where $\sigma_m^X(S)$ is the number of nodes reachable from S in the possible world X. Consider the Bernoulli random variable $path(S, u)$ which is 1 if there is a (directed) path from a node in S to node u and is 0 otherwise. Let $path_X(S, u)$ denote its outcome in possible world X. Then we can rewrite the influence spread as

$$\sigma_m(S) = \sum_{X \in G} \Pr(X) \sum_{u \in V} path_X(S, u) = \sum_{u \in V} \sum_{X \in G} \Pr(X) path_X(S, u). \qquad (4.2)$$

From the definition of expectation, we can rewrite this as

$$\sigma_m(S) = \sum_{u \in V} \mathbb{E}(path(S, u)) = \sum_{u \in V} \Pr(path(S, u) = 1). \qquad (4.3)$$

In other words, the influence spread is simply the sum of activation probabilities of all nodes, given the seed set. Thus, building a model for predicting the influence spread can be reduced to predicting node activation probability. A natural approach to estimating $\Pr(path(S, u) = 1)$ for given S, u is to measure the fraction of actions that node u performed for which the set of initiators was exactly S. However, given any reasonably large set of action propagation traces, for most node sets S, it would be extremely rare to find actions for which S was the exact set of initiators: i.e., each node in S performed the action before any of its in-neighbors and no other nodes satisfy this property. In other words, we are hit by extreme sparsity!

Fortunately, we can circumvent this difficulty by not estimating the node activation probability, but by directly predicting the influence spread. To do this, we ask of each node u that performed an action a, which nodes influenced u to perform this action and to what extent, i.e., we derive an *influence credit* for every ancestor of u that performed a before u. By aggregating these credits over all actions, we can estimate the net influence flow from an arbitrary set S to an arbitrary node u.

The simplest scheme for credit distribution is to give equal credit to each in-neighbor of u that performed an action before u. Precisely, let $G(a) = (V(a), E(a))$ be the projection of the network G on action a: $V(a)$ contains nodes that performed action a and $E(a)$ is the set of all arcs between them, such that $(x, y) \in E(a)$ iff $(x, y) \in E$ and x performed a before y. Let $N^{in}(u, a)$ be the set of in-neighbors of u in $G(a)$. Then the *direct credit* given by u to a node $v \in N^{in}(u, a)$ is $\gamma_{v,u}(a) = 1/|N^{in}(u, a)|$.

A more sophisticated scheme for assigning direct credits is to weigh in the following empirical observations [Goyal et al., 2010]: (i) influence decays exponentially over time and (ii) influenceability varies across users. Accordingly, we may define direct credit as

$$\gamma_{v,u}(a) = \frac{infl(u)}{|N^{in}(u, a)|} \cdot \exp\left(-\frac{t(u, a) - t(v, a)}{\tau_{v,u}}\right). \qquad (4.4)$$

Here, $\tau_{v,u}$ is the average time taken for actions to propagate from user v to user u, while $infl(u)$ denotes the user influenceability, that is, how prone the user u is to accept the influence from its social peers. Influenceability is defined as the fraction of actions that u performs under the influence of at least one of its in-neighbors, say v, i.e., u performs the action, say a, such that $t(u, a) - t(v, a) \leq \tau_{v,u}$; this is normalized by $|N^{in}(u, a)|$ to ensure that the sum of direct credits assigned to neighbors of u for action a is at most 1. Let $\mathbb{L}$ denote the action log consisting of triples of the form (u, a, t) denoting that user u performed action a at time t. Then both $infl(u)$ and $\tau_{.,u}$ can be learned from $\mathbb{L}$.

Regardless of how direct credits are assigned, since influence may propagate down multiple paths, we need to aggregate influence credits. Thus, we define the *total credit* given to node v by node u for action a as

$$\Gamma_{v,u}(a) = \sum_{w \in N^{in}(u,a)} \Gamma_{v,w}(a)\gamma_{w,u}(a). \tag{4.5}$$

The base case is $\Gamma_{u,u}(a) = 1$.

How can we calculate the influence credit for a *set* of nodes S? Clearly, if $u \in S$, $\Gamma_{S,u}(a) = 1$. If not, $\Gamma_{S,u}(a) = \sum_{w \in N^{in}(u,a)} \Gamma_{S,w}(a)\gamma_{w,u}(a)$.

Example 4.1   Consider the graph shown in Figure 4.1 as the propagation graph $G(a)$ corresponding to action a. The arcs are labeled with equally assigned direct credits $1/|N^{in}(u, a)|$, for each node u, e.g., $\Gamma_{v,u}(a) = \Gamma_{v,v}(a) \cdot \gamma_{v,u}(a) + \Gamma_{v,t}(a) \cdot \gamma_{t,u}(a) + \Gamma_{v,w}(a) \cdot \gamma_{w,u}(a) + \Gamma_{v,z}(a) \cdot \gamma_{z,u}(a) = 1 \cdot 0.25 + 0.5 \cdot 0.25 + 1 \cdot 0.25 + 0.5 \cdot 0.25 = 0.75$. Let $S = \{v, z\}$. Then, $\Gamma_{S,u}(a) = \Gamma_{S,w}(a) \cdot \gamma_{w,u}(a) + \Gamma_{S,v}(a) \cdot \gamma_{v,u}(a) + \Gamma_{S,t}(a) \cdot \gamma_{t,u}(a) + \Gamma_{S,z}(a) \cdot \gamma_{z,u}(a) = 1 \cdot 0.25 + 1 \cdot 0.25 + 0.5 \cdot 0.25 + 1 \cdot 0.25 = 0.875$.   ∎

In order to estimate the influence spread achieved by a seed set S, we need to aggregate S's influence credit across all actions in the log and over all users. For a pair of nodes v, u, define the net influence flow from v to u as $\kappa_{v,u} = 1/|\mathcal{A}_u| \sum_{a \in \mathcal{A}} \Gamma_{v,u}(a)$. It's the average credit v gets from u for actions performed by u. This generalizes straightforwardly to a set of nodes S: $\kappa_{S,u} = 1/|\mathcal{A}_u| \sum_{a \in \mathcal{A}} \Gamma_{S,u}(a)$. Notice that since the credit distribution model is not a probabilistic model, $\kappa_{S,u}$, the net influence flow from S to u that is estimated by the model, takes the place of $\Pr(path(S, u) = 1)$. Thus, the influence spread predicted by this model for a given seed set S is $\sigma_{cd}(S) = \sum_{u \in V} \kappa_{S,u}$.

Given a network and an action log, we can attempt to find a seed set with size under a given budget k that achieves the maximum influence spread as predicted by the credit distribution model. Goyal et al. [2011a] show that this problem is NP-complete but the influence spread function continues to be monotone and submodular, thus affording the $(1 - 1/e)$-approximation to the optimum in polynomial time. However, there are two major differences with the traditional approach. Firstly, there is no need for expensive Monte Carlo simulations. The influence spread predicted by the CD model can be computed exactly and efficiently. Secondly, and as a result of the above, there is no additional penalty of ε to the approximation factor unlike in the traditional approach.

Goyal et al. [2011a] develop a scalable algorithm influence maximization based on the preceding ideas. By experimenting on the Flixster and Flickr data sets, they found the following: (i) the data-based algorithm is several orders of magnitude faster than the traditional learning and simulation approaches using the IC and LT models, e.g., on a subset of 13K nodes and 192K arcs from the Flixster data set, the greedy algorithm with lazy evaluations using the IC and LT models takes 40 and 25 h, respectively, to find 50 seeds, whereas the data-based approach takes 3 min. Similarly, on a subset of 15K nodes and 1.2M arcs from the Flickr dataset, greedy with lazy evaluations for the IC model ran for 27 days without picking a single seed and for the LT model it managed to find only 17 seeds in that time. By contrast, the data-based approach found 50 seeds in 6 min; and (ii) spread estimation by the data-based approach achieves a superior accuracy compared to that estimated by both IC and LT models, and IC model in turns does worse than the LT model in the data sets tested. We refer the reader to [Goyal et al., 2011a] for further details.

4.2 COMPETITIVE INFLUENCE MODELING AND MAXIMIZATION

So far we only studied information or influence diffusion for a single product or idea in a social network, and we refer to this as *single-item* diffusion. In reality, it is often the case that many different pieces of information, ideas, products, and innovations are propagating concurrently in a social network, and we refer to these as *multi-item* diffusions. If each concurrent diffusion does not interfere with other diffusions, the models and results we have described for single-item diffusion can be directly applied to multi-item diffusions. However, concurrent diffusions may interfere with each other, competing for a scarce resource such as attention (in the case of an idea), or disposable income (in the case of a product). For example, if one has been influenced by friends and has already bought a mobile phone from a particular brand, one is less likely to buy another mobile phone in the short run, even under a strong influence from other people.

The competing nature of multi-item diffusions requires extensions to existing diffusion models, new problem formulations and new methods in algorithm design. We refer to such multi-item diffusions with competitive nature as *competitive influence diffusions* and the corresponding models as *competitive diffusion models*. A number of studies in the literature have modeled competitive influence diffusions and addressed various maximization problems under this context [Bharathi et al., 2007, Borodin et al., 2010, Budak et al., 2011, Chen et al., 2011, He et al., 2012, Kostka et al., 2008, Pathak et al., 2010, Trpevski et al., 2010].

In this section, we summarize and generalize some of the results appeared in the literature and present extensions to the IC and LT models to accommodate multi-item diffusions, define two different versions of maximization problems under competitive influence diffusions, and discuss algorithmic techniques to achieve scalable solutions to these problems. Many extensions are possible for modeling multi-item diffusions; we only discuss some variants and leave the investigation of other variants to interested readers. For convenience, in the most part of this section we only consider the diffusions of two competing items, which we conveniently refer to as the *positive opinion* and the *negative opinion*, respectively. Many results on modeling and algorithms can be easily extended to more than two competing items.

4.2.1   MODEL EXTENSIONS FOR COMPETITIVE INFLUENCE DIFFUSION

We refer to the class of models extending the independent cascade model as the *competitive independent cascade (CIC)* models, and models extending the linear threshold model as *competitive linear threshold (CLT)* models.

We first specify the class of CIC models. Consider a social graph $G = (V, E)$. Each node has three possible states: *inactive*, *positive*, and *negative*. The two latter states are referred to as *active* states. A node may change from the inactive state to an active state, which is referred to as the node being *activated*, but it does not change from an active state back to the inactive state. This property is called *progressiveness*, a property inherited by CIC and CLT models from their progressive classical counterparts (IC and LT). A node changing to the positive state is called *positively activated* and a node changing to the negative state is called *negatively activated*. A general model may allow transitions from the positive state to the negative state or viceversa, but in this section we only consider transitions from the inactive state to one of the active states (node activation), without allowing other transitions after node activation.

Let S_0^+ be the seed set for the positive opinion and S_0^- be the seed set for the negative opinion, with $S_0^+ \cap S_0^- = \emptyset$.[2] Suppose that the positive opinion propagates according to influence probability $p^+(u, v)$, and the negative opinion propagates according to influence probability $p^-(u, v)$, for every arc $(u, v) \in E$. If the positive and negative opinions propagate independently without any competition, we could simply use the IC model with parameters S_0^+ and $p^+(u, v)$'s for the positive diffusion and the IC model with parameters S_0^- and $p^-(u, v)$'s for the negative diffusion, and study them independently. The interference and competition of the two diffusions come from the model restriction that once a node is positively or negatively activated, it will not change its state any more. Therefore, a negatively (resp. positively) activated node blocks the dif-

---

[2]Requiring $S_0^+ \cap S_0^- = \emptyset$ is for the ease of presentation. If $S_0^+ \cap S_0^- \neq \emptyset$, a tie-breaking rule is needed for the seeds. An equivalent way is to view that each node v has two special shadow in-neighbors, one positive shadow v^+ and one negative shadow v^-. The shadow nodes do not have any in-neighbors themselves. The influence probability on arcs are 1 for both arcs (v^+, v) and (v^-, v). Positive seeds can only be selected among positive shadow nodes while negative seeds can only be selected among negative shadow nodes. Thus, positive and negative seeds are disjoint. The influence spread only counts the active normal nodes, excluding shadow nodes. At time 0, if a node v has both a positive shadow seed and a negative shadow seed, then a tie-breaking rule (to be discussed shortly for normal cases of concurrent activation by positive and negative seeds) is applied to determine the state of v. With this equivalent description, there is no need to treat the case of $S_0^+ \cap S_0^- \neq \emptyset$ separately and all results apply to this case as well.

fusion of the positive (resp. negative) opinion, causing the diffusion pattern of both to be different from the pattern when they propagate independently without competition.

Definition 4.2 Class of competitive independent cascade models. A *competitive independent cascade (CIC) model* contains the social graph $G = (V, E)$, the positive and negative influence probabilities $p^+(\cdot)$ and $p^-(\cdot)$ on all arcs, and the positive and negative initial seed sets S_0^+ and S_0^- with $S_0^+ \cap S_0^- = \emptyset$ as the input, and generates the positive and negative active sets S_t^+ and S_t^- for all $t \geq 1$ by the following randomized operation rule. At every time step $t \geq 1$, first set S_t^+ to be S_{t-1}^+ and S_t^- to be S_{t-1}^-; next for every inactive node $v \notin S_{t-1}^+ \cup S_{t-1}^-$, for every node $u \in N^{in}(v) \cap (S_{t-1}^+ \setminus S_{t-2}^+)$, u executes a *positive activation attempt* by flipping an independent coin with success probability $p^+(u, v)$; if successful we add u into a *positive successful attempt set* $A_t^+(v)$ for node v. Symmetrically, for every node $u \in N^{in}(v) \cap (S_{t-1}^- \setminus S_{t-2}^-)$, u executes a *negative activation attempt* by flipping an independent coin with success probability $p^-(u, v)$; if successful we add u into a *negative successful attempt set* $A_t^-(v)$ for node v; if $A_t^+(v) \neq \emptyset$ while $A_t^-(v) = \emptyset$, v is positively activated and is added into S_t^+; if $A_t^+(v) = \emptyset$ while $A_t^-(v) \neq \emptyset$, v is negatively activated and is added into S_t^-. If both $A_t^+(v)$ and $A_t^-(v)$ are nonempty, then we need to apply a *tie-breaking rule* (to be defined next) to determine whether v is positively activated or negatively activated, and then add v into S_t^+ or S_t^- accordingly.

Basically, CIC models follow the IC model in the independent activation process. A new issue that any CIC model needs to address is the *tie-breaking rule*, that is, when both positive successful attempt set $A_t^+(v)$ and negative successful attempt set $A_t^-(v)$ as defined in Definition 4.2 are nonempty, what is the final state of node v? Below, we summarize two variants of the tie-breaking rule that have appeared in the literature.

- Fixed probability tie-breaking rule TB-FP(ϕ). With a fixed probability ϕ, v becomes positive, and with probability $1 - \phi$ v becomes negative. The special cases of this rule include TB-FP(1) meaning *positive dominance* [Budak et al., 2011], TP-FP(0) meaning *negative dominance* [He et al., 2012], and $\phi = 1/2$ meaning *uniformly random selection* [Borodin et al., 2010]. Note that in purely model perspective positive dominance and negative dominance are symmetric, but when coupled with an optimization objective (e.g., maximizing positive influence spread or minimizing negative influence spread), they are no longer symmetric.

- Proportional probability tie-breaking rule TB-PP. Node v is positive with probability $\frac{|A_t^+(v)|}{|A_t^+(v)| + |A_t^-(v)|}$, and v is negative with probability $\frac{|A_t^-(v)|}{|A_t^+(v)| + |A_t^-(v)|}$. Note that this is equivalent to the model in which we randomly permute all of v's in-neighbors $N^{in}(v)$ first, and then when we need to break a tie on v, we find the node u in $A_t^+(v) \cup A_t^-(v)$ that is ordered first in the permutation order, and assign the state of u as v's state. Chen et al. [2011] propose a model that uses this tie-breaking rule.

Other options for this rule are possible. For example, Bharathi et al. [2007] introduce continuous time in node activation so that the probability of two nodes activating one node at the same time is zero, thus avoiding a explicit tie-breaking definition.

The class of competitive linear threshold (CLT) models can be similarly defined. The general idea is the same as above except positive opinion and negative opinion both diffuse via a linear threshold model with an independent set of parameters. In particular, positive diffusions have positive influence weights $w^+(u, v)$'s and negative diffusions have negative influence weights $w^-(u, v)$. A tie-breaking rule needs to be specified for the case where the influences from a node's positive and negative neighbors both pass the node's threshold in the same time step.

Definition 4.3 Class of competitive linear threshold models. A *competitive linear threshold (CLT) model* contains the social graph $G = (V, E)$, the positive and negative influence weights $w^+(\cdot)$ and $w^-(\cdot)$ on all arcs, and the positive and negative seed sets S_0^+ and S_0^- as the input, and generates the positive and negative active sets S_t^+ and S_t^- for all $t \geq 1$ by the following randomized operation rule. Initially, each node $v \in V$ selects a positive threshold θ_v^+ and a negative threshold θ_v^- independently and uniformly at random in the range $[0, 1]$, and this selection is independent of all other threshold selections. At every time step $t \geq 1$, first set S_t^+ to be S_{t-1}^+ and S_t^- to be S_{t-1}^-; next for every inactive node $v \notin S_{t-1}^+ \cup S_{t-1}^-$, determine if its positive activation attempt is successful (i.e., $\sum_{u \in S_{t-1}^+ \cap N^{in}(v)} w^+(u, v) \geq \theta_v^+$), and if its negative activation attempt is successful (i.e., $\sum_{u \in S_{t-1}^- \cap N^{in}(v)} w^-(u, v) \geq \theta_v^-$); if the former is successful but not the latter, add v into S_t^+ and v is *positively activated*; if the latter is successful but not the former, add v into S_t^- and v is *negatively activated*. If both activation attempts are successful, we use a tie-breaking rule to determine the activation polarity.

The fixed probability tie-breaking rule TB-FP(ϕ) described earlier also applies to CLT, that is, when both positive and negative activation attempts are successful, with a fixed probability ϕ, v becomes positive, and with probability $(1 - \phi)$, v becomes negative. Note that the proportional probability tie-breaking rule TB-PP only applies to CIC models, not CLT models. Borodin et al. [2010] also propose several other variants of linear threshold models combining positive and negative diffusions, which we omit from further discussion in this section.

Similar to the original IC and LT models, we can use equivalent live-arc graph models to help understand the CIC and CLT models, as we now explain. Both the CIC and CLT models follow the same theme in which positive and negative opinions diffuse separately, but they interact according to two rules: (a) if one opinion arrives at a node first, then that opinion wins on that node; and (b) if both opinions arrive at a node at the same time, then a certain tie-breaking rule is applied. Based on this theme, we can device the following live-arc graph model to reflect competitive diffusion process. We describe the live-arc graph model for CIC and CLT models together, since they share most of the modeling aspects. The only difference is that the proportional probability tie-breaking rule only applies to the CIC models. We will make it clear from the context in the following definition.

Definition 4.4   Live-arc graph model for competitive influence diffusion.   Given a CIC or a CLT model, we first generate a positive live-arc graph G_L^+ and a negative live-arc graph G_L^- independently, according to the equivalent live-arc graphs for the IC or LT model, respectively, as given in Definitions 2.5 and 2.10. Next, we need to fix the random choices for the tie-breaking rule as follows. For the fixed probability rule TB-FP(ϕ), each node flips an independent coin with bias ϕ and stores its positive and negative state in a variable τ_v. For the proportional probability rule TB-PP (for CIC models), each node v fixes a random order π_v among all its in-neighbors in G_L^+ and G_L^-. Then we recursively define positive and negative active sets S_t^+ and S_t^- for any $t \geq 1$ as follows. First, S_t^+ includes S_{t-1}^+ and S_t^- includes S_{t-1}^-. Next, for any $v \notin S_{t-1}^+ \cup S_{t-1}^-$, if v is reachable from S_{t-1}^+ in one step in G_L^+ (i.e., $d_{G_L^+}(S_{t-1}^+, v) = 1$) but not reachable from S_{t-1}^- in one step in G_L^- (i.e., $d_{G_L^-}(S_{t-1}^-, v) > 1$), then v is in S_t^+; symmetrically, if v is not reachable from S_{t-1}^+ in one step in G_L^+ but reachable from S_{t-1}^- in one step in G_L^-, then v is in S_t^-. Finally, if v is reachable from S_{t-1}^+ in one step in G_L^+ and reachable from S_{t-1}^- in one step in G_L^-, we use predetermined tie-breaking outcome to decide the state of v. In particular, for the fixed probability rule, we use the tie-breaking outcome τ_v as the state of v; for the proportional probability rule (for CIC models), among all nodes in $S_{t-1}^+ \cup S_{t-1}^-$ that can reach v in one step, we find the first node in the random order π_v and set v's state to be the state of this node.

It is easy to see that the above live-arc graph model is equivalent to the corresponding CIC or CLT models, because it simply pre-determines certain random outcomes and then describes exactly what the diffusion process would be when these randomness are fixed. The following theorem formally states their equivalence, and its formal verification is left for the interested readers to fill in.

Theorem 4.5   *The live-arc graph model for a competitive influence diffusion model defined in Definition 4.4 is equivalent to the corresponding CIC or CLT models with the corresponding tie-breaking rule.*

4.2.2   MAXIMIZATION PROBLEMS FOR COMPETITIVE INFLUENCE DIFFUSION

Given a positive seed set S_0^+ and a negative seed set S_0^-, let $\sigma^+(S_0^+, S_0^-)$ denote the *positive influence spread*, which is the expected number of positive nodes after the diffusion ends, and let $\sigma^-(S_0^+, S_0^-)$ denote the *negative influence spread*, which is the expected number of negative nodes after the diffusion ends (again we omit explicit notations of the social graph, the diffusion model and the specific model parameters since it would be made clear from the context).

We consider two maximization problems, *influence maximization under competition* and *influence-blocking maximization under competition*, both specified from the perspective of the positive opinion, since positive and negative diffusions are symmetric in our setting.

Influence Maximization under a Competitive Diffusion Model

This problem corresponds to a situation where, for example, a company knows the current status of diffusion of the competing product or opinion, and it needs to select its own seed set to maximize its own coverage, considering the influence over users by its competitor. Formally:

Problem 4.6   Influence maximization under a competitive diffusion model   Given a social graph G, a competitive diffusion model on G for positive and negative opinions, a negative seed set S_0^-, and an integer k, the *influence maximization* problem under this competitive diffusion model is to find a positive seed set $S_0^+ \subseteq V \setminus S_0^-$ with at most k seeds, such that the positive influence spread of S_0^+ given negative seeds S_0^-, $\sigma^+(S_0^+, S_0^-)$, is maximized. That is, compute set $S_0^{+*} \subseteq V \setminus S_0^-$ such that

$$S_0^{+*} = \operatorname*{argmax}_{S_0^+ \subseteq V \setminus S_0^-, |S_0^+| = k} \sigma^+(S_0^+, S_0^-).$$

Note that when the negative seed set $S_0^- = \emptyset$, the above problem becomes the original influence maximization problem under the single-item diffusion model (Problem 3.1). Therefore, the hardness result given in Section 3.1 also applies to influence maximization for the competitive diffusion models. In particular, under both CIC and CLT models, influence maximization is NP-hard.

Following the greedy approach for the single-item influence maximization problem, we would like to investigate the submodularity of influence spread functions under the competitive diffusion models, in the hope to apply greedy approach again to achieve constant approximation of the optimal solution. However, the diffusion dynamics change and submodularity is no longer guaranteed to hold, but under certain special cases, submodularity still holds. Next we will provide relevant results concerning influence maximization under the competitive diffusion models.

We first show that monotonicity on positive and negative influence spread still holds.

Theorem 4.7   *Given any negative seed set S_0^-, the positive influence spread $\sigma^+(S_0^+, S_0^-)$ is monotone with respect to the positive seed set S_0^+, for both CIC and CLT models. Symmetrically, given any positive seed set S_0^+, the negative influence spread $\sigma^-(S_0^+, S_0^-)$ is monotone with respect to the negative seed set S_0^-.*

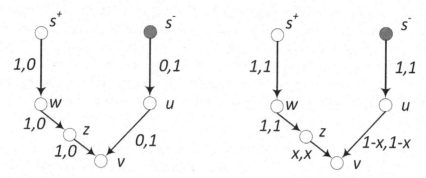

(a) for the general CIC and CLT models   (b) for the homogeneous CLT models

Figure 4.2: Examples showing that positive influence spread is not submodular in a competitive diffusion model. For the two numbers next to an arc, the first number is the weight for the positive diffusion while the second number is the weight for the negative diffusion. The gray node s^- in each figure is the fixed negative seed.

Proof (sketch). This is easy to see by the equivalence to the live-arc graph model (Theorem 4.5). When the live-arc graph together with the tie-breaking outcomes are predetermined, we can see that the states of all nodes are deterministically decided in the live-arc graph model of Definition 4.4. Thus, one just needs to prove that when S_{t-1}^+ grows and/or S_{t-1}^- shrinks, S_t^+ cannot shrink in the live-arc graph model, which is straightforward for both tie-breaking rules.   □

However, submodularity does not hold in general for CIC and CLT models.

Theorem 4.8   *There exist instances in which, given a negative seed set S_0^-, the positive influence spread $\sigma^+(S_0^+, S_0^-)$ is not submodular in either CIC or CLT models. Symmetrically, there exist instances in which, given a positive seed set S_0^+, the negative influence spread $\sigma^-(S_0^+, S_0^-)$ is not submodular in the above models.*

Proof. We use the counter example shown in Figure 4.2(a) to show the case for the positive influence spread. It is similar to the example used by Borodin et al. [2010]. Node s^- is the single negative seed. For positive seed sets, we consider $\emptyset$, $\{s^+\}$, $\{u\}$, and $\{s^+, u\}$. For arc weight assignment, weights $1, 0$ on an arc mean that it only propagates positive influence but not negative influence. In the CIC models, this is achieved by assigning positive influence probability of the arc to 1 and negative influence probability of the arc to 0, while in the CLT models it is achieved by assigning positive influence weight to 1 and negative influence weight to 0. Weights $0, 1$ are assigned symmetrically. In this example, no tie-breaking rule is needed for any node, and thus the example applies to any tie-breaking rule.

Then it is easy to see that (a) $\sigma^+(\emptyset, \{s^-\}) = 0$; (b) $\sigma^+(\{s^+\}, \{s^-\}) = 3$ (nodes s^+, w and z are positive while v is negative because the negative influence s^- reaches v first); (c) $\sigma^+(\{u\}, \{s^-\}) = 1$ (only node u is positive); and (d) $\sigma^+(\{s^+, u\}, \{s^-\}) = 5$ (nodes s^+, w, z, u and v are all positive). Thus, $\sigma^+(\{u\}, \{s^-\}) - \sigma^+(\emptyset, \{s^-\}) = 1 < 2 = \sigma^+(\{s^+, u\}, \{s^-\}) - \sigma^+(\{s^+\}, \{s^-\})$, i.e., the marginal contribution of u on positive influence spread given positive seed set $\emptyset$ is smaller than the marginal contribution of u given positive seed set $\{s^+\}$, which means positive influence spread is not submodular. $\square$

Intuitively, what the example of Figure 4.2(a) shows is a key difference in diffusion dynamics between the competitive diffusion models and the single-item diffusion models. In single-item diffusions, the way a new seed node contributes to the marginal influence spread is by reaching additional nodes. However, in competitive diffusion, a new positive seed may also contribute to marginal positive influence spread by *blocking* the influence of a negative seed (e.g., node u blocks the negative influence of node s^- to node v in Figure 4.2(a)), while allowing the positive influence to reach more nodes (e.g., the positive influence from node s^+ reaches node v after the negative influence from s^- is blocked by u in Figure 4.2(a)). Since the blocking of negative influence has to work together with positive influence from certain positive seeds, the blocking effect may not generate larger marginal influence when working with a smaller positive seed set, making positive influence spread not submodular.

Theorem 4.8 shows that positive (or negative) influence spread is not submodular in the general competitive diffusion models. Some restricted models, however, are indeed submodular. We say that a CIC model is *homogeneous* if on every arc $(u, v) \in E$, $p^+(u, v) = p^-(u, v)$, that is, the diffusion properties of all arcs are the same for positive and negative influence (this model is due to Budak et al. [2011]). We show below that the homogeneous CIC model with positive or negative dominance tie-breaking rule preserves the submodularity property.

Theorem 4.9   *In a homogeneous CIC model with positive dominance TB-FP(1), negative dominance TB-FP(0), or proportional probability TB-PP tie-breaking rule, given a negative seed set S_0^-, the positive influence spread function is submodular. Symmetrically, given a positive seed set S_0^+ the negative influence spread function is submodular.*

Proof. We still use the argument based on live-arc graphs, but we do not need the independent generation of positive and negative live-arc graphs as given in Definition 4.4. Instead, for each arc $(u, v) \in E$, we sample it with probability $p^+(u, v) = p^-(u, v)$ and generate one live-arc graph G_L. The idea is that during the diffusion of the positive and negative influence in graph G, on each arc at most one opinion propagates through the arc and it cannot happen that both positive and negative opinions propagate on the arc. Therefore, each arc (u, v) can be sampled once (since they have the same positive and negative influence probability), and whether it propagates positive or negative influence depends on whether u is positively or negatively activated. We prove the theorem for positive and negative dominance tie-breaking rules first, and then prove the case for proportional probability tie-breaking rule.

Note that in the above live-arc graph model, when positive and negative seed sets as well as the tie-breaking outcomes are fixed, the final states of all nodes are fixed deterministically. When fixing a live-arc graph G_L, let $\Phi^+(S_0^+, S_0^-)$ be the final set of positive nodes in G_L after the diffusion ends, when the positive and negative seed sets are S_0^+ and S_0^- respectively. By the live-arc graph model, it is straightforward to verify that for any $S \subseteq T$, $\Phi^+(S, S_0^-) \subseteq \Phi^+(T, S_0^-)$, under any fixed tie-breaking outcome.

Let us consider first the positive or negative dominance tie-breaking rule. In this case, the tie-breaking outcomes for all nodes as described in Definition 4.4 are the same for all nodes — τ_v for all nodes are either all positive or all negative.

Let S and T be two positive seed sets with $S \subseteq T \subseteq V \setminus S_0^-$ and a node $u \in V \setminus (S_0^- \cup T)$. Consider a node $v \in \Phi^+(T \cup \{u\}, S_0^-) \setminus \Phi^+(T, S_0^-)$. Recall that $d_G(S, v)$ denotes the graph distance from set of nodes S to v in graph G, and $d_G(u, v) = d_G(\{u\}, v)$ (again if $v \in S$, $d_G(S, v) = 0$). We analyze below the relationships among $d_{G_L}(u, v)$, $d_{G_L}(T, v)$, and $d_{G_L}(S_0^-, v)$, and show that $d_{G_L}(u, v) < d_{G_L}(T, v) \leq d_{G_L}(S_0^-, v)$.

Consider first the positive dominance tie-breaking rule. In this case, we must have $d_{G_L}(T \cup \{u\}, v) \leq d_{G_L}(S_0^-, v)$. Otherwise, suppose $d_{G_L}(S_0^-, v) < d_{G_L}(T \cup \{u\}, v)$. Consider any shortest path P^- from some node in S_0^- to v with length $d_{G_L}(S_0^-, v)$. For any node w on path P^-, we have $d_{G_L}(S_0^-, w) < d_{G_L}(T \cup \{u\}, w)$. Then by the live-arc graph model, all nodes w on P^- must be negative, which contradicts the fact that v is on path P^- and $v \in \Phi^+(T \cup \{u\}, S_0^-)$. Then consider a path P^+ from some node in $T \cup \{u\}$ to v with length $d_{G_L}(T \cup \{u\}, v)$. If the starting node of path P^+ is not u, then we know that for every node w on path P^+, $d_{G_L}(T, w) \leq d_{G_L}(S_0^-, w)$. Since we have positive dominance tie-breaking rule, this implies that all nodes w on path P^+ are positive when T is the positive seed set, which contradicts to the fact that v is on path P^+ and $v \notin \Phi^+(T, S_0^-)$. Therefore, path P^+ has to be started from node u, which means $d_{G_L}(u, v) < d_{G_L}(T, v)$.

Now consider the negative dominance tie-breaking rule, the argument for which is similar. In this case, we must have $d_{G_L}(T \cup \{u\}, v) < d_{G_L}(S_0^-, v)$, because otherwise v would be negative. Again consider a path P^+ from some node in $T \cup \{u\}$ to v with length $d_{G_L}(T \cup \{u\}, v)$. It must be the case that P^+ starts with node u, because otherwise v would be positive even when T is the seed set. Therefore, path P^+ has to be started from node u, which again implies $d_{G_L}(u, v) < d_{G_L}(T, v)$.

Now for set $S \subseteq T$, with the above argument, we have $d_{G_L}(u, v) < d_{G_L}(S_0^-, v)$, and thus $v \in \Phi^+(S \cup \{u\}, S_0^-)$. Moreover, since $d_{G_L}(T, v) \leq d_{G_L}(S, v)$, it is clear that $v \notin \Phi^+(S, S_0^-)$. Therefore, $v \in \Phi^+(S \cup \{u\}, S_0^-) \setminus \Phi^+(S, S_0^-)$. That is, we have $\Phi^+(T \cup \{u\}, S_0^-) \setminus \Phi^+(T, S_0^-) \subseteq \Phi^+(S \cup \{u\}, S_0^-) \setminus \Phi^+(S, S_0^-)$. This means that, when fixing a live-arc graph, the marginal contribution of u given T is at most the marginal contribution of u given S. When summing over all possible live-arc graphs, we conclude that the submodularity holds, for the case with positive or negative dominance tie-breaking rule.

Now let us consider the case of proportional probability tie-breaking rule. The proof follows the same general structure as the above: we show that for any $v \in \Phi^+(T \cup \{u\}, S_0^-) \setminus \Phi^+(T, S_0^-)$, we can find a path P^+ from u to v such that even if u is the only positive seed, all nodes on path P^+ are still positive, which implies the key relation $\Phi^+(T \cup \{u\}, S_0^-) \setminus \Phi^+(T, S_0^-) \subseteq \Phi^+(S \cup \{u\}, S_0^-) \setminus \Phi^+(S, S_0^-)$ whenever $S \subseteq T$, which in turn implies submodularity. The detailed proof, however, is more involved, as explain below. Recall that for the proportional probability tie-breaking rule, in the live-edge graph model (Definition 4.4) for each node w we fix an ordering of its in-neighbors in π_v.

Consider a node $v \in \Phi^+(T \cup \{u\}, S_0^-) \setminus \Phi^+(T, S_0^-)$. In the following, we construct a shortest path P^+ in G_L from u to v such that all nodes on the path are positive when $T \cup \{u\}$ is the positive seed set. Starting from v, if v has only one active in-neighbor w at the step before v is activated, then w must be positive, and we select w as the predecessor of v on path P^+. If v have multiple active in-neighbors at the step before v is activated (either all of them are positive or some of them are negative), then among them select node w that is ordered first in π_v as the predecessor of v on path P^+. This node w must be positive, since otherwise according to the proportional probability tie-breaking rule v would be negative. We follow the same rule to find the path backwards until it hits one of the positive seeds in $T \cup \{u\}$. All nodes on path P^+ must be positive. Moreover, by the live-arc graph model, it is clear that P^+ is a shortest path from $T \cup \{u\}$ to v.

Let w_0 be the positive seed at the beginning of path P^+. We claim that even if w_0 is the only positive seed, all nodes on path P^+ are still positive. Suppose, for a contradiction, that some node on P^+ turns negative when w_0 is the only positive seed. Let w be the first node on path P^+ from w_0 that is negative. This means that there is a shortest path P^- from S_0^- to w on which all nodes are negative. The length of path P^- must be the same as the length of sub-path from w_0 to w on path P^+, because (a) if the former is larger, then w must be positive, and (b) if the former is smaller, then w would be negative even when $T \cup \{u\}$ is the positive seed set. Thus proportional probability tie-breaking rule TB-PP is applied at w. Let x be the predecessor of w on path P^+ and y be the predecessor of w on path P^-. According to TB-PP, y must be ordered before x in the order π_v. Now consider that $T \cup \{u\}$ is the positive seed set, in which case w turns positive by our construction of P^+. The shortest path from $T \cup \{u\}$ to w are of the same length as path P^-, since P^+ is a shortest path from $T \cup \{u\}$ to v and w is on P^+. This means that when $T \cup \{u\}$ is the seed set, both x and y are still in-neighbors of w that activate w. In this case, y must still be negative, because if y turns positive, since y is ordered before x, our construction of path P^+ would not select x as w's predecessor. When y is negative, again since y is ordered before x and w is positive, it implies that there must be another in-neighbor z of w that is positive and activates w and is ordered before y, but this means that z would be selected when constructing path P^+.

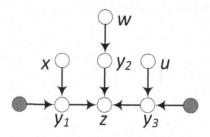

Figure 4.3: Example showing that positive influence spread is not submodular in the homogeneous CIC model with tie-breaking rule TB-FP(ϕ), $0 < \phi < 1$. The gray nodes are fixed negative seeds, and all arcs have influence probability 1.

Thus, whether or not y is positive we reach a contradiction, which means that our claim that all nodes in P^+ remains positive when w_0 is the only positive seed is true.

The above claim immediately implies that $w_0 = u$, because otherwise, $w_0 \in T$, and we have $v \in \Phi^+(\{w_0\}, S_0^-) \subseteq \Phi^+(T, S_0^-)$, contradicting to our assumption that $v \notin \Phi^+(T, S_0^-)$. Now that $w_0 = u$, we have $v \in \Phi^+(\{w_0\}, S_0^-) = \Phi^+(\{u\}, S_0^-) \subseteq \Phi^+(S \cup \{u\}, S_0^-)$. Moreover, since $S \subseteq T$, we have that $v \notin \Phi^+(T, S_0^-)$ implies $v \notin \Phi^+(S, S_0^-)$. Therefore, $v \in \Phi^+(S \cup \{u\}, S_0^-) \setminus \Phi^+(S, S_0^-)$. This concludes the proof that $\Phi^+(T \cup \{u\}, S_0^-) \setminus \Phi^+(T, S_0^-) \subseteq \Phi^+(S \cup \{u\}, S_0^-) \setminus \Phi^+(S, S_0^-)$, which implies submodularity for the proportional probability tie-breaking rule. $\square$

The above theorem shows submodularity for the homogeneous CIC model with positive dominance, negative dominance, or proportional probability tie-breaking rule. For the general fixed probability tie-breaking rule TB-FP(ϕ) with $0 < \phi < 1$, the homogeneous CIC model may be not submodular, as shown by the following theorem.

Theorem 4.10   *In a homogeneous CIC model with fixed probability tie-breaking rule TB-FP(ϕ) and $0 < \phi < 1$, there exist instances in which, given a negative seed set S_0^-, the positive influence spread function is not submodular in general.*

Proof. Figure 4.3 is an example showing that homogeneous CIC model with tie-breaking rule TB-FP(ϕ) with $0 < \phi < 1$ is not submodular. The gray nodes are fixed negative seeds, and all arcs have influence probability 1.

For any node v in the graph, let $ap_v^+(S)$ denote the positive activation probability of node v when S is the positive seed set. Let $S = \{w\}$, $T = \{w, x\}$. For node z in the graph, we verify below that $ap_z^+(T \cup \{u\}) - ap_z^+(T) > ap_z^+(S \cup \{u\}) - ap_z^+(S)$ when $0 < \phi < 1$. In fact, we have $ap_z^+(S) = ap_z^+(T) = ap_z^+(S \cup \{u\}) = \phi$, while $ap_z^+(T \cup \{u\}) = \phi^2 + (1 - \phi^2)\phi$. For the last equality, we use the following useful computation fact. For any node v in the graph (with arc influence probabilities on all arcs being 1), if all in-neighbors of v are activated at the same step (or not activated at all), and the activation events of all in-neighbors of v are mutually independent, then

$$ap_v^+(S) = \prod_{u \in N^{in}(v)} ap_u^+(S) + \left(1 - \prod_{u \in N^{in}(v)} ap_u^+(S) - \prod_{u \in N^{in}(v)} (1 - ap_u^+(S))\right) \phi. \qquad (4.6)$$

The first additive term on the right-hand side means that all in-neighbors of v are positive, in which case v must be positive. The second additive term means that some in-neighbors are positive and some are negative, in which case tie-breaking rule TB-FP(ϕ) is applied and v is positive with probability ϕ. Note that the graph in Figure 4.3 is a tree, so the activation events of all in-neighbors of z are mutually independent. Moreover, all in-neighbors of z are all activated at the same time (if activated at all), and thus Equation (4.6) is applicable to node z. Then, together with the easy fact that $ap_{y_1}^+(T \cup \{u\}) = ap_{y_3}^+(T \cup \{u\}) = \phi$ and $ap_{y_2}^+(T \cup \{u\}) = 1$, we obtain $ap_z^+(T \cup \{u\}) = \phi^2 + (1 - \phi^2)\phi$.

Therefore, $(ap_z^+(T \cup \{u\}) - ap_z^+(T)) - (ap_z^+(S \cup \{u\}) - ap_z^+(S)) = \phi^2 + (1 - \phi^2)\phi - \phi = \phi^2(1 - \phi) > 0$ when $0 < \phi < 1$, which implies that $ap_z^+(\cdot)$ is not submodular. This should be enough to show that there exists a graph with non-submodular positive influence spread function, because we can always attach a large number of nodes to z such that the overall positive influence spread is dominated by the positive activation probability of node z multiplied by the number of nodes attached to z. However, for the example in Figure 4.3, it is also easy to argue that the non-submodularity of $ap_z^+(\cdot)$ directly implies the non-submodularity of the positive influence spread function in the same graph. This is because, for any node v in the graph other than z, either u cannot reach v, in which case u has no marginal contribution to the positive activation probability of v, or T cannot reach v, which means u's marginal contribution to the positive activation probability of v given S or T as positive seed set must be the same. Hence, any change on u's marginal contribution to the positive influence spread must be due to the change of u's marginal contribution to node z. Therefore, the non-submodularity of $ap_z^+(\cdot)$ implies the non-submodularity of the positive influence spread function in the same graph. $\square$

Note that the example graph in Figure 4.3 is also an example showing that if nodes may use different dominance tie-breaking rules, the positive influence spread may be not submodular. In particular, if node z uses negative dominance rule, while all other nodes use positive dominance rule, the submodularity does not hold.

Theorem 4.9 establishes submodularity for homogeneous CIC models under certain tie-breaking rules. Unfortunately, for the CLT models, making them homogeneous does not recover submodularity. A CLT model is *homogeneous* if for every arc $(u, v) \in E$, $w^+(u, v) = w^-(u, v)$ (but each node still has two independently sampled threshold values θ_v^+ and θ_v^-). The positive influence spread in the homogeneous CLT model is still not submodular, regardless of the tie-breaking rule, as shown by the following example.

Example 4.11   The example graph in Figure 4.2(b) shows that the positive influence spread in the homogeneous CLT model is not submodular. No tie-breaking rule is needed at any node, and thus it applies to any tie-breaking rule. One can verify that $\sigma^+(\{u\}, \{s^-\}) - \sigma^+(\emptyset, \{s^-\}) = 2 - x$, while $\sigma^+(\{s^+, u\}, \{s^-\}) - \sigma^+(\{s^+\}, \{s^-\}) = 5 - (3 + x^2) = 2 - x^2$. Thus for any $0 < x < 1$, submodularity does not hold.   ∎

There are other possibilities of extending LT model to competitive influence, but many of them do not satisfy submodularity (see [Borodin et al., 2010] for more model variants). One exception to this is the K-LT model recently proposed by Lu et al. [2013], where the authors extend the LT model to a competitive setting while retaining submodularity. We discuss this in more detail in Section 4.2.4.

In general, when we have submodularity for positive influence spread, such as the homogeneous CIC models under certain tie-breaking rules, we could apply the greedy approach to obtain approximation algorithms for the influence maximization problem, similar to the single-item case. However, when submodularity does not hold, influence maximization problem is still quite open, and so far one can only rely on heuristics without theoretical guarantee.

Influence-Blocking Maximization under a Competitive Diffusion Model

Another possible optimization objective is to minimize the coverage of the competing product or opinion. This is especially the case when a negative opinion or a rumor about a company or political party is propagating, and the company or party tries to spread positive and true information to reduce the spread of the rumor as much as possible. For this purpose, we define *negative influence reduction* of a positive seed set S_0^+ given a negative seed set S_0^- to be the difference between the negative influence spread when there are no positive seeds and the negative influence spread when nodes in S_0^+ are positive seeds, and we denote it as $\rho^-(S_0^+, S_0^-)$. That is, $\rho^-(S_0^+, S_0^-) = \sigma^-(\emptyset, S_0^-) - \sigma^-(S_0^+, S_0^-)$.

Problem 4.12   Influence-blocking maximization under a competitive diffusion model   Given a social graph G, a competitive diffusion model on G for positive and negative opinions, a negative seed set S_0^-, and an integer k, the *influence-blocking maximization* problem under this competitive diffusion model is to find a positive seed set $S_0^+ \subseteq V \setminus S_0^-$ with at most k seeds, such that the negative influence reduction of S_0^+ given negative seeds S_0^-, $\rho^-(S_0^+, S_0^-)$, is maximized. That is, compute set $S_0^{+*} \subseteq V \setminus S_0^-$ such that

$$S_0^{+*} = \operatorname*{argmax}_{S_0^+ \subseteq V \setminus S_0^-, |S_0^+| = k} \rho^-(S_0^+, S_0^-).$$

Influence-blocking maximization defined above includes the *immunization problem* often studied in the epidemiology literature as a special case. The immunization problem is to find a set of k nodes to immunize so as to block the spread of a disease as much as possible. In our model, if the disease is the negative opinion, the immunized nodes hold the positive opinion, and positive opinion does not diffuse in the network, e.g., the positive influence probabilities are zero in the CIC models or the positive influence weights are zero in the CLT models, then the influence-blocking maximization problem becomes the immunization problem.

Influence-blocking maximization has a different objective from the influence maximization problem, and thus its hardness needs to be investigated independently.

Theorem 4.13   *Influence-blocking maximization in both CIC and CLT models is NP-hard.*

Proof. See Theorem 4.1 and its proof in [Budak et al., 2011] for the CIC models, and Theorem 4.1 and its proof in [He et al., 2012] for the CLT models.   □

To overcome the NP-hardness result, again we would like to investigate the monotonicity and submodularity of the negative influence reduction function $\rho^-(\cdot, S_0^-)$. Comparing to the case for influence maximization, an interesting difference is that in the general CLT models, the negative influence reduction function $\rho^-(\cdot, S_0^-)$ is actually monotone and submodular.

Theorem 4.14   *The negative influence reduction function $\rho^-(\cdot, S_0^-)$ is monotone and submodular in the CLT models.*

Proof. See Theorem 4.2 and its proof in [He et al., 2012], which is for the case of negative dominance in the tie-breaking rule TB-FP(0). For the general fixed probability tie-breaking rule TB-FP(ϕ), as claimed in the paper, one can extend the proof by pre-determining the tie-breaking outcomes of all nodes and properly adjusting the proof to show that it works for TB-FP(ϕ) for any $\phi \in [0, 1]$.   □

Given the above result, we can apply the greedy approach to provide an approximation algorithm for the influence-blocking maximization problem under the CLT models. He et al. [2012] further extend the LDAG algorithm of [Chen et al., 2010] and apply dynamic programming method to devise a scalable heuristic algorithm CLDAG for the influence-blocking maximization problem.

For the CIC models, the situation is similar to the case of influence maximization, as given below.

Theorem 4.15   *The negative influence reduction function $\rho^-(\cdot, S_0^-)$ is submodular in the homogeneous CIC models with tie-breaking rule TB-FP(0), TB-FP(1), or TB-PP.*

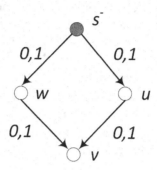

Figure 4.4: An example showing that negative influence reduction is not submodular in the non-homogeneous CIC model. For the two numbers next to an arc, the first number is the positive influence probability while the second number is the negative influence probability. The gray node s^- is the fixed negative seed.

Proof. The monotonicity and submodularity of homogeneous CIC model with TB-FP(1) (i.e., positive dominance) is shown by Budak et al. [2011]. We can actually use the live-arc graph model and link the influence-blocking maximization problem in this case to the influence maximization problem to show the result for other tie-breaking rules, as we explain below.

Given a live-arc graph G_L as described in the proof of Theorem 4.9 and a negative seed set S_0^-, the set of nodes that is negative when there is no positive seeds in G_L is exactly the set of nodes reachable from S_0^- in G_L, $R_{G_L}(S_0^-)$. For any node $v \in R_{G_L}(S_0^-)$, when some positive seeds are added, v is either positive or negative, but cannot be inactive, because positive and negative influence use the same diffusion graph G_L. This property implies that the negative influence reduction of a positive seed set S in G_L is $\sum_{v \in R_{G_L}(S_0^-)} i_v(S)$, where $i_v(S)$ is an indicator function with value 1 if v is positive in G_L and 0 if v is negative, given S as positive seeds and S_0^- as negative seeds. This means that it is sufficient to show the monotonicity and submodularity of $i_v(S)$ for all $v \in R_{G_L}(S_0^-)$. In the proof of Theorem 4.9, we have shown that $\Phi^+(T \cup \{u\}, S_0^-) \setminus \Phi^+(T, S_0^-) \subseteq \Phi^+(S \cup \{u\}, S_0^-) \setminus \Phi^+(S, S_0^-)$. One can easily verify that this implies that for every node $v \in V$, $i_v(S)$ is submodular. Monotonicity of $i_v(S)$ can also be verified following the proof of Theorem 4.7. □

The following example shows that the general non-homogeneous CIC models as well as homogeneous CIC with TB-FP(ϕ) and $0 < \phi < 1$ do not have submodularity property for negative influence reduction.

Example 4.16 The non-submodularity for the general non-homogeneous CIC case is shown by a simple example in Figure 4.4. In the example, positive influence does not propagate at all and only negative influence propagates. We have $\rho^-(\emptyset, \{s^-\}) = 0$, $\rho^-(\{w\}, \{s^-\}) = \rho^-(\{u\}, \{s^-\}) =$

1, and $\rho^-(\{w, u\}, \{s^-\}) = 3$. That is, when only one of w and u are positive seeds, they can only save themselves but not v, but when both of them are positive seeds, the also save v. Therefore, $\rho^-(\{w, u\}, \{s^-\}) - \rho^-(\{w\}, \{s^-\}) = 2 > 1 = \rho^-(\{u\}, \{s^-\}) - \rho^-(\emptyset, \{s^-\})$, and thus $\rho^-(\cdot, \{s^-\})$ is not submodular.

For the homogeneous CIC with TB-FP(ϕ) and $0 < \phi < 1$, we can use the same example in Figure 4.3 to show that it is not submodular. It is easy to notice that the negative influence reduction in the example in Figure 4.3 is exactly the same as the sum of positive activation probabilities of z, y_1, and y_3. Therefore, it is easy to verify that the negative influence reduction is not submodular with the fixed probability tie-breaking rule TB-FP(ϕ) when $0 < \phi < 1$. ∎

The example shown in Figure 4.4 is exactly the situation that arises in case of the immunization problem, where positive seeds do not propagate influence and they can only block negative influence. The example shows that immunization is not submodular and it could be a very hard problem to solve optimally.

From the example, we can also discern a key difference between the CIC and CLT models in terms of influence-blocking effect. For the CIC models, if a positive seed cannot propagate influence, then it may be completely useless in blocking the negative influence to a node if negative influence has an alternative path to the node (e.g., in Figure 4.4, s^- has two paths to v so only blocking one path is useless for protecting v). However, for the CLT models, even if a positive seed cannot propagate positive influence (all positive influence weights are zero), by occupying a position as a neighbor of a node, it may still reduce the negative influence to the node (e.g., in Figure 4.4, if w is a positive seed, and arcs (w, v) and (u, v) have equal negative influence weights, then w blocks half of the negative influence from s^- to v even if w does not propagate positive influence). It is this key difference that makes negative influence reduction model submodular in the CLT model but not submodular in the CIC model.

4.2.3 ENDOGENOUS COMPETITION

In the competitive diffusion models discussed so far, the negative opinion competing with the positive opinion is from an external source, such as a business competitor. However, it is also possible that negative opinions are generated internally, due to the defects of the products or services being promoted in the network. For example, a person may be influenced by the recommendation from his friend to try out a restaurant, but he may happen to be served a badly prepared dish and dislike the restaurant, and start to spread bad opinions about the restaurant to his friends. This could happen for a wide range of products and services. We call this kind of competitive diffusion between positive and negative opinions where the negative opinion emerges during the diffusion of positive opinion due to product or service defects the *endogenous competition*. In contrast, we refer to the previously modeled competitive diffusion where negative opinion is originated from some external source as *exogenous competition*.

Chen et al. [2011] model the influence diffusion of such endogenous competition by extending the IC model. The idea is to add a quality factor q in the IC model, such that when a node v is activated by a positive node u, v becomes positive with probability q and with probability $1 - q$ it turns to negative opinion (e.g., hitting a problem and disliking the product). Negative nodes also propagate negative influence in the same way as positive influence, but when a node is activated by a negative neighbor, it will always be negative and will not turn positive, reflecting the "negativity bias" phenomenon that is commonly seen and has been studied in social psychology (e.g., Rosin and Royzman [2001]). The exact model is given below.

Definition 4.17   Independent cascade model for endogenous competition.   The independent cascade model for endogenous competition, also referred to as the IC-N model, has a social graph $G = (V, E)$, arc influence probabilities $p(u, v)$ for every $(u, v) \in E$, a seed set S_0, and a quality factor $q \in [0, 1]$ as input, and generates positive and negative active sets S_t^+ and S_t^- for all $t \geq 0$ by the following randomized operation rule. We denote $S_t = S_t^+ \cup S_t^-$ for all $t \geq 1$. Initially, for each node $u \in S_0$, flip an independent coin such that with probability q, u is positive and in S_0^+ and probability $(1 - q)$, u is negative and in S_0^-. At time step $t \geq 1$, first set S_t^+ to S_{t-1}^+ and S_t^- to S_{t-1}^-; then for every inactive node $v \in V \setminus S_{t-1}$, we randomly permute all its just activated in-neighbors $N^{in}(v) \cap (S_{t-1} \setminus S_{t-2})$, and let each node u in this set try to activate v one by one following the permutation order, with success probability $p(u, v)$. If v is activated, let u be the first in the permutation order that successfully activates v. If u is negative, then v is negative; if u is positive, then v is positive with probability q and negative with probability $1 - q$; and we add v to S_t^+ or S_t^- accordingly.

We can see that if we only look at the active sets S_t's, they are generated exactly in the same way as in the IC model. If $q = 1$ IC-N is also reduced to the IC model. When $q < 1$, IC-N is a homogeneous diffusion model in that positive and negative opinions diffuse on an arc with the same probability. However, their activation behavior is different: nodes activated by negative nodes are always negative, but nodes activated by positive nodes may be positive or negative depending on the quality factor q. This is to match the scenarios in which if an individual accepts the negative influence about a product or service, then he will not try out the product or service, while if he accepts the positive influence, he will try the product or service and then he may have a chance to dislike it and turn negative. For the tie-breaking rule, IC-N model uses the proportional probability tie breaking rule as we explained for the CIC models.

Chen et al. [2011] show that IC-N model has the following important property, which is the key for both proving submodularity and algorithm design.

Lemma 4.18   (Lemma 2.1 of [Chen et al., 2011])   *Suppose that in a social graph $G = (V, E)$, all arcs have influence probability 1. Then given a seed set S_0, the probability that a node $v \in V$ is positive after the diffusion process, denoted $pap(v, S_0, q)$, is given by*

$$pap(v, S_0, q) = q^{d_G(S_0, v)+1}.$$

The above property asserts that the positive activation probability of nodes decreases exponentially as their distance to the seed set increases, if all arcs deterministically propagate the influence.

For the IC-N model, let $\sigma^+(S_0)$ denote the *positive influence spread* given seed set S_0, which is the expected number of positive nodes after the diffusion process ends. Using the above property, we can show that the positive influence spread is monotone and submodular.

Theorem 4.19 (Theorem 2.1 of [Chen et al., 2011]).   *The positive influence spread function $\sigma^+(\cdot)$ is monotone and submodular.*

Proof (sketch). The proof is still based on the live-arc graph model. One key point is to fix the randomness on the arcs to generate a live-arc graph, but not fix the randomness for determining the positive or negative state of a node based on quality factor q. Instead, use Lemma 4.18 to directly argue for monotonicity and submodularity. See the proof of Theorem 2.1 in [Chen et al., 2011] for details. □

Based on the submodularity of the model and the MIA algorithm of [Wang et al., 2012], Chen et al. [2011] propose the efficient MIA-N algorithm to solve the problem of maximizing the positive influence spread for the IC-N model. Due to the competition between positive influence and negative influence, more involved dynamic programming method is used in MIA-N to facilitate influence computation on the MIA tree structure.

In addition to the above, the authors also provide a theoretical analysis of the quality sensitivity in influence maximization. That is, how sensitive is the influence maximization problem for different quality factors. They show that, if one always uses one fixed quality factor q for influence maximization, then in the worst case it is possible that the actual optimal influence spread is $\Theta(\sqrt{n/k})$ larger than the optimal influence spread under q, where n is the number of nodes and k is the number of seeds selected.

Furthermore, they also discuss several model extensions, such as each node having different quality factors, allowing non-homogeneous arc diffusions, using different objectives such as the difference between positive influence spread and negative influence spread, etc. They show that in most extensions submodularity no longer holds.

4.2.4 A NEW FRONTIER – THE HOST PERSPECTIVE

Most of the studies in information propagation, with or without competition, implicitly assume that the players, e.g., the companies running a campaign, have unfettered access to the underlying social network. This means they have access to the network as well as to the underlying influence probabilities or at the very least to a large enough action log from which either influence probabilities can be learned or spread can be predicted directly (see Section 4.1). This is an unrealistic assumption. The online social networking site may be operated by a third party (such as Facebook) and companies running marketing campaigns need its explicit permission to access the network. The permissions may be established using formal contracts. This suggests a new business opportunity for the owner of the social network who can offer *seed selection as service*. For a fee, it selects the seeds on behalf of (the competing) companies. We call the social network owner the *host*. A majority of the studies in competitive influence maximization ignore the role played by the host and typically focus on strategies one of the companies can adopt in order to maximize its gains. As shown by Lu et al. [2013], the role played by the host is fundamental.

A natural setting is one in which each company C_i that intends to run a campaign specifies a budget, a number k_i. Each company pays a fee to the host which we can reasonably assume is monotone in the number of seeds, i.e., the more seeds desired, the larger the fee. Once all companies specify their budget, the host uses an algorithm and its network and influence probabilities to choose seeds effectively. Next, it allocates these seeds to the various companies according to their specified budget. From a business perspective, it is in the best interest of the host to ensure the seeds are selected such that the collective expected number of adoptions across all companies is maximized and at the same time the seeds are allocated to companies in a fair manner. An intuitive metric for measuring fairness is the *amplification factor*, informally referred to as *bang-for-the-buck*, defined as the ratio of the influence spread over the number of seeds, $\sigma(S_0)/|S_0|$, where S_0 is the seed set selected for a company. If the host allocates the seeds arbitrarily, it may result in wide variance in the amplification factor, leading to resentful clients. This motivates the need for fair allocation from a business perspective.

The K-LT Propagation Model

It should be noted that the host perspective can be adopted in the context of any competitive propagation model. Lu et al. [2013] propose an extension to the LT model for capturing competition, called K-LT. They show that unlike previous competitive propagation models in the literature, the K-LT model satisfies certain desirable properties. We define the model next.

Definition 4.20 K-LT model for competitive influence diffusion. The input to the model consists of a directed graph $G = (V, E)$ along with influence weights $w(u, v)$ (or simply w_{uv}) on all arcs $(u, v) \in E$, and a number K representing the number of competing companies, denoted $\{C_1, ..., C_K\}$. A propagation or campaign in this model proceeds as follows. Each company C_i specifies a budget k_i to the host and wants to promote its product. For simplicity, we use C_i to also denote the product of that company. The host selects $\sum_{1 \leq i \leq K} k_i$ seeds and allocates the seed set S_0^i to company C_i where $|S_0^i| = k_i$ and S_0^i's are pairwise disjoint. Once the seeds are allocated every seed $u \in S_0^i$ becomes C_i-active at time $t = 0$, by definition, i.e., it adopts product C_i. All non-seeds u choose a random threshold $\theta_u \in [0, 1]$. For any time $t \geq 1$, let S_t^i be the set of nodes that are C_i-active, $i \in \{1, ..., K\}$, and let $S_t = S_t^1 \cup S_t^2 \cup \cdots \cup S_t^K$. Each activation step consists of two phases. At any time $t \geq 1$, in the first phase, a node u becomes active if the net inflow of influence from all active nodes as of time $t - 1$ exceeds the node threshold θ_u, i.e.,

$\sum_{v \in S_{t-1} \cup N^{in}(u)} w_{vu} \geq \theta_u$. In the second phase, still at time t, node u decides which product to adopt: it adopts product C_i with probability equal to the ratio of the total inflow of influence from its neighbors that just became active at time $t - 1$ w.r.t. C_i, over the total inflow of influence from all neighbors that just became active (w.r.t. any product) at time $t - 1$, i.e., the probability of u adopting C_i is $\sum_{v \in S_{t-1}^i \setminus S_{t-2}^i} w_{vu} / \sum_{v \in S_{t-1} \setminus S_{t-2}} w_{vu}$ (by convention $S_{-1}^i = S_{-1} = \emptyset$).

Notice that when u is not an in-neighbor of v, $w_{uv} = 0$ by definition, so the probability calculated in the second phase is based on active in-neighbors of u. Also notice that, essentially, ties are broken using proportional probabilities.

Observe that the adoption probability is defined based on nodes activated in the previous instant. One reason for this is that it captures recency effects, as it is known that influence decays over time and consumers are likely to rely on recent information about adoption by their neighbors rather than old information [Hogg and Szabó, 2009, Peng and Mu, 2011, Zhao et al., 2003]. An alternative definition of adoption probability might be $\sum_{v \in S_{t-1}^i} w_{vu} / \sum_{v \in S_{t-1}} w_{vu}$, i.e., the ratio of net incoming influence of neighbors that are C_i-active at time $t - 1$ to that of neighbors active at time $t - 1$. This definition treats the influence of all neighbors alike regardless of how long ago the neighbor activated and does not account for recency effects. This definition is in fact adopted in the WPCLT model proposed by Borodin et al. [Borodin et al., 2010]. We discuss the pros and cons of the two different choices below, but first we define a few core notions. Let $\mathbf{S} = \{S_0^1, ..., S_0^K\}$ be a seed set allocation, i.e., the set of seed sets assigned to the K companies. We use $\mathbf{S}_{-i}$ to denote the set of seed sets allocated to all companies but C_i, i.e., $\mathbf{S}_{-i} = \{S_0^1, ..., S_0^{i-1}, S_0^{i+1}, ..., S_0^K\}$.

Definition 4.21   Influence spread for the K-LT model.   We use $\sigma_i(S_0^i, \mathbf{S}_{-i})$ to denote the expected number of nodes that are C_i-active, given the seed set allocation $\mathbf{S}$. We define $\sigma_{all} = \sum_{i=1}^K \sigma_i(S_0^i, \mathbf{S}_{-i})$, i.e., the sum of expected numbers of nodes activated with different products.

First, as noted by Borodin et al. [2010], the WPCLT model has some counter-intuitive properties. Allocating more seeds for a company may sometimes result in that company's influence spread going down! This strange behavior stems from the possibility under this model that seeding of some nodes by a company may allow multiple "activation attempts" by seeds of a different company, as illustrated by the following example.

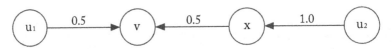

Figure 4.5: Graph for Example 4.22.

Example 4.22   Multiple activation attempts.   Consider the network of Figure 4.5, taken from Lu et al. [2013], and two companies with seed sets $S_0^1 = \{u_1\}$ and $S_0^2 = \emptyset$. Suppose the random thresholds chosen by v and x, θ_v and θ_x, fall into $(0.5, 1)$. It is easy to see that no non-seed node will become active at any time. Now consider adding the seed u_2 to S_0^2, i.e., $S_0^2 := \{u_2\}$. Now, at time step 1, x is active w.r.t. company C_2 (as $w_{u_2,x} = 1 > \theta_x$) and v remains inactive (as $w_{u_2,v} = 0.5 < \theta_v$). Then, at time step 2, v becomes influenced as the total incoming weight is now 1, and then it will become active w.r.t. company C_1 or C_2 each with probability 0.5. ∎

Notice that adding a seed to company C_2 ends up helping its competition C_1. The activation attempt by u_1 fails at step 1. Since u_1 is considered "contagious" indefinitely in the future, at time 2, u_1 gets to make a second attempt at activating v and succeeds this time thanks to the newly added seed u_2 for company C_2. This behavior may be undesirable and is at the core of WPCLT's lack of monotonicity and submodularity: Borodin et al. [2010] give examples showing that influence spread under the WPCLT model is neither monotone nor submodular, making it hard to approximate. On the other hand, it can be shown [Lu et al., 2013] that the K-LT model retains these desirable properties of monotonicity and submodularity. More precisely, we have the following.

Theorem 4.23   *Under the K-LT model, the influence spread function $\sigma_i(S_0^i, \mathbf{S}_{-i})$, with $\mathbf{S}_{-i}$ fixed, is monotone and submodular in S_0^i.*

This result is proved by developing a competitive version of the live-arc graph model, which we define next.

Definition 4.24   Live-arc graph model for the K-LT competitive diffusion model.   The competitive version of the live-arc graph model is defined analogously to the classical one: every node v picks at most one of its incoming arcs at random, picking arc (u, v) with probability w_{uv} and picking no incoming arc with probability $1 - \sum_{x \in N^{in}(v)} w_{xv}$. Remove all incoming arcs for each of the seed nodes. A non-seed node is C_i-reachable if there is a live path from a node in S_0^i to that node. Each set of such random choices of in-neighbors is a possible world X and let $R_X(S_0^i)$ denote the set of C_i-reachable nodes in X. The expected number of C_i-reachable nodes is just $\sum_X \Pr(X) R_X(S_0^i)$.

Note that in a live-arc graph (i.e., a possible world), each node has at most one incoming arc and the seeds have no incoming arcs, and thus each non-seed node can be reached by at most one seed node, and thus reachable sets $R_X(S_0^i)$'s for all i's are pairwise disjoint in any possible world. We can show that the K-LT model is equivalent to the competitive live-arc graph model above. It is easy to see the influence spread under the latter model is monotone and submodular.

Note that the K-LT model is different from the CLT model in Definition 4.3, and the live-arc graph model defined above is different from the live-arc graph model for CIC and CLT in Definition 4.4. The CLT and its corresponding live-arc graph model consider two independent and competing campaigns, and the two campaigns only compete on which one reaches inactive nodes first. The K-LT model and its corresponding live-arc graph model, on the other hand, essentially model a combined diffusion of all campaigns as one diffusion process, and the final state of an activated node is determined at random in proportion to the contribution to the node's activation by each of the competing campaigns.

Returning to the main technical problem, the host must select the seeds such that the overall influence spread is maximum and allocate them to the companies such that the *bang for the buck* for different companies is as close to each other as possible. We formalize this below.

Definition 4.25 Amplification factor.   We define the *amplification factor* of company C_i as the average influence spread it gets per seed, i.e., $\alpha_i = \sigma_i(S_0^i, \mathbf{S_{-i}})/k_i$, where k_i is the budget of company C_i.

We remark that although the definition refers to companies, it should be understood that they could instead be political parties or any organization, etc., depending on the application at hand. The first problem is seed selection.

Problem 4.26 Overall influence maximization   Given a directed graph $G = (V, E)$ with pairwise arc weights, budgets $k_1, k_2, \ldots, k_K \in \mathbb{Z}_+$ with $\sum_{i=1}^{K} b_i \leq |V|$, select a seed set $S_0 \subseteq V$ of size $\sum_{i=1}^{K} k_i$, such that σ_{all} is maximized.

It can be shown that under both K-LT and WPCLT models, the overall influence spread can be reasoned about by "collapsing" all companies into one and focusing on maximizing its influence spread. More precisely, we have:

Proposition 4.27   *Given a directed graph $G = (V, E)$ with arc weights, and K pair-wise disjoint subsets $S_0^1, S_0^2, \ldots, S_0^K$ of V, then under both the K-LT model and the WPCLT model, letting $S_0 = S_0^1 \cup \ldots \cup S_0^K$, we have*

$$\sigma_{all} = \sigma_{LT}(S_0),\tag{4.7}$$

where σ_{LT} is the influence spread function for the classical LT model.

The implication is that all the techniques developed for seed selection under the classical LT model, including greedy approximation using Monte Carlo simulation as well as various efficient high quality heuristics are now available for solving the above problem. We can now focus on the second and the main challenging problem, where given a set of seed nodes, they need to be allocated to the companies in the fairest possible manner. We formalize fairness by insisting that the amplification factor offered by the host to the different companies should be as close to each other as possible. One way of realizing this is to say that the maximum amplification factor, $\alpha_{max} := max_{1 \leq i \leq K} \alpha_i$ should be minimized. The intuition is that minimizing α_{max} will balance

---

Algorithm 12 Needy-Greedy: Greedy allocation of seeds to K companies.

Input: S_0 (order in non-increasing order of $\delta_u, u \in S_0$) and $k_i, \forall i \in \{1, \ldots, K\}$.
Output: A K-partition of S_0, with $|S_0^i| = k_i, \forall i$.

1: Initialize $S_0^i \leftarrow \emptyset, \forall i$
2: **for** each $u \in S_0$ **do**
3:      $T \leftarrow \{i \mid i \in \{1, 2, \ldots, K\}, |S_0^i| < k_i\}$
4:      $j \leftarrow \operatorname{argmin}_{i \in T}\{\sigma_i(S_0^i, \mathbf{S_{-i}})/k_i\}$
5:      $S_0^j \leftarrow S_0^j \cup \{u\}$
6: **end for**

---

out the various amplification factors. This min-max objective is a natural choice and has been widely adopted in resource allocation and load balancing [Kleinberg and Tardos, 2006].

Problem 4.28 Fair seed allocation (FSA) Given a directed graph $G = (V, E)$ with pair-wise arc weights, budgets $k_1, k_2, \ldots, k_K \in \mathbb{Z}_+$, a seed set $S_0 \subseteq V$ with $|S_0| = \sum_{i=1}^{K} k_i$, find a partition of S_0 into K disjoint subsets $S_0^1, S_0^2, \ldots, S_0^K \subseteq S_0$, such that $|S_0^i| = k_i, i \in \{1, \ldots, K\}$, and the maximum amplification factor of any company is minimized.

It can be shown that the above problem is NP-hard, by reduction from the 3-PARTITION problem. In spite of this hardness result, we can devise a very effective heuristic algorithm. The algorithm is based on the notion of adjusted marginal gain, defined as follows. In the classical LT setting, given a seed set S_0, the *adjusted marginal gain* of a node $u \in S_0$ is defined as $\delta_u = \sigma_{LT}^{V-S_0+u}(\{u\})$, i.e., the influence spread of node u in the subgraph of G induced by node u along with all non-seeds. We have the following.

Theorem 4.29 *Consider an allocation of seed sets, where the seed set $S_0^i \subseteq S_0$ is assigned to company C_i and the remaining seeds $S_0 \setminus S_0^i$ are allocated arbitrarily to other companies (denoted by $\mathbf{S_{-i}}$). Then under the K-LT model,*

$$\sigma_i(S_0^i, \mathbf{S_{-i}}) = \sum_{u \in S_0^i} \delta_u. \tag{4.8}$$

The theorem says that the influence spread for any company C_i can be calculated simply by adding up the adjusted marginal gains of the seeds it has been allocated, ignoring details of allocation to other companies. This is a powerful result and forms the centerpiece of our efficient algorithm for FSA.

We can pick the seeds using any approach for influence maximization for LT. We order the seeds in non-increasing order of the adjusted marginal gains. We start with an empty allocation and start allocating seeds in a "needy greedy" fashion, as shown in Algorithm 12. Maintain all companies for which the budget has not been reached. Among them, allocate the next seed to the company with the least average influence spread so far, until all companies are allocated up to their budget. It turns out that the FSA problem is NP-hard even when $K = 2$. However, this case admits a pseudo-polynomial time optimal algorithm, based on dynamic programming. This allows us to gauge the performance of the Needy-Greedy algorithm compared to the optimal solution for the special case $K = 2$.

Baselines: Two baseline algorithms that can be considered are Random and Alternating. Random assigns seeds to the K companies uniformly at random, subject to the budget constraints. Alternating first orders the K companies according to a randomly chosen permutation. Then it assigns seeds to them in a round robin fashion, following the order.

The algorithms are run on three real data sets: Epinions, Flixster, and NetHEPT. An important metric on which the algorithms are compared is the *relative error* incurred by the algorithm w.r.t. the best possible amplification factor, $\alpha_{ideal} = \sigma_{all} / \sum_{i=1}^{K} k_j$. Intuitively, this is theoretically the fairest possible solution, since every company is offered the exact same amplification factor α_{ideal}. In practice, it may not be possible to realize this owing to network structure, arc influence probabilities, etc. Yet, it offers a bound on the best possible. Relative error of a seed allocation algorithm is defined by comparing the maximum amplification factor α_{max} achieved by the algorithm with α_{ideal}. More precisely,

$$RelativeError(\alpha_{max}) = \frac{\alpha_{max} - \alpha_{ideal}}{\alpha_{ideal}} \times 100\% , \qquad (4.9)$$

where α_{max} is the maximum amplification factor achieved by a given allocation algorithm. Lu et al. [2013] show the following. For the case $K = 2$, the dynamic programming approach achieves the best relative error, depending on the precision chosen. Needy-Greedy achieves a relative error close to that of dynamic programming and is often three orders of magnitude faster than dynamic programming on the data sets tested. While the baseline algorithms take about the same running time as Needy-Greedy, they suffer from a relative error that is at least an order of magnitude higher. We refer the reader to [Lu et al., 2013] for details of the proofs as well as extensive experimental analysis.

We close this section by noting that the perspective of a host, the network owner, is a fundamental aspect of a successful viral marketing campaign. This is so even when there is no competition. Most of the existing literature on competitive viral marketing has ignored the important role played by the host. Incorporating host in the equation takes an important step in closing the gap between influence maximization (competitive or otherwise) and real-world viral marketing. Further investigation is necessary to make it possible to transfer the technology embodied in the rich body of techniques to the practical viral marketing world.

4.3   INFLUENCE, ADOPTION, AND PROFIT

The majority of the research literature on influence maximization considers an idealized setting where being influenced is typically equated with product adoption, and influence spread is treated synonymously with revenue or profit. There has been recent efforts at distinguishing between these notions, and this section briefly describes some of these works. Note that these distinctions are orthogonal to whether one considers competition in the campaign.

4.3.1   INFLUENCE VS. ADOPTION

Much of the work on influence maximization tacitly assumes that whenever a user is influenced about a product or an innovation, she will immediately buy or adopt it and will encourage her social peers to adopt it. However, an influenced user may not necessarily adopt a product, say because she does not have the opportunity yet, but has formed an opinion about it anyway based on experience of her friends. Furthermore, she may decide to share this opinion with other friends. In the epidemiology setting, this would be similar to being infected by a disease, and hence, potentially transmitting it to others, but not having any symptoms.

On the other hand, a user who adopts a product may not like it and hence may decide to not encourage her friends to adopt it, at least not to the extent as another user who adopted the product and liked it (she may even try to discourage further adoptions, as in the endogenous competition case of Section 4.2.3). Thus, adoption is not necessarily the same as influence in general and experience with a product is an important factor to take into account in modeling adoption and influence explicitly. As an example, Bob buys a new gadget and does not like it because of certain features he thinks are lacking. He describes them in his blog. Sally follows Bob's tech blogs seriously and decides not to buy the gadget herself. Similarly, Mary watches a movie and likes it. Her friend John respects her taste in movies, but does not have the time to watch it just yet; nevertheless, he tells his friends about it, some of who decide to watch it.

In a nutshell, an adopting user's opinion (degree of endorsement) plays a key role in determining the likelihood of her friends adopting it; and even a non-adopter may act as an *information bridge* and share her opinion with her friends, thus contributing to influence propagation and even adoption. Bhagat et al. [2012] propose a Linear Threshold model with Colors (LT-C) for capturing influence and adoption, based on the degree of endorsement by users. Is there empirical evidence supporting the distinction between adoption and influence? As pointed out by the authors, in the Flixster data set, a social movie rating web site, in addition to the usual numerical ratings, there are special "ratings"—"want to see it" and "not interested." These correspond to users who have not adopted (i.e., watched the movie) but either promote or inhibit the product w.r.t. further adoption. Similar special ratings also exist in the MovieLens data set. Inspired by these observations and intuitions, they propose the LT-C model, which is illustrated in Figure 4.6, taken from Bhagat et al. [2012], as a state diagram.

A user is in one of the *inactive, active, adopt, tattle, promote,* or *inhibit* states. In the inactive state, she has not formed an opinion on the product. She reaches the active state once influenced by her neighbors. Let A be the set of neighbors of a given node v who are active and let $f_v(A)$ be a monotone function that returns the net influence of the active users A on v. If $f_v(A) \geq \theta_v$, where $\theta_v \in [0, 1]$ is a threshold randomly chosen by user v, then v becomes active. As in the classical

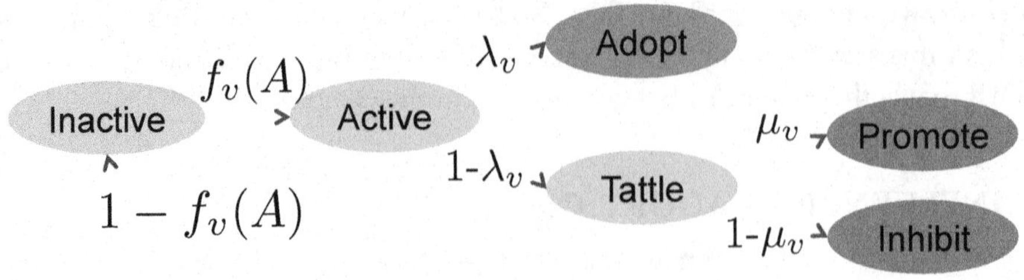

Figure 4.6: LT-C model with colored end states: adopt–green, promote–blue, inhibit–red.

LT model, $_v$ is a measure of how much incoming influence it takes for v to become influenced, or active. In the context of a social rating system, one possible way to define the function f is as follows:

$$f_v(A) = \frac{\sum_{u \in A} w_{uv}(r_{u,i} \quad r_{min})}{r_{max} \quad r_{min}}, \tag{4.10}$$

where r_{max} and r_{min} represent the maximum and minimum ratings in the system, respectively. $(r_{u,i} \quad r_{min})$ is a measure of user u's endorsement of the product i, $(r_{max} \quad r_{min})$ capturing the highest possible endorsement, and w_{uv} is the influence weight on arc (u, v) in the LT model. Once a user is in the active state, she has the necessary information to form an opinion on the product. She may decide to adopt and rate the product or to share her opinions without adopting the product, i.e., to enter the tattle state. Similarly, once she enters the tattle state, she may share positive or negative opinions on the product, i.e., enter the promote, or inhibit state. These choices are governed by probabilistic parameters ϕ_v and $_v$, which are specific to a user v. It is worth noting that only inactive, adopt, promote, and inhibit states are observable. The other internal states are not. In this model, we are interested in maximizing adoption as opposed to just influence spread. More precisely, we use $\tau(S)$ to denote the *coverage*, i.e., the expected number of nodes in the adopt state at the end of a propagation, given a set of seed nodes S. The problem then is that given a seed budget k, find up to k nodes that maximize $\tau(S)$ under the LT-C model. Bhagat et al. [2012] show that this problem is NP-hard and that $\tau()$ is monotone and submodular. Consequently, the greedy algorithm can once again be used in order to obtain a polynomial time $(1 \quad 1/e)$-approximation to the optimal solution.

They show how the node parameters ϕ_v, $_v$, as well as the arc weights $w_{u,v}$, can be learned from given ratings data sets. They validate their model on the movie rating data sets Flixster and MovieLens and music rating data set last.fm. They compare the coverage predicted by the LT-C model with that predicted by the following natural baselines: (i) the classical LT model; (ii) LT-Ratings: the LT-C model without the tattle state, i.e., all active (aka influenced) nodes adopt the product and provide ratings according to Eq. 4.10; and (iii) LT-Tattle: LT-C model with ratings ignored, i.e., all adopting and promoting users are assumed to rate the product at r_{max} and all

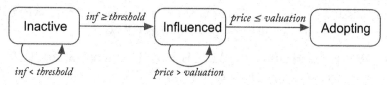

Figure 4.7: Node states in the LT-V model, adapted from [Lu and Lakshmanan, 2012].

inhibiting users rate it at r_{min}, while the actual ratings in the data set are ignored. They show that LT-C by far is the most accurate in predicting actual coverage. We refer the reader to that paper for a comprehensive coverage of this topic as well as extensive experiments and analysis.

4.3.2 INFLUENCE VS. PROFIT

The pricing of a product plays a significant role in its adoption by users. Even when a user is influenced enough to want to buy a product, she only buys it if her own internal valuation of the product exceeds the price she is offered. In fact, studies in management science (e.g., Kalish [1985]) show that product purchase proceeds in two stages: (i) first, the user becomes aware of the product and then (ii) based on the price, she decides whether to buy it. Of these, it is only in the first stage where awareness of a product spreads because of influence. Once this propagation is complete, different considerations take over. Every user has her own valuation of a product, reflecting how much it is worth to her. It is only when this exceeds the price she is offered that she decides to buy it. Figure 4.7 shows the state diagram from Lu and Lakshmanan [2012] that depicts the salient points above.

We now describe the LT-V model from [Lu and Lakshmanan, 2012] that incorporates the above aspect. As in the classical LT model, a user is in the *inactive* state and stays there until the net inflow of influence exceeds the user's own internal threshold, at which point the user reaches the *influenced* state. From this state, the user reaches the *adopting* state only if the offer price is no more than the user's own valuation of the product. We will see later how valuation is determined. It is assumed that only adopting states are visible so only users in this state can influence their neighbors. Influence propagates as per the classical LT model, governed by arc weights, which need to be learned from available data. Let $G = (V, E)$ be a social graph along with influence weights $w : E \rightarrow [0, 1]$. A price offering can be regarded as a vector in $[0, 1]^V$, where we assume the price is in the unit interval w.l.o.g. The expected profit can then be expressed as $\pi : 2^V \times [0, 1]^V \rightarrow \mathbb{R}$, i.e., given a seed set S and a price vector $\vec{\wp} \in [0, 1]^V$, $\pi(S, \vec{\wp})$ returns the expected profit resulting from the propagation followed by product adoption. In reality, it costs to seed nodes, so for any fixed price vector $\vec{\wp}$, the function $\pi(S, \vec{\wp})$ is not monotone in S. Intuitively, $\pi(S, \vec{\wp})$ can be seen as the *difference* between the revenue obtained from all adopting users buying the product (in expectation) and the cost of seeding the $|S|$ users (e.g., from rebates, cost of mailing ads and coupons), making the function non-monotone. In view of this, the right way to formulate the profit maximization problem is as follows.

Problem 4.30   Profit maximization (PROMAX) [Lu and Lakshmanan, 2012]   Given an instance of the LT-V model consisting of a graph $G = (V, E)$ with influence weights $w : E \to [0, 1]$, find the optimal pair of a seed set S and a price vector $\vec{\wp}$ that maximizes the expected profit $\pi(S, \vec{\wp})$.

Notice that there is no budget associated with the size of S. Since π is non-monotone in S, it is reasonable to try to find the best seed set S, regardless of size, that maximizes the expected profit. A fundamental distinction between profit maximization and influence maximization is that unlike the latter, the former calls for making non-boolean decisions in that for each node, we need to decide not only whether to seed it but also what price to offer it.

Several questions arise. How do users pick their valuations? How do they respond to price offering? Who knows about the valuations? The LT-V model [Lu and Lakshmanan, 2012] makes the *independent private value* (IPV) assumption [Kleinberg and Leighton, 2003, Shoham and Leyton-Brown, 2009]: users' valuations are drawn independently at random from a certain distribution. Each user holds her valuation private and does not reveal it. She only interacts by responding to a price offering by either adopting a product or declining the offer. This assumption is motivated by reasons of privacy and trust. The underlying distribution of user valuations can be learned from historical sales data. A second key assumption is that users are *price-takers* who respond myopically to the price they are offered solely based on their privately held valuation and the offer price.

A restricted special case of PROMAX is of theoretical interest, mainly as a stepping stone to understand the development of PROMAX. This corresponds to the assumption that the valuation of every user is a fixed constant $\wp \in (0, 1]$. That is, every user picks this valuation with probability 1. For simplicity, assume that the offer price for every seed node is 0, i.e., the seeds are given a free sample.[3] All other users are charged price $\wp$. Let $h_L(S)$ denote the expected number of adopting nodes according to the LT-V model. Then the expected profit is

$$
\begin{aligned}
\hat{\pi}(S) &= \wp \cdot (h_L(S) - |S|) - c_a |S| \\
&= \wp \cdot h_L(S) - (\wp + c_a) |S|,
\end{aligned}
\tag{4.11}
$$

where c_a is a constant seeding cost per node. Notice that the expected profit is a function of just the seed set S as that uniquely determines the pricing for all nodes. It is easy to see that $\hat{\pi}(\cdot)$ is non-monotone: $\hat{\pi}(\emptyset) = 0 < \hat{\pi}(\{u\})$ and $\hat{\pi}(V) < 0$. If we had charged the seeds the "full" price of $\wp$, $\hat{\pi}(\cdot)$ would still be non-monotone. The only difference is the maximum of this function. In this setting, we want to find the best set of seeds that maximizes the expected profit, thus the number of seeds k is not given as input but is to be determined as part of a solution. It is shown in [Lu and Lakshmanan, 2012].

Theorem 4.31   *Finding a seed set S that maximizes $\hat{\pi}(S)$ is NP-hard.*

---

[3]Technically, we can charge price $\wp$ to the seeds and our results still carry over.

Algorithm 13 U-Greedy($G = (V, E)$, $\hat{\pi}$)

Input: Graph $G = (V, E)$ with influence weights, seeding cost c_a and "full price" $\wp$.
Output: Greedy approximation to the optimal seed set.
  1: $S \leftarrow \emptyset$
  2: **while** true **do**
  3:     $u \leftarrow \text{argmax}_{u_i \in V \setminus S} [\hat{\pi}(S \cup \{u_i\}) - \hat{\pi}(S)]$
  4:     **if** $\hat{\pi}(S \cup \{u\}) - \hat{\pi}(S) > 0$ **then**
  5:         $S \leftarrow S \cup \{u\}$
  6:     **else**
  7:         *break*
  8:     **end if**
  9: **end while**
 10: Output S

The proof is by reduction from Minimum Vertex Cover. It is easy to see that $\hat{\pi}(\cdot)$ is submodular as it is a non-negative linear combination of the submodular functions $h_L(S)$ and $-|S|$. We can use the following variant of the greedy algorithm, which we call U-Greedy (for unbudgeted greedy) for finding a good set of seeds. The algorithm keeps adding any seed with the maximum marginal gain that is positive, to the current set of seeds until no longer possible.

As shown by Feige et al. [2007], using randomized local search we can obtain a 2/5-approximation for the problem of maximizing general non-monotone submodular functions. In our case, this would lead to a time complexity $O(|V|^3 |E|/\varepsilon)$, where $(1 + \varepsilon/|V|^2)$ is the per-step improvement factor in the search. By contrast, the function $\hat{\pi}$ is the difference between a monotone submodular function and a linear function, and our unbudgeted greedy approach (Algorithm 13 U-Greedy) has time complexity $O(|V|^2|E|)$ and a better approximation ratio, which is slightly lower than $1 - 1/e$, shown next.

Theorem 4.32   *Given an instance of the restricted* ProMax *problem under the LT-V model consisting of a graph $G = (V, E)$ with influence weights $w : E \to [0, 1]$ and objective function $\hat{\pi}$, let $S^g \subseteq V$ be the seed set returned by Algorithm 13, and $S^* \subseteq V$ be the optimal solution. Then,*

$$\hat{\pi}(S^g) \geq (1 - 1/e) \cdot \hat{\pi}(S^*) - \Theta(\max\{|S^g|, |S^*|\}). \tag{4.12}$$

Typically, the size of S tends to be a fraction of $h_L(S)$, the expected number of adopting nodes and thus the approximation ratio afforded by U-Greedy is expected to be much better than using randomized local search. It can be shown that for the general LT-V model, the function $\pi(S, \vec{\wp})$ is submodular in S for any fixed price vector $\vec{\wp}$. The proof is more involved than that of Theorem 2.13. We can also show that computing $\pi(S, \vec{\wp})$ for any given S and $\vec{\wp}$ is #P-hard. As in the classical case, we can estimate this to an arbitrarily high precision by running Monte Carlo simulations sufficiently many times. What algorithms can we use for finding good seed sets in the general case? It turns out we can devise good algorithms using U-Greedy as a basis.

Baselines: The first baseline, called All-OMP, is obtained by running U-Greedy to obtain a seed set and then adjusting the price in a second phase. The price charged is *optimal myopic price* (OMP), calculated as follows. Let $X \in [0, 1]$ denote the random variable corresponding to the price offered to a node u_i. Then the expected revenue resulting from that node's adoption is $X(1 - F_i(X))$ where $F_i(\cdot)$ is the distribution function associated with the valuation of node u_i and $(1 - F_i(X))$ is the probability that the valuation of node u_i is more than X. Let $\wp_i^m$ denote the optimal value of X that maximizes this expected revenue. Notice that this optimization is local to node u_i and completely ignores the network effect. All-OMP charges the price $\wp_i^m$ to node u_i, regardless of whether it is a seed or not.

All-OMP loses sight of the fact that there is a probability $F_i(\wp_i^m)$ with which a seed node u_i may decline the offer. As a result, that seed is essentially "wasted." Not only do we miss out on the revenue that might have come from it, worse yet, we miss out on the network effect from that node's adoption. Motivated by this, we can design a second baseline, which goes to the extreme of offering a full discount to the seed nodes, thereby ensuring all of them adopt. So, seed nodes pay no price and all other nodes pay their corresponding OMP. We call this baseline FFS, for free for seeds.

Clearly, both baselines make ad hoc choices w.r.t. pricing in that the network structure is not taken into account. A more sophisticated algorithm, called PAGE, for Price Aware GrEedy, adjusts the prices charged to the seed nodes in a greedy manner. Initially, every node is a candidate to be a seed and we initialize the price vector so as to charge OMP to all nodes. Then for each node u_i, find the best adjustment $\wp_i^*$ to its current price $\wp_i^m$ which brings the maximum improvement to π, keeping prices offered to all other nodes fixed. Then greedily pick the node u_j whose best adjustment $\wp_j^*$ brings the maximum marginal gain among all remaining nodes, update its offer price to $\wp_j^*$ and add it to the set of seeds. Repeat this until we can no longer find a seed for which a price adjustment leads to a positive marginal gain. At the end of this procedure, we leave the offer prices of all non-seeds unchanged at their OMP values. An important point is that computing the expected profit $\pi(\cdot, \cdot)$ exactly is #P-hard. The proof of this result is analogous to a similar result for computing the influence spread for the LT model. We can circumvent this difficulty as in the classical case by running Monte Carlo simulations. The reader is referred to [Lu and Lakshmanan, 2012] for more details of PAGE as well as for a detailed empirical analysis of the various algorithms on three real data sets Epinions, Flixster, and NetHEPT. The authors show that PAGE outperforms the baselines under a variety of conditions, both on running time and on the expected profit achieved.

We close this section by noting that optimizing (expected) product adoption and/or profit in the context of competitive viral marketing is a fruitful direction for future research.

4.4   OTHER EXTENSIONS

There have been many studies on various optimization problems based on the stochastic diffusion models such as the IC and LT models, and it is still a very active research area with new research results coming out constantly while many problems remain open and many new directions remain to be explored. We conclude this chapter with a brief survey on a number of recent extensions and studies related to influence modeling and influence maximization.

Time-critical influence maximization.   One natural extension is to consider time-critical influence maximization, that is, maximizing influence spread within a certain time constraint. Chen et al. [2012] and Liu et al. [2012] independently propose time-delayed diffusion models and algorithms for time-critical influence maximization problem. The algorithm is greedy-based, since the objective function is still monotone and submodular, and they also propose different improvements to make the algorithm scalable. Goyal et al. [2012] also consider time aspect, but they consider the problem MINTIME, which is to minimize the time span of achieving a certain required influence spread given a certain budget constraint on the seed set. They show that bi-criteria or tri-criteria optimizations in the IC model (allowing slacks on seed set size, influence spread, and/or time span) are hard when the slacks are small unless $NP \subseteq DTIME(n^{O(\log\log n)})$,[4] and provide a positive result on tri-criteria approximation when the slacks allowed are above certain level.

Seed minimization.   The dual problem of influence maximization is the seed minimization problem, which tries to minimize the size of the seed set that could achieve certain level of influence spread. Seed minimization problem contains set cover as a special case, which is known to be hard to approximate within a factor of $(1 - \epsilon) \ln n$ unless $NP \subseteq DTIME(n^{O(\log\log n)})$ Feige [1998]. Goyal et al. [2012] show that a bi-criteria greedy algorithm is possible for the seed minimization problem if the influence spread function $\sigma(\cdot)$ is monotone and submodular. In particular, they study the seed minimization problem with non-uniform and non-negative node cost $c(v)$, and cost of a seed set S is $c(S) = \sum_{v \in S} c(v)$. They show that if the target influence spread is η and the corresponding minimum cost seed set is S^*, then for any shortfall $\varepsilon > 0$, there is a greedy solution to find a seed set S such that $\sigma(S) \geq \eta - \varepsilon$ and $c(S) \geq c(S^*)(1 + \ln(\eta/\varepsilon))$. Chen [2008] studies the seed minimization problem for the fixed threshold model (Definition 2.19), and show that it is not approximable within a poly-logarithmic factor unless $NP \subseteq DTIME(n^{polylog(n)})$.

Participation maximization.   Another type of maximization problems, called *participation maximization*, utilize social influence diffusion for seed allocations to support multiple diffusions, where each node can only serve as seeds for a small number of diffusions ([Ienco et al., 2010, Sun et al., 2011]). For example, Sun et al. [2011] consider the context of online discussion forums, where there are multiple discussion threads, and users who write a post on a thread may influence the readers of the thread to generate more posts in the thread. When a user logs into

---

[4]DTIME(t) denotes the class of languages that have a deterministic algorithm that runs in time t.

the system, the system would like to recommend several discussion threads in which the user may likely to respond and generate further interests and responses on the thread. The users who are recommended to a particular thread are the seeds of the thread. They propose a user posting model based on the IC diffusion model, and prove that diffusion in every thread is submodular. However, the maximization problem is not on one thread, but to maximize the total number of participants on all threads, and thus the name participation maximization. Sun et al. link participation maximization to social welfare maximization with submodular functions [Dobzinski and Schapira, 2006, Vondrák, 2008], apply greedy algorithm proposed in the literature and also propose fast heuristics to solve the participation maximization problem. Ienco et al. [2010] study the similar problem in the context of microblogging services, where the system recommends a small number of ongoing topics (called *memes*) to a user to increase the total participation on all topics. Different from recommender systems, these works rely on social influence diffusion, and thus the objective is not only to match a thread or a meme to a user who would most likely be interested by the thread or meme, but also has the potential to generate a diffusion cascade in the network. Participation maximization may also find applications in advertisement placement or targeting in social networks.

Adaptive influence maximization.   Influence maximization may also be done in an adaptive way. That is, one may select one or several seed nodes first, observe the cascade result of these seeds, and then based on the cascade results adaptively select subsequent seeds to achieve more effective influence maximization result. Golovin and Krause [2011] define the general framework of adaptive submodularity and study the adaptive influence maximization problem as an application of their framework. Under the independent cascade model, they define the *full-adoption feedback model*, in which one could observe the complete cascade of current seeds before selecting future seeds. They show that independent cascade model with the full-adoption feedback is adaptive submodular, and thus an adaptive greedy algorithm could achieve $(1 - 1/e)$ approximation of the optimal adaptive algorithm.

Influence maximization with non-submodular influence spread functions.   Almost all influence maximization related problems appeared in the literature so far rely on the greedy approach for submodular function maximization. When the diffusion model is not submodular, either hardness of approximation results are shown or it is still open on how to solve these problems effectively. For example, for the fixed threshold model (Definition 2.19), Kempe et al. [2003] show that it is hard to approximate the influence maximization problem in this model to any non-trivial ratio unless NP=P, while Chen [2008] show that the dual seed minimization problem is hard to approximate to any poly-logarithmic ratio unless $NP \subseteq DTIME(n^{polylog(n)})$. Polynomial algorithms are only available for special classes of graphs such as trees [Chen, 2008] or bounded tree-width graphs [Ben-Zwi et al., 2009]. The only work we are aware of that solves a non-submodular maximization problem related to influence diffusion for general graphs is a very recent work by Goldberg and Liu [2013]. Their diffusion model is similar to the fixed threshold model, with one crucial difference: to activate a node v, it not only counts the immediate active neighbors of v but all active nodes that are connected to v through only activate nodes in determining whether the count has exceeded the threshold of v. The motivation of this model is adopting networking technology (e.g., IPv6), in which a node adopting the new technology benefits not only from its immediate neighbors that also adopt the new technology, but from all nodes in the network that it can connect to using the new technology. They study the seed minimization problem to activate all nodes in the network with the new technology. Interestingly, this particular version of the problem allows a linear-programming based approximation algorithm with the approximation ratio $O(r\ell \log n)$, where n is the number of nodes, r is the diameter of the graph, and ℓ is the number of different threshold values used by all nodes. However, their approach is limited to the particular problem formulation. When we change the problem such that the targeted influence spread is a fraction of the total number of nodes, or when we change the problem from seed minimization to influence maximization, their technique does not directly apply. Therefore, while non-submodular diffusions behaviors often exist in reality, it is still widely open on how to deal with optimization problems beyond submodular function maximization techniques.

Active friending and intermediate node selection problem.   In a recent work, Yang et al. [2013] propose the problem of *active friending* in a social network such as Facebook. When a source node s in the network wants to make friend with another target node t that does not share common neighbors with s, the platform provider could suggest at most k intermediate nodes between s and t for s to make friends first, so that in the end s could send t a friending request when they have some common friends. The optimization problem is to find k intermediate nodes that in the end maximize the probability of t accepting the friending request from s. They also use IC model for influence diffusion. Different from the influence maximization problem where k seed nodes need to be selected, the active friending problem need to select k intermediate nodes through which the immediate friends of s (the actual seeds of the diffusion) could pass on the influence to the target node t. [Yang et al., 2013] show that the problem is NP-hard, and the objective function is not submodular. They then use the MIA structure proposed by [Wang et al., 2012] to simplify the problem and find solutions in the MIA tree structure.

Game theoretic analysis for competitive influence diffusion.   For competitive influence diffusion, one may also study the strategic game perspective of the problem, where the competitors are players and their strategies are selecting seeds in the network. A few studies have investigated the game perspective of competitive influence diffusion ([Goyal and Kearns, 2012, Tsai et al., 2012]). Tsai et al. [2012] study the zero-sum game in which the negative opinion tries to maximizes its influence while the positive opinion tries to minimize the influence of the negative opinion. They utilize the results in influence-blocking maximization and propose heuristic algorithms to compute mixed strategies for the positive side to adopt. Goyal and Kearns [2012] study the nonzero-sum game in which both sides try to maximize their own influence spread. They use a stochastic diffusion model that bears similarity with the general threshold model but are technically different. They show results on the price of anarchy, which indicates the lost in social welfare when the two sides behave selfishly, and the budget multiplier, which indicates whether the initial difference in the budgets will lead to a larger difference in market share in the end. Game theoretic study of competitive diffusion is a promising area for many future researches.

Leveraging peer influence where there is no social network.   There are social systems without an explicit network where users tend to influence each other. A notable example of such a system is a recommender system [Ricci et al., 2011]. Based on the past history of experiential feedback from users, the system builds a model for various users' taste profile and uses it to recommend items to them. Recommender systems (RS) are quite popular today and form the backbone of the business of companies like Amazon and Netflix. Taking Amazon as an example, various products are sold using their online system. Amazon makes use of users' past purchase patterns to recommend various products for them to buy whenever they are about to buy some product. Users "influence" each other in that their purchase history and tastes influence what gets recommended to other users. How can we leverage this influence? Goyal and Lakshmanan [2012] propose a new business model for a RS owner like Amazon. It can offer "seed selection" as a service to product manufacturers. For a fee, it can strategically choose k users such that if they were to like a product and provide good ratings for it, the ratings would affect the RS's model such that the product would get recommended to many other users. The authors study the problem of choosing k users to maximize the number of other users to whom the RS would recommend the product. It should be noted that the operational recommender system is left intact and untouched. For RS using user-based and item-based collaborative filtering [Ricci et al., 2011], they show that the problem is NP-hard and is also NP-hard to approximate within a factor of $1/|V|^{1-\varepsilon}$ for any fixed $\varepsilon > 0$, where V is the set of users in the system. In spite of this negative result, they show that seeding a small number of users using relatively simple heuristics can still bring substantial benefits in terms of the other users to whom a product is recommended by the RS. Interesting avenues of future research include developing more sophisticated heuristics, heuristics to work with model-based RS such as matrix factorization [Ricci et al., 2011], and methods for deploying this kind of service in an operational RS which is far more complex than just a recommender algorithm.

CHAPTER 5

Learning Propagation Models

Most of the studies on information propagation and influence maximization in social networks assume the following information is available. (1) A social network $G = (V, E)$ whose nodes correspond to users or entities and whose arcs are directed.[1] (2) A propagation model which describes just how information or influence diffuses over the network, more precisely, how information or influence propagates to a node from its neighbors. (3) A function $p : E \rightarrow [0, 1]$ that associates a parameter $p(u, v)$ (or simply p_{uv}) with arc (u, v) capturing the influence u exerts over v. The p_{uv}'s are key parameters of the propagation model. These studies focus on the problem of how to find a small number of seed nodes to activate at start, such that the expected number of network nodes that are activated when the propagation saturates is maximum.

In case of the IC model, the parameters p_{uv}'s are arc influence probabilities. In case of the LT model, they are arc influence weights, although by virtue of equivalence to the live-arc graph model, they do have a probabilistic interpretation. When we do not commit to a model, we refer to p_{uv} as arc parameters, with the understanding that they may refer to arc influence probabilities for the IC model or arc influence weights for the LT model.

These studies make several assumptions. (1) The arc parameters p_{uv} capturing influence probabilities of nodes on their neighbors are known. (2) These probabilities remain constant over time. (3) When a user performs an action, it is solely due to influence exerted from its neighbors. This amounts to a kind of *closed world assumption*: other sources of information are assumed to be not present. For example, a user may watch and rate the movie *Oblivion* because of its inherent popularity and not necessarily because of neighbors' influence. Similarly, when buying a product, a user may consult external sources of information like newspapers, online customer reviews etc. The closed world assumption ignores the influence of such external sources.

In this chapter, we describe early and influential work that has been conducted on addressing the limitations imposed by the above assumptions.

5.1 BASIC MODELS

Early work in influence maximization assumes that pairwise influence probabilities are given as input. Since real world social network data do not come with such probabilities, these works tend to assign these probabilities in ad hoc and arbitrary ways. We briefly review them next and refer the reader to Kempe et al. [2003] for more details. In the *uniform model*, one simply assumes all

---

[1]Occasionally, we will consider networks that are undirected in this chapter. Following convention, we associate the term edge with undirected graphs and use the term arc to indicate directed edges in a directed graph.

influence probabilities to be a constant (say 0.01). This does not distinguish between relationships (i.e., edges), i.e., all nodes exert the same amount of influence on their neighbors. Besides, it does not discriminate between the neighbors of a given node, i.e., a node exerts the same influence on all its neighbors. Clearly, both of these assumptions are questionable.

In the so-called *trivalency model*, the first limitation is partly addressed. Instead of assuming all nodes are equally influential, influence probabilities are drawn uniformly at random from a predetermined set of probabilities, e.g., $\{0.001, 0.01, 0.1\}$. As with the uniform model, neighbors of a node are not discriminated. For instance, all neighbors of a node may be influenced with probability 0.001. The idea of this model is that nodes whose (outgoing) influence is 0.001 can be thought of low influence nodes, with 0.01 corresponding to medium influence and 0.1 to high influence.

In both the uniform and trivalency models, the influence probabilities are independent of the network structure. In the *weighted cascade* model, we define the probability associated with an arc (u, v) as $p_{uv} = 1/d_{in}(v)$, where $d_{in}(v)$ is the in-degree of node v. This model has a greater resolution than the above two models in distinguishing between nodes: nodes with a low in-degree experience a higher influence from each of their in-neighbors than those with a high in-degree. Probabilities are thus not simply chosen from a constant set of values. Furthermore, a node does not necessarily exert the same influence on all its out-neighbors, since their in-degrees may be different. Despite these advantages, this model still suffers from the fact that there is no basis for the way in which influence probabilities are computed. The probabilities are computed from the network structure rather than any evidence of past influence among nodes.

5.2 IC MODEL

In an early pioneering work, Saito et al. [2008] studied the problem of learning influence probabilities, with a focus on the IC propagation model.[2] More specifically, they studied the following problem. Let $G = (V, E)$ be a (directed) social network. Define an *information diffusion episode* to be a sequence of node sets $\langle D(0), D(1), ..., D(T) \rangle$, with $D(i) \cap D(j) = \emptyset$, $i \neq j$. Here T is the length of the episode. At time t, the nodes in $D(t)$ become active for the first time. [3] The nodes $D(0)$ are active to start with and can be thought of as seeds that effected the episode. Each episode offer some evidence of the extent to which influence of an active node succeeded (or failed) in activating its inactive out-neighbor at the next time instant. The question is *given a set of such episodes $S = \{D_1, ..., D_n\}$, how can we learn the influence probabilities?* For a given node u, let $N^{out}(u) = \{v \mid (u, v) \in E\}$ denote its children and let $N^{in}(u) = \{v \mid (v, u) \in E\}$ denote its parents.[4] Influence (for performing actions) flows from nodes to their children. In

---

[2]Gruhl et al. [2004] was an earlier work on this problem, but we prefer to discuss the more rigorous approach of Saito et al. [2008] here.

[3]In previous chapters, we use notation S_t to denote the active set at time t. Conceptually, it is similar to the notation $D(t)$ here. However, technically S_t is a random set generated by a particular influence diffusion model given some seed set S_0, while $D(t)$ is the set of *observed* active nodes at time t. Thus, we use different notations for them.

[4]We use the terms parents and in-neighbors as well as children and out-neighbors interchangeably.

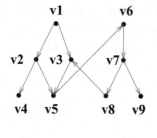

User	Time
v_1	5
v_2	10
v_3	10
v_4	15
v_5	15

User	Time
v_6	8
v_7	12
v_8	16
v_9	17

Figure 5.1: Directed social network and node activation times.

an episode $\langle D_s(0), ..., D_s(T_s)\rangle$, for a node $v \in D_s(t+1)$, one of the nodes in $N^{in}(v) \cap D_s(t)$ must have succeeded in activating v. Observe that we can assume without loss of generality that $N^{in}(v) \cap D_s(t)$ is non-empty, for every $v \in D_s(t+1)$. Given an episode where this is not true, we can always consider that all nodes $v \in D_s(t+1)$ which do not have any parent in $D_s(t)$ start a *new* episode where those nodes are defined to be active at time 0. Figure 5.1 shows an example social network and a table summarizing the times at which different nodes activated. We can model this information in the form of one or more episodes. E.g., we can define two episodes: $D_1(0) = \{v_1\}$, $D_1(1) = \{v_2, v_3\}$, $D_1(2) = \{v_4, v_5\}$ and $D_2(0) = \{v_6\}$, $D_2(1) = \{v_7\}$, $D_2(2) = \{v_8, v_9\}$. Alternatively, we can model this information as one episode by setting $D(0) = \{v_1, v_6\}$, $D(1) = \{v_2, v_3, v_7\}$, $D(2) = \{v_4, v_5, v_8, v_9\}$. Observe the direction of the arcs in relation to the definitions of these episodes.

Given an episode D_s, the probability that a node w becomes active at time $t+1$ is given by

$$P_w^s(t+1) = 1 - \prod_{v \in N^{in}(w) \cap D_s(t)} (1 - p_{vw}). \tag{5.1}$$

This corresponds to the probability that at least one of the parents of w that were active at time t succeeded in activating w, under the independent cascade model, where each parent of a node gets one shot at trying to activate the node and the attempts are made in an arbitrary order and happen at time step t. Let $C_s(t) = \bigcup_{\tau \le t} D_s(\tau)$ denote the set of nodes that are active at time t in an episode D_s. Then the likelihood of observing the episode D_s, w.r.t. $\theta = \{p_{vw}\}$ is given by

$$L(\theta; D_s) = \left(\prod_{t=0}^{T_s-1} \prod_{w \in D_s(t+1)} P_w^s(t+1)\right)\left(\prod_{t=0}^{T_s-1} \prod_{v \in D_s(t)} \prod_{w \in N^{out}(v) \setminus C_s(t+1)} (1 - p_{vw})\right). \tag{5.2}$$

The intuition is that for an arc (v, w), if $w \in D_s(t+1)$, we know that one of the parents of w that was active at time t must have succeeded whereas if $w \notin D_s(t+1)$, we know that all parents of w that were active at time t surely failed. These are the only signals from the episode D_s that we can use to learn the probability p_{vw}. In particular, the cases (a) $v \in D_s(t)$ and $w \in C_s(t)$ and (b) $v \notin D_s(t)$ have no bearing on the influence probability p_{vw}. Taking the joint probability of the likelihood of observing the set of episodes $S = \{D_1, ..., D_n\}$ simultaneously w.r.t. θ and taking log of the likelihood, we get

$$L(\theta) = \sum_{s=1}^{n} \log L(\theta; D_s) = \sum_{s=1}^{n} \sum_{t=0}^{T_s-1} \left(\sum_{w \in D_s(t+1)} \log P_w^s(t+1) + \sum_{v \in D_s(t)} \sum_{w \in N^{out}(v) \backslash C_s(t+1)} \log(1 - p_{vw}) \right). \tag{5.3}$$

For a node w, the time it became active in an episode D_s is known. Let t_w^s be this time. Thus, in the equation above, $P_w^s(t+1)$ can be replaced simply by P_w^s since the time of activation is known and can be suppressed. This yields

$$P_w^s = 1 - \prod_{v \in D_s(t_w^s-1) \cap N^{in}(w)} (1 - p_{vw}). \tag{5.4}$$

Thus, the problem of learning influence probabilities according to the IC model from a given set of episodes is formalized as that of learning θ that maximizes Eq. (5.3). Since this is difficult to optimize analytically, Saito et al. [2008] solve this by taking recourse to Expectation Maximization (EM). Let $\hat{p}_{vw}$ denote the current estimate of p_{vw} and $\hat{P}_w^s$ denote the value of P_w^s calculated using Eq. (5.4) with the current estimates $\hat{\theta} = \{\hat{p}_{vw}\}$. Consider the latent variables corresponding to a parent v that became active at time t succeeding or failing to activate its children w at time $t + 1$. The activation attempt succeeds with probability $\hat{p}_{vw}/\hat{P}_w^s$ and fails with probability $1 - \hat{p}_{vw}/\hat{P}_w^s$. Then the expected value of the log likelihood function w.r.t. the conditional distribution of these latent variables, given the set of episodes $S = \{D_1, ..., D_n\}$ and the current estimate of the parameters $\hat{\theta}$ is given by

$$Q(\theta|\hat{\theta}) = \sum_{s=1}^{n} \sum_{t=0}^{T_s-1} \sum_{v \in D_s(t)} \left(\sum_{w \in N^{out}(v) \cap D_s(t+1)} \left(\frac{\hat{p}_{vw}}{\hat{P}_w^s} \log p_{vw} + \left(1 - \frac{\hat{p}_{vw}}{\hat{P}_w^s}\right) \log(1 - p_{vw}) \right) + \sum_{w \in N^{out}(v) \backslash C_s(t+1)} \log(1 - p_{vw}) \right). \tag{5.5}$$

Let S_{vw}^+ (S_{vw}^-) be the subset of episodes in S for which the activation attempt by a node v on its child w succeeded (resp., failed). More precisely, S_{vw}^+ is the set of episodes in which $v \in D_s(t)$ and $w \in D_s(t + 1)$, where $(v, w) \in E$. Similarly, S_{vw}^- is the set of episodes in which $v \in D_s(t)$ and $w \notin C_s(t + 1)$ (and $(v, w) \in E$).

By equating the derivative w.r.t. p_{vw} to zero, we can derive

$$p_{vw} = \frac{1}{|\mathcal{S}_{vw}^+| + |\mathcal{S}_{vw}^-|} \sum_{D_s \in \mathcal{S}_{vw}^+} \frac{\hat{p}_{vw}}{\hat{P}_w^s}. \tag{5.6}$$

Notice that in general it is not necessary that $|\mathcal{S}_{vw}^+| + |\mathcal{S}_{vw}^-| = n$, where $n = |\mathcal{S}|$ is the given number of episodes. To learn the influence probabilities we simply iteratively evaluate Equations (5.5) and (5.6).

To summarize, given a set of episodes each consisting of sets of nodes that activated at successive time points, we can formulate the problem of learning arc influence probabilities as an expectation maximization problem of maximizing the likelihood of observing the given episodes. This method was proposed by Saito et al. [2008] for the IC model and shown to work well over a real small network data set consisting of approximately 12,000 nodes and 80,000 arcs. The approach uses available evidence of influence for learning the probabilities and is elegant in that it uses the EM algorithm.

However, it has been recognized that: (i) this approach does not scale to large social networks consisting of millions of nodes and many more arcs, and (ii) it produces influence networks having many arcs whose contribution to the likelihood of the data is minuscule. The first problem requires parallelization and/or a different method for the estimation. The second problem can be alleviated by a post-processing method such as SPINE [Mathioudakis et al., 2011], which sparsifies the vector of parameters in an IC model.

Concretely, SPINE first computes a sub-set of the arcs in the original model to create an IC model having non-zero likelihood for the data. In their experiments, on graphs having up to a million arcs, the reduced model has 17–42% of the original arcs, but a much lower likelihood. Next, the algorithm greedily adds the arcs that lead to the maximum increase of likelihood of the data, until the same likelihood as the entire model is reached, with 30–69% of the arcs of the original model. This sparsification process is independent of the specific learning algorithm used to create the original IC model.

5.3 THRESHOLD MODELS

In this section, we describe a method for learning influence parameters w.r.t. an underlying threshold model. In their seminal paper, Kempe et al. [2003] introduced a *generalized threshold* (GT) propagation model as a generalization of both IC and LT models. The method we discuss in this section is based on the GT model. In the GT model, as in the LT model, every node v chooses a threshold $\theta_v \in [0, 1]$ at random. The net influence of the active neighbors on a node is governed by a monotone function $f_v : 2^{N^{in}(v)} \to [0, 1]$, where $N^{in}(v)$ is the set of all in-neighbors of v. If $S \subseteq N^{in}(v)$ is the set of in-neighbors of v active at time t, then $f(S)$ captures their net influence on v: accordingly, v becomes active at time $t + 1$ if $f(S) \geq \theta_v$ (Definition 2.16). Let p_{uv} be the weight associated with arc (u, v). Clearly, $f(\cdot)$ is a function of the weights associated with the incoming arcs of a node. Goyal et al. [2010] studied the problem of learning the arc weights from an input data set consisting of a social network along with action propagation traces. We describe their method next.

Technically, the parameters associated with arcs in the LT model are weights. However, recall that they get their probabilistic interpretation by virtue of the equivalence between the LT model and the corresponding live-arc graph model (Theorem 2.11 in Chapter 2). In the following, for convenience, we will refer to arc weights as arc probabilities. The main observation is that while arc probabilities are not available in real data sets, both the underlying social network and a log of actions performed by users are available. We can leverage this information to learn arc probabilities. As we will see, the times at which actions are performed play a key role in the learning, where we include among actions the formation of social ties or arcs. Let $G = (V, E, \mathcal{T})$ denote an undirected social graph (V, E) along with a function $\mathcal{T} : E \to \mathbb{N}$ that for every edge says when the edge was formed. We suppose the underlying graph is undirected for simplicity. The method discussed easily extends to directed graphs. Let $\mathcal{A}$ be a universe of actions. The relation $actions(User, Action, Time) \subseteq V \times \mathcal{A} \times \mathbb{N}$ represents a log of all actions performed by users in the network. A tuple $(u, a, t) \in actions$ means user u performed action a at time t. For simplicity, assume a user performs any action at most once. Denote by $\mathcal{A}_u$, $\mathcal{A}_{u\&v}$, and $\mathcal{A}_{u|v}$ the sets of actions performed by u, by u and v, by u or v, respectively, and let $\mathcal{A}_{u2v}$ be the set of actions that were propagated from u to its out-neighbor v, i.e., they are performed by both u and v, but performed by u earlier. Clearly, $|\mathcal{A}_{u|v}| = |\mathcal{A}_u| + |\mathcal{A}_v| - |\mathcal{A}_{u\&v}|$.

Definition 5.1   Action propagation.   We say that an action $a \in \mathcal{A}$ propagates from user u to v iff: (i) $(u, v) \in E$; (ii) $\exists (u, a, t_u), (v, a, t_v) \in actions$ with $t_u < t_v$; and (iii) $\mathcal{T}(u, v) \leq t_u$. When this holds we write $prop(a, u, v, \Delta t)$, where $\Delta t = t_v - t_u$.

Both u and v must have performed the action in that order and after the arc (u, v) is formed. The above notion leads to a natural notion of a propagation graph.

Definition 5.2   Propagation graph.   Given a social network and an action log, each action a induces a propagation graph $PG(a) = (V(a), E(a))$, defined as follows. $V(a) = \{v \mid \exists t : (v, a, t) \in actions\}$; there is an arc $u \xrightarrow{\Delta t} v$ in $E(a)$ whenever $prop(a, u, v, \Delta t)$ holds.

A propagation graph corresponding to an action is a directed acyclic graph, consisting of all users who performed that action. Since arcs in this graph have a temporal constraint, cycles are impossible. In fact, a propagation graph can be viewed as a set of episodes in the sense of the previous section. Figure 5.2, top, depicts an example undirected social network and an action log. The edge labels indicate the times at which the edges were formed. There are three distinct actions a, b, c performed by the users. The corresponding action propagation graphs are shown in Figure 5.2, bottom. Notice that even though there is an edge between y and z in the network, there is no arc between them in the action propagation graph for action a, since the edge (y, z) was formed (at time 12) *after* user y performed action a (at time 10). In this way, the action log

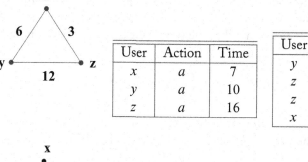

User	Action	Time
x	a	7
y	a	10
z	a	16

User	Action	Time
y	b	13
z	b	14
z	c	7
x	c	15

Figure 5.2: Undirected social network, action log, and action propagation graphs.

together with the social network can be regarded as a set of action propagation traces or cascades, represented in the form of action propagation graphs. This is the evidence we have and we would like to mine this data to learn a function $p : E \rightarrow [0, 1] \times [0, 1]$ that assigns probabilities p_{uv} and p_{vu} with both directions of an edge $(u, v) \in E$.

5.3.1   STATIC MODELS

Let us first consider the case where arc probabilities remain constant over time. Even though this is not the most realistic case, it is instructive to start with this case and develop a methodology that works with the case where probabilities may vary with time. Let v be any node in the network and suppose S is the set of its neighbors which are currently active. In particular, assume these neighbors are activated after they became v's neighbors. Recall that the GT model posits that the net influence of a set of active neighbors S on a node v is a monotone function of S. Let us model this using the threshold function $f_v(S)$ of the GT model (see Definition 2.16). Intuitively, $f_v(\cdot)$ can be regarded as a function of the arc probabilities $\{p_{uv} \mid u \in S\}$. Since it is meant to be used in the context of influence maximization, the function $f_v(\cdot)$ needs to be consistent with the propagation models used for influence maximization. As discussed in Chapter 2, these propagation models typically satisfy two key properties: monotonicity and submodularity. In order to be compatible with these propagation models, we require that $f_v(\cdot)$ satisfy the following properties: (i) monotonicity: $f_v(S) \leq f_v(T)$, whenever $S \subseteq T$; and (ii) submodularity: for $S \subseteq T$ and $x \in V \setminus T$, $f_v(T \cup \{x\}) - f_v(T) \leq f_v(S \cup \{x\}) - f_v(S)$. These requirements should not be confused with the corresponding properties of the influence spread functions associated with propagation models. The above requirements are purely local: we merely require that the set function f_v satisfy these properties. There are various options for defining $f_v(\cdot)$ so as to guarantee these properties. A simple and natural choice is to assume that the probabilities of v's neighbors in S influencing v are independent of each other. This leads to[5]

$$f_v(S) = 1 - \prod_{u \in S}(1 - p_{uv}). \tag{5.7}$$

It can be shown that $f_v(\cdot)$ defined above is monotone and submodular (see Goyal et al. [2010] for a proof; see also the paragraph following Theorem 2.17). In addition, this function has the nice property of being incrementally computable. More precisely, suppose S is a current set of active neighbors of v. Suppose we have already computed $f_v(S)$ and that a new neighbor $w \notin S$ has become active. We can compute $f_v(S \cup \{u\})$ as

$$f_v(S \cup \{u\}) = 1 - (1 - p_{wv}) \times \prod_{u \in S}(1 - p_{uv})$$
$$= f_v(S) + (1 - f_v(S))p_{wv}. \tag{5.8}$$

That is, $f_v(S \cup \{w\})$ can be computed solely in terms of $f_v(S)$ and p_{wv}.

We remark that the above is just one way of defining $f_v(S)$ that guarantees the above properties of (local) monotonicity, submodularity, and incremental computation. The framework allows the learning of arc probabilities as long as any such definition of $f_v(S)$ is available.

We next discuss three simple ways of modeling the influence of v's active neighbors on v. We can model influence using a Bernoulli distribution. An active neighbor u of v has a fixed probability of influencing v and activate it. Each attempt at activation is a Bernoulli trial. The maximum likelihood estimate (MLE) of the success probability is just the ratio of the number of actions that propagated from u to v over the number of actions performed by u, i.e.,

$$p_{uv} = \frac{|\mathcal{A}_{u2v}|}{|\mathcal{A}_u|}. \tag{5.9}$$

The Jaccard index is quite commonly used for measuring the similarity between two sets, defined as the number of items common between the sets over those that belong to either set. Adapted to our setting, this yields

$$p_{uv} = \frac{|\mathcal{A}_{u2v}|}{|\mathcal{A}_{u|v}|}. \tag{5.10}$$

Both the Bernoulli and the Jaccard approaches treat each arc probability individually. More specifically, possible influence of other users in activating a node is ignored when calculating the

---

[5]Technically, $f_v(S)$ defined in Equation (5.7) is a threshold function in the GT model. However, according to the GT model v is activated when $f_v(S) \geq \theta_v$ where θ_v is drawn uniformly at random from $[0, 1]$, which implies that the probability that v is activated is also $f_v(S)$. Thus, we sometimes also refer to $f_v(S)$ as the (joint) probability that v's active in-neighbors successfully activate v.

arc probability of (u, v). This can be addressed by considering that the "credit" for making v perform an action a is equally shared by all neighbors u of v which performed action a before v did but after u became a neighbor of v. More precisely, let S be the set of all neighbors of v, regardless of when they became v's neighbors. Define

$$credit_{uv}(a) = \frac{1}{\sum_{w \in S} I(\mathcal{T}(w, v) \leq t_w(a) \& t_w(a) < t_u(a))}, \tag{5.11}$$

where $\mathcal{T}(w, v)$ and $t_w(a)$ are the times at which the edge (w, v) is formed and user w performs action a respectively, and I is the indicator function. We can now inject partial credits into either of the approaches discussed above. For example, using the Bernoulli approach with partial credits, we can estimate the arc probability as follows:

$$p_{uv} = \frac{\sum_{a \in \mathcal{A}} credit_{uv}(a)}{|\mathcal{A}_u|}. \tag{5.12}$$

Arc probability using Jaccard index with partial credits can be estimated similarly. So far, we have discussed how to estimate individual arc probabilities using a variety of static models. In order to validate these models, we need to calculate the joint probability of a set of active neighbors on a given node. This can be done using Equation (5.7). An important issue in validation is computational efficiency, as our intention is to learn the arc probabilities and validate them over very large data sets. We will return to this issue when discussing validation.

5.3.2 DOES INFLUENCE REMAIN STATIC?

Intuitively speaking, we expect influence to change with time. For example, when we hear about a smart phone from friends who bought and reviewed it, at first we feel the urge to try it out ourselves. But with time, it is plausible that this urge, and hence the influence exerted by friends in the context of this specific action, may decay. While this example is intuitive, we would like to ask whether there is real evidence suggesting that influence changes with time. We briefly discuss the results of one of the measurements by Goyal et al. [2010] on a real data set: they measured the number of actions that propagated between pairs of neighbors in Flickr at various time intervals. Figure 5.3, taken from Goyal et al. [2010], shows the number of propagated actions against the time elapsed between the performance of the action between the neighbors. The distribution is shown at three levels of granularity: every 10 min during the first hour, every hour during the first week, and every week in case of actions that propagated with a large delay. In all cases, we can clearly observe that a great majority of actions propagated within a short time elapse and there is an exponential decay in the number of actions propagated as the time elapsed increases, confirming our intuition that influence decays with time.

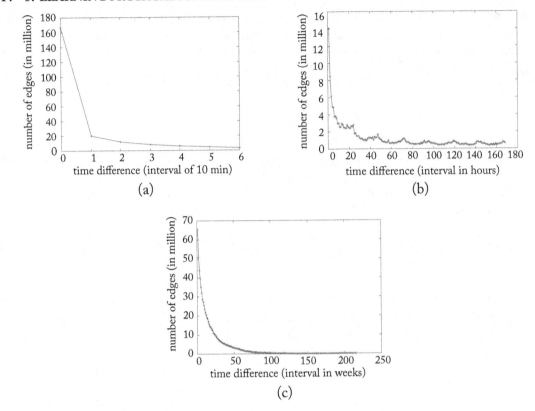

Figure 5.3: Frequency of common actions vs the time difference between two users performing actions: (a) every 10 min, during the first hour; (b) every hour, during the first week (without considering the cases in which the time difference is less than one hour, i.e., the cases in (a)); and (c) the rest of the dataset with weekly granularity

5.3.3 CONTINUOUS TIME MODELS

Motivated by the above observations, we can model arc probability as a continuous decaying function of time:

$$p_{uv}^t = p_{uv}^0 e^{-\frac{t-t_u}{\tau_{uv}}} . \tag{5.13}$$

Here, p_{uv}^0 is the maximum strength of u's influence on v, realized immediately after u performs the action, i.e., at $t = t_u$ and p_{uv}^t decays exponentially thereafter. The parameter p_{uv}^0 can be estimated using any of the static models—Bernoulli or Jaccard—with or without partial credits. The parameter τ_{uv} can be thought of as a *mean life time*, corresponding to the expected time elapse between the time u performs an action and when v follows suit, and can be estimated as

$$\tau_{uv} = \frac{\sum_{a \in \mathcal{A}} (t_v(a) - t_u(a))}{|\mathcal{A}_{u2v}|}. \tag{5.14}$$

We can now estimate the joint probability of influence of a set of active neighbors on a node v as the following time-based threshold function:

$$f_v^t(S) = 1 - \prod_{u \in S} (1 - p_{uv}^t). \tag{5.15}$$

Notice that $f_v^t(S)$ is a piecewise continuous function: as a new neighbor of v becomes activated, it causes a sharp increase in $f_v^t(\cdot)$. After that it decays until the next neighbor becomes active at which point there is a jump in its value. We say that v is activated provided $\max_t \{f_v^t(\cdot)\} \geq \theta_v$, where θ_v is the activation threshold of v. Calculating $\max_t \{f_v^t(\cdot)\}$ requires that we calculate $f_v^t(\cdot)$ every time a new neighbor is activated. Since $f_v^t(\cdot)$ is a continuous function of time, these calculations have to be from the scratch and cannot be done incrementally. Since we would like to perform model validation efficiently, it is desirable that the joint probabilities of neighbors on a given node be computable incrementally. This is addressed next.

5.3.4 DISCRETE TIME MODELS

In order to achieve incremental computability, we approximate continuous time models by positing that a newly active node remains contagious, i.e., capable of activating its neighbors, over a fixed interval of time. Once that window elapses, it loses its contagiousness, i.e., it cannot activate its neighbors any more. More precisely, a newly activated node u has a fixed probability p_{uv} of activating its neighbor v over the time interval $[t_u, t_u + \tau_{uv}]$, where t_u is the time u becomes active and τ_{uv} is a parameter. This leads to an important issue that S should only account for contagious neighbors, not just active neighbors. Specifically, if an active neighbor w just became non-contagious, we can update the probability to

$$f_v(S \setminus \{w\}) = \frac{f_v(S) - p_{wv}}{1 - p_{wv}}. \tag{5.16}$$

Thus, the discrete time model represents a compromise between accuracy and efficiency. It is more accurate than static models by explicitly taking the effect of tie into account. It is less accurate than continuous time models but has the advantage of incremental computability. We close this section by noting that the constant probability p_{uv} can be estimated using any of the static models: Bernoulli, Jaccard, or their partial credit variants. As an example, p_{uv} for Bernoulli with partial credits can be estimated as

$$p_{uv} = \frac{\sum_{a \in \mathcal{A}_u} \frac{1}{\sum_{w \in N^{in}(v)} I(0 < t_v(a) - t_w(a) < \tau_{wv})}}{|\mathcal{A}_u|}. \tag{5.17}$$

In these two sections, we have discussed 12 models in all: a model can be static or time aware and a time aware model may be continuous time or discrete time. The constant (in case of static) or the maximum (in case of time aware) probability with which an active node influences its neighbor, can be estimated using Bernoulli or Jaccard or their partial credit variants. In later sections, we discuss how to learn the parameters associated with these models from training data and also discuss the validation of models. Before that, we turn to a basic question.

5.3.5 ARE ALL OBJECTS EQUALLY INFLUENCE PRONE?

There is an implicit assumption in our discussion so far that all users are equally prone to influence and similarly all actions are equally subject to influence. Is this a realistic assumption? There are experimental results [Goyal et al., 2010] that help us approach these questions quantitatively. There can be at least three reasons for a user performing an action. She may be influenced by external factors (e.g., main stream media, water cooler conversations, etc.) and may hence feel motivated to perform the action. Or she may be an active initiator of actions, acting on her own often without being influenced by other users. Alternatively, she may be genuinely influenced by her social network contacts. How can we tell?

Users who are initiators of actions and who are more influenced by external factors are unpredictable or less influenceable. So, we define an *influenceability score* representing how influenceable a user is, as the ratio between the number of actions for which we have evidence that the user was influenced, over the total number of actions performed by the user. More precisely, we define:

$$infl(v) = \frac{|\{a \mid \exists v, \Delta t : prop(a, u, v, \Delta t) \& 0 \leq \Delta t \leq \tau_{uv}|}{|\mathcal{A}_u|}. \tag{5.18}$$

We can model the value of the parameter τ_{uv}, used in discrete time models and in the above equation in any appropriate way. One possibility is to define it as the average time elapsed in an action propagating from user u to v:

$$\tau_{uv} = \frac{\sum_{a \in \mathcal{A}} (t_v(a) - t_u(a))}{|\mathcal{A}_{u2v}|}, \tag{5.19}$$

where $t_u(a)$ is the time at which u performs a. Intuitively, we expect that users with a high value for $infl(u)$ may exhibit a high degree of being influenced by their neighbors compared to those with a low influenceability score.

Likewise, we define the *influence quotient* of actions to distinguish actions for which there is evidence of influence propagation from the rest:

$$infl(a) = \frac{|\{u \mid \exists v, \Delta t : prop(a, u, v, \Delta t) \& 0 \leq \Delta t \leq \tau_{uv}|}{|\mathcal{U}_a|}, \tag{5.20}$$

Algorithm 14 Learning – Phase I

Input: Graph $G = (V, e)$ and action log.

Output: Information needed to derive influence weights, influence quotient, influenceability score, and parameters for discrete and continuous time models.

1: **for** each action a in the training set **do**
2:      $current\_table \leftarrow \emptyset$
3:      **for** each user tuple $< v, a, t_v >$ in chronological order **do**
4:        update $\mathcal{A}_v$
5:        $parents \leftarrow \emptyset$
6:        **for** each user $u : (u, a, t_u) \in current\_table$ && $(u, v) \in E^{t_u}$ **do**
7:          **if** $t_u < t_v$ **then**
8:            update $\mathcal{A}_{u2v}$
9:            update τ_{uv}
10:           insert u into $parents$
11:         **end if**
12:         update $\mathcal{A}_{u\&v}$
13:       **end for**
14:       **for** each parent $u \in parents$ **do**
15:         update $credit_{uv}$
16:       **end for**
17:       add (v, a, t_v) to $current\_table$
18:     **end for**
19: **end for**

---

where $\mathcal{U}_a$ is the set of users who perform action a. We expect that for actions with high $infl(a)$, predictions (based on influence models) of users performing those actions will be more reliable compared to other actions.

5.3.6   ALGORITHMS

Given a social network along with an action log, we would like to learn parameters of the models proposed in the preceding subsections. The social network can contain millions of nodes and edges and the action log may contain tens of millions of tuples. Besides, all models involve a huge number of parameters: at the very least they all involve arc probabilities associated with all arcs. Thus, it is important for both training and testing (validation) to be performed efficiently. To facilitate efficient processing, we assume the action log is grouped by action id and each group is sorted by the time stamp.

Algorithm 14 describes an algorithm for learning the models. It should be noted that it is a general algorithmic framework for learning any (in fact, all) of the 12 models discussed earlier

---

Algorithm 15 Learning - Phase II

Input: Graph $G = (V, e)$ and action log.

Output: Information needed to derive influence weights, influence quotient, influenceability score, and parameters for discrete and continuous time models.

1: **for** each action a in training set **do**
2:      *current_table* $\leftarrow \emptyset$
3:      **for** each user tuple $< v, a, t_v >$ in chronological order **do**
4:          *parents* $\leftarrow \emptyset$
5:          **for** each user $u : (u, a, t_u) \in$ *current_table* && $(u, v) \in E^{t_u}$ **do**
6:              **if** $0 < t_v - t_u < \tau_{uv}$ **then**
7:                  increment A_{u2v}
8:                  insert u in *parents*
9:              **end if**
10:          **end for**
11:          **for** each parent $u \in$ *parents* **do**
12:              update $credit_{uv}^{\tau_{uv}}$
13:          **end for**
14:          **if** *parents* $\neq \emptyset$ **then**
15:              update *infl*(v)
16:          **end if**
17:          add (v, a, t_v) in *current_table*
18:      **end for**
19: **end for**

---

from the input training dataset. It makes one pass over the data, processing action log tuples one by one. For the current tuple (v, a, t_v), whenever there is a previously visited tuple (u, a, t_u) with $t_u < t_v$ and there exists an edge (u, v) which is formed before time t_v, we consider that the action potentially propagated from u to v and update all relevant parameters. When considering partial credits, we also update the credits.

Learning user influenceability score and action influence quotient requires τ (learned from first scan) and this requires a second scan of the action log. Similarly, learning parameters of discrete time models also requires τ beforehand. The second phase of the learning algorithm, described in Algorithm 15, is similar to Algorithm 14, except in Step 6 we require that $t_v - t_u \leq \tau_{uv}$. For simplicity, we just show how *infl*(v) is computed; handling of *infl*(a) is similar. Notice that *infl*(v) is updated whenever we find at least one neighbor from which v is influenced.

5.3.7 EXPERIMENTAL VALIDATION

We briefly discuss the experiments conducted by Goyal et al. [2010] and their findings. For complete details of the experiments as well as efficient algorithms for validating multiple models, the reader is referred to that paper.

Experiments were conducted on the Flickr dataset, which at that time contained a social network with 6.2 million users having 71 million edges between them. Using "joining a group" as an action and projecting the network on those users who joined at least one group, a subgraph with 1,450,347 users and 40,562,923 edges was obtained. Among the multiple connected components in this graph, the largest one has 1,319,573 users and 40,450,082 edges, and accounts for over 90% nodes and 99.72% edges and is what is used in the experiments. The total number of tuples in action log after the filtering is 35,967,169. In the experiments, the dataset is split into training and test based on actions such that each action can appear completely either in training or in test dataset.

Comparison of different models in terms of prediction accuracy is done using ROC curves. An ROC curve plots the true positive rate (TPR) against the false positive rate (FPR), where TPR = TP/(TP+FN) and FPR = FP/(FP+TN). Here TP (TN) is the number of true positives (negatives) and FN (FP) is the number of false negatives (positives). In our setting, we define these quantities as follows. TP is the number of cases when user performs the action, at least one of its neighbors performs the action before it and model estimates it performs the action. FP is the number of cases when user does not perform the action, at least one of its neighbors performs action and model estimates it performs the action. Similarly, TN is the number of cases when user doesn't perform the action, and at least one of its neighbors performs the action and the model estimates it does not perform the action. Finally, FN is the number of cases when the user performs the action, at least one of its neighbors performs the action before it and the model estimates it does not perform the action. ROC curves are well recognized for their effectiveness in comparing different binary classification models [Provost et al., 1998] and thus it makes sense to use them for comparing models that predict whether a user will perform an action. In an ROC curve, the closer the hump of the curve to the point (0, 1) the better the performance.

The results reported in [Goyal et al., 2010] show that among the static models, Bernoulli performs slightly better than Jaccard, with partial credits having a slight advantage over the vanilla versions. We focus on the relative performance between static and time aware models and on the effect of taking user and action influenceability into account. Figure 5.4 compares static and time aware models and clearly demonstrates that time aware models perform much better than static models. Figures 5.5 and 5.6 depict the ROC curves for different slices of user influenceability and action influenceability. These figures are taken from Goyal et al. [2010]. Here, each point in an ROC curve corresponds to a distinct value of node threshold θ_v, where all nodes are set to the same threshold. The plots confirm the intuition that larger user influenceability and larger action influence quotient lead to a more accurate prediction of influence.

With the aid of time aware models, it is possible, in addition, to predict the most likely *time* at which a user will perform an action. We refer the reader to [Goyal et al., 2010] for details.

5.3.8 DISCUSSION

In this chapter, we have discussed two major approaches for learning influence parameters. In this section, we briefly discuss their limitations and important open problems. In the first approach, discussed in Section 5.2, we need to assume available evidence of influence is broken down and preprocessed into a set of episodes. Each episode is a sequence of pairwise disjoint sets of nodes of the form $(D(0), ..., D(T))$, where T is the episode length. Since in available real datasets, episodes are not explicitly available, we must construct them from an action log. Intuitively, we can associate an episode with each action. Since the time stamps associated with actions may be real numbers, we need to discretize them appropriately in order to partition network nodes into disjoint subsets corresponding to episodes. Then we can consider that $D(i-1)$ consists of nodes that perform an action at (discretized) time $i-1$ and $D(i)$ consists of nodes which perform the action at time i which have a neighbor (if the network is undirected) or a predecessor (if the network is directed) in $D(i-1)$. We give a simple example illustrating the issues involved in doing this.

Consider again Figure 5.2 where we focus on the episode D we may associate with action a. Suppose all edges in the network are present in the beginning, for simplicity. All three nodes perform action a, x being the earliest among them so it must be in $D(0)$. Nodes y, z cannot be put in $D(0)$ since their neighbor x performed it before them. Putting them in $D(0)$ will force us to ignore their neighbor's influence on them. Similarly, y, z cannot both be in $D(1)$ since y performs the action before z and is a neighbor of z, leading us to set $D(1) = \{y\}$ and $D(2) = \{z\}$. Under the model discussed in Section 5.2, we will end up ignoring the influence x may have exerted on z to perform a since only neighbors in the *previous* time step are considered. It is easy to see that there is no perfect partition of the nodes into discrete time steps which accounts for the influence of all neighbors of each node in performing action a. It is worth noting that this difficulty remains even if the network is made directed. It remains an open problem how to transform an action log into the best fitting set of episodes such that a model learned from them yields high quality predictions.

A second limitation of this approach is scalability. Indeed, once the input data is transformed into a set of episodes, the model is learned by means of expected minimization. Since the model involves several millions of parameters corresponding at the very least to arc probabilities, learning all of them iteratively by means of EM does not scale well. Distributed computing frameworks like MapReduce may offer some promise. Further discussion on this theme can be found in [Bonchi, 2011].

While the approach presented in Section 5.2 is geared for the IC model, Section 5.3 presents an approach designed for threshold based models. The latter is a frequentist approach to learning parameters and has been shown to scale very well to very large social networks. It is intriguing to ask whether a more machine learning-based approach can be developed for threshold based propagation models which is at once accurate and scalable.

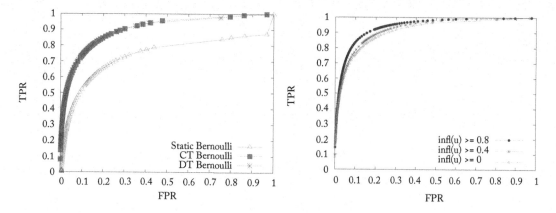

Figure 5.4: ROC comparisons of Static, CT, and DT Models.

Figure 5.5: ROC curves for different slices of user influenceability.

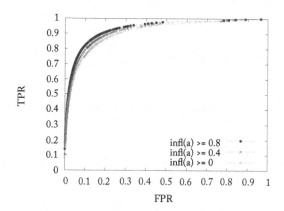

Figure 5.6: ROC curves for different slices of action influenceability.

CHAPTER 6

Data and Software for Information/Influence: Propagation Research

Research on information and influence propagations is motivated by real-world applications. The availability of real-world datasets from such applications, or datasets that closely resemble them, is of utmost importance. Data is important to validate models about how viral phenomena unravel in practice under a variety of conditions.

This chapter describes classes of datasets that have been used by authors in this field. It also provides pointers to specific instances of such datasets. Finally, it briefly outlines packaged software that researchers have produced to be used by other researchers—while there are not many examples, as this research field progresses we expect more tools will be developed.

6.1 TYPES OF DATASETS

Datasets for this research must contain the elements that the models described in Chapter 2 require. First, a *social graph* $G = (V, E)$ representing social connections. Second, a family of ℓ action traces $S_t^{(i)}$, where $i = 1, \ldots, \ell$ and $S_0^{(i)}$ is the seed set of action i, and $S_t^{(i)}$ for $t \geq 1$ is the set of active nodes for action i at time t.

Social networks. While the models we have described do not require symmetric social networks, in practice many online social networks are symmetric. This is the case with platforms where users must confirm or acknowledge that they are friends with the initiator of a friend request.

In some cases, social networks are not explicitly recorded by the platforms from which the data originates, or can not be directly observed. In those cases, it is common to infer the connections from interactions between users, e.g., whenever two users interact beyond a certain threshold, exchanging more than k messages, they are considered to be connected in G.

Action traces. Any change that can be observed in the state of individuals in the network can be considered an action. Sometimes these actions are explicit choices of individuals, such as deciding to switch to a different mobile phone provider (e.g. [Dasgupta et al., 2008]). A variety of other state changes can also be considered as actions, such as catching a disease or gaining weight (e.g. [Christakis and Fowler, 2007]).

Real datasets describing propagation phenomena may or may not include *attribution* information. Attribution information is a family of functions $P_{i,t} : D_i(t) \rightarrow 2^{(\cup_{t' < t} D_i(t'))}$ for $t \geq 1$, where as in Chapter 5 $D_i(t)$ is the set of nodes active at time t for action (or episode) i. Function $P_{i,t}$ is such that $v \in P_{i,t}(u)$ if and only if node v was among the ones that triggered the node u which activated at time t. In this case v is said to be a *parent* of u for action i at time t. In most datasets that include attribution information, for any given action there is a single parent for every active node.

Currently, publicly available datasets containing both a social network and action traces are relatively rare. Researchers typically resort to using datasets for which one of the two parts is missing and need to be inferred or synthesized.

Another option is to use proprietary or closed datasets, however, the exclusive use of proprietary datasets is being shunned upon in recent years. First-tier conferences including KDD and SIGMOD among others, are including increasingly stronger language in their call for papers, asking for reproducibility of research results. This does not prevent researchers from using proprietary datasets, but it often conditions that on the existence of alternative public datasets in which at least part of the experimental results can be reproduced.

6.2   PROPAGATION OF INFORMATION "MEMES"

The most common type of dataset used for research on information propagation corresponds to textual corpora from which propagation of information "memes" can be inferred. "Meme" is a term coined by Dawkins [1990] to indicate a cultural entity: an idea, behavior, or style, that an observer might consider a *replicator*. The specific form that observable "memes" can take in real-world datasets depends on the platform/system from which data are collected by researchers.

6.2.1   MICROBLOGGING

Microblogging is a well-established paradigm for online social networking sites, in which users are able to upload small pieces of content (links to web pages, photos, videos, or short pieces of text) that can be voted upon and/or "shared" by other users. Microblogging ocassionaly generates information cascades in which the number of people exposed to a given piece of content is large –the content is said to "go viral" in social media marketing parlance.

The social network in microblogging platforms is typically non-symmetrical, as users are encouraged to *follow* other users, who may or may not want to reciprocate this connection. Examples of highly-visited microblogging platforms (according to Alexa[1]) include Facebook, Twitter, LinkedIn, Sina Weibo, and Pinterest, among many others.

The seed set $D_i(0)$ for an action i corresponds to people who first posted a content item into what is known as their *timeline*. Every time a user u logs into a microblogging platform, she is shown a subset of items posted into the timelines of users that are being followed by u. In

[1]http://www.alexa.com/

addition to browsing this content, there are simple (often one-click) mechanisms for *re-posting* an existing message.

In this setting, action traces originated by cascades of re-posts are often explicitly attributed. In practice, however, the linkage between a user posting an item and its parent is not present in the publicly-available data. This happens often with third-party clients for online social networking sites that tend to generate a new post instead of a re-post linked to the parent element, such as in the case of third-party clients for Twitter.

Sampling issues. The availability of APIs to access microblogging data has been one of the factors that have boosted the development of this area, but often these datasets are not complete. For instance, as of 2013, Twitter offers through its free API a uniform random sample of 1% of the tweets. This is problematic for researchers, as given this sampling method the information of any large cascade is almost certainly incomplete. There are methods to alleviate this problem, such as the one described by Sadikov et al. [2011].

6.2.2 NEWSPAPERS/BLOGS/ETC.

"Memes" can also be extracted automatically from textual corpora. Tracking their spread can be made easier if there are explicit links (citations/references) among documents. For instance, academic papers contain citations to other papers—those citations can be interpreted as explicit attributions of the propagation of an idea.

However, outside academic research, citations tend to be rare. For instance, blog postings—and other online media such as online news articles and general web pages—rarely cite the previous works they build upon, as shown by Adar and Adamic [2005]. In these cases, attribution for propagations needs to be inferred from other factors, for instance by taking into account the timestamp of the documents and assuming that a meme can propagate only from an older document to a newer document.

But even when propagations are explicitly attributed, characterizing computationally memes can be a daunting task. In the case of media, for instance, sometimes memes can be obvious, as in the case of an emerging popular music star whose name suddenly appears in many news articles in a collection. Other times, memes can be subtle, such as changes in the way a certain subject is framed; an interesting case in the USA is the evolution of "waterboarding" from "torture" to "enhanced interrogation technique" documented by Desai et al. [2010].

A straightforward solution is to define a "meme" as a small set of words or a phrase, as in [Gruhl et al., 2004]. Unfortunately, in practice this often yields a mixture of actions that are either too broad or too narrow. For instance, if we select news articles containing the phrase "French president" we may be selecting multiple stories that are unrelated to each other, as a person may be involved in a number of topics at the same time. On the other hand, if we select news articles containing "nuclear disarmament, we may miss related documents containing other terms such as "nuclear proliferation," etc.

Something similar happens in the case of social media that supports free-form tagging for content (e.g., with "hashtags") or URL links embedded in the content. With some exceptions, tags tend to be too broad, while URLs tend to be too narrow, as the same meme/story/event may be represented by more than one URL ([Wu et al., 2011]). To overcome these problems, methods such as LDA (latent dirichlet allocation) can be applied to detect topics in collections of documents or social media postings, as in [Zhao et al., 2011].

Alternatively, a solution that has been proposed for detecting memes is to start by locating "bursty" [Kleinberg, 2002] words or phrases, i.e., words or phrases that increase significantly in frequency at a given time. Once such an example is found, a method for improving precision can be applied, e.g., by demanding every document to include one extra word or phrase from a set of related terms, as in the system described by Mathioudakis and Koudas [2010].

Another solution is to consider that at every timestep, a meme can suffer small modifications. This method has been applied to the tracking of online petition letters (and their variants) as studied by Liben-Nowell and Kleinberg [2008]. An influential work in this space is the *meme tracker* system, described by Leskovec et al. [2009]. Meme tracker infers likely paths of transmission for a set of memes, starting from a list of timestamped documents, and assuming that memes can "mutate" every time they are copied.

6.3   PROPAGATION OF OTHER ACTIONS

Besides memes, there are a variety of other types of actions for which propagation data is sometimes available.

6.3.1   CONSUMPTION/APPRAISAL PLATFORMS

The consumption of products has always had a social component, as attested by the numerous trends and fashions in clothing and other industries. Online shopping is increasingly becoming a "social" activity, a phenomenon that also affect brick-and-mortar shops as many consumers go online to find recommendations for products they intend to buy [Hu and Liu, 2004]. Websites such as Pinterest (http://www.pinterest.com/) among many others, allow users to browse and *curate* collections of products and interests.

Many users also share publicly—and sometimes automatically—the media products they consume. This is done through sites like http://kindle.amazon.com/ and http://goodreads.com/ for books, http://getmiso.com/ and http://intonow.com/ for TV shows, and http://last.fm/ for music, among many others.

These online platforms currently include social networking features that allow users to "follow" a set of users, and receive notifications when one of those users listens to a new album or reads a new book. Users are thus exposed to lists of items consumed by other users, as well as occasional ratings and reviews posted by them.

In this context, consuming or appraising a product becomes an action that can generate a propagation cascade. The links among users plus the sequence of products each user consumes, and/or posts an opinion on, constitute a rich (and potentially profitable) dataset to study propagation phenomena.

For instance, Bhagat et al. [2012] analyze data about films from Flixster and data about music preferences from Last.fm. Huang et al. [2012] use data from a Chinese media appraisal platform named Douban and the GoodReads book-reading social network.

In most cases, propagations are implicitly attributed—we do not know especifically who was the cause that user consumed a product, we just know the temporal sequence of these actions. However, in some cases there is evidence that allows to track attribution, such as in platforms that have an explicit "recommend to a friend" feature. This is the case of *@cosme*, a platform for recommendation of cosmetic products whose data has been used for research by Matsuo and Yamamoto [2009].

6.3.2   USER-GENERATED CONTENT SHARING/VOTING

Platforms to share user generated content often allow some mechanisms for social networking. For instance, photo sharing site Flickr allows users to declare (non-symmetrically) people to be "family" or "friends." In this specific case, Cha et al. [2009] studied whether these links affect the decision of adding a photo as a "favorite." Anagnostopoulos et al. [2008] studied whether the adoption of a certain tag by users when describing their photos affects their social connections. Something similar happens in user voting sites such as Digg or Reddit where there are explicit friendship links and the main action is to vote on content, as studied by Lerman [2007].

6.3.3   COMMUNITY MEMBERSHIP AS ACTION

There are many online platforms that allow users to form online groups or communities. Some researchers have considered the action of becoming a member of a group to be influenced by the social network connections of users. The hypothesis is that there is to some extent a "bandwagon effect," in which if many of the connections/friends of a user join a community, the user is also likely to join.

For instance, in blogging platform Livejournal, a user is a blogger who can declare that s/he wants to "join" a community around a topic. Such actions has been correlated with the actions of connections/friends in the same blogging platform [Goyal et al., 2011a].

The definition of community can be quite flexible. In the academic world, a "community" may be represented by a journal, a conference, or even a topic. Publishing a paper on that community means becoming a member, and the social network can be inferred from past co-authorship relationships. This type of dataset was used by Backstrom et al. [2006], using data from DBLP, and Tan et al. [2010], using data from ArnetMiner.

A community can also be a group of readers of a website, such as the people who follow a particular blog through an RSS feed. This is the case of the research by Java et al. [2007] performed on blog reading platform *Bloglines* (http://www.bloglines.com/). The social network are explicit ties among readers, and an action is to subscribe to an RSS feed.

6.3.4 CROSS-PROVIDER DATA

Large Internet companies have user bases in the order of tens or hundreds of millions of users. When those companies offer a variety of services to users, the activity records from these users on the different services can be linked through site-wide user-ids. This allows them to extract the network from connections among users in one product, and track their actions in another product.

In Singla and Richardson [2008] researchers used Microsoft data from instant messaging platform MSN Messenger, together with searches in the Microsoft search engine Bing. Their conclusion was that users who are friends in the messaging platform do tend to issue similar queries. Something similar was done by Goyal et al. [2008] who used the social network of Yahoo! Instant Messenger users, and joined it with information about movies appraised by the users in Yahoo! Movies.

Using cross-provider data may have at least two caveats. First, even if the terms of services allow for it, some users may be surprised or turned off by the fact that their actions in two different (from their perspective) platforms are being correlated. Second, given that the same users can have multiple online *personas*, the nature of the platforms should be similar, e.g., if the social networking platform is oriented mostly to entertainment or gaming, the other platform should also have the same tone (and not be, e.g., a professional-oriented site).

6.3.5 PHONE LOGS

The mining of logs from (mobile) phone conversations has been mostly motivated by one specific application: reducing "churning," which is short-term switching among phone providers. In this setting, the social network is inferred by phone calls, i.e., two users are connected if they exchange many phone calls, and the action is "switching to another phone provider" or ceasing to use the phone network, as studied by Dasgupta et al. [2008].

Despite strong privacy protections around this type of data, some phone datasets are available. For instance, Nokia offers a dataset for academic labs (not industrial ones) http://research.nokia.com/page/12000. Another dataset, more publicly available, covers exchanges of phone calls and SMS messages among 5 million users in Ivory Coast (http://www.d4d.orange.com/home).

6.4 NETWORK-ONLY DATASETS

In the previous sections we have included several datasets in which the action traces are available but the social network needs to be inferred. In this section we outline datasets for which the social network is available and actions traces need to be synthesized. Despite the obvious drawbacks of using synthetic action traces, the validation of some methods in the literature has required large-scale networks for which real action traces are not available.

6.4.1   CITATION NETWORKS

Citation networks can be extracted from a variety of sources, including academic publication repositories and patent repositories. Patents are particularly attractive because they include as many citations as academic papers, and have the additional benefit that in jurisdictions like the USA the documents are in the public domain – unlike most scientific articles.

The blogosphere (the Web of blogs), linked data repositories (such as Freebase and DBPedia), and the entire Web have also been used as citation networks. Large collections of this type are widely available; for instance Amazon offers currently a crawl of the Web containing 5×10^9 pages.

6.4.2   OTHER NETWORKS

Network data are widely available across a variety of domains.

In the domain of transportation, there are multiple publicly-available datasets containing roads, railways, or air travel routes. In the domain of communications, there are detailed descriptions of the communication networks connecting Internet autonomous systems, connections among peer-to-peer applications, etc. In the biological domain, there are protein interaction networks, metabolic networks, and entire maps of neuronal connections of simple organisms.

In the domain of collaborative production, there are several online collections of works for which it is possible to infer a co-authorship or collaboration network. We have mentioned collaborations among scientists (e.g., the NetHEPT dataset described in Section 3.2.2, which is available at `http://research.microsoft.com/en-us/people/weic/graphdata.zip`), the same applies to actors, dancers, musicians and athletes in team sports, whose information is available from specialized databases. A special case are Wikipedia editors, given that its platform logs almost all the activities of editors. These include co-editing the same article, sending messages to each other through their user profiles, and discussing about an article on an article discussion page. A number of networks can be inferred from these exchanges.

In general, almost any online platform in which users can declare explicitly their "friends" or connections can provide to a certain extent with information that is relevant to study information propagation: online forums and online games are obvious examples of this.

Some example repositories in which the networks described above can be found include `http://snap.stanford.edu/data/`, `http://www-personal.umich.edu/~mejn/netdata/`, and `http://networkdata.ics.uci.edu/`

6.5   OTHER OFF-LINE DATASETS

Before the information technology revolution, social scientists collected information through direct observation in the field. One of the earliest examples of off-line social networks available is a study of the participation of 18 women in 14 social activities over 9 months in the South of the US [Davis et al., 1941]. A more well-known example is a field work done by Zachary [1977] observing acquaintances between members of a Karate Club of 34 members (dataset available at `http://networkdata.ics.uci.edu/data.php?id=105`). Interestingly, the club splitted in two during the observation period, providing a natural experiment that has been used to benchmark graph partitioning algorithms, e.g., [Girvan and Newman, 2002].

There are many more examples of "off-line" social networks and they are very varied. For instance, the already mentioned dataset of medical records of 12,067 patients during 32 years studied by Christakis and Fowler [2007], a romantic network of relationships among 288 highschool students obtained by Bearman et al. [2004], and a network of presumed acquaintances links between 74 terrorist suspects analyzed by Krebs [2002].

Multiple datasets of this type can be found in the listing of UCINET IV datasets (`http://vlado.fmf.uni-lj.si/pub/networks/data/ucinet/ucidata.htm`).

6.6   PUBLISHING YOUR OWN DATASETS

This is an evolving area and many new datasets are available every year. Publishing a new dataset generates a social good and increases the scientific impact of those who make such datasets available. We briefly outline three steps in a data release: construction, anonymization, and licensing.

First, the construction of each new dataset must be documented in detail. The researcher(s) that release a dataset can not foresee all the different settings in which the dataset will be used. Different settings may require to understand different ways in which the biases of the data must be accounted for. Hence, every sampling, filtering, and processing step must be carefully explained.

Second, personally identifiable information must be removed from the data, even if the collection is sampled from publicly available data.

Third, a license must be chosen. For datasets that do not contain any sensitive or proprietary information, the best is to use a wide disclaimer of warranties and to allow maximum freedom when using the dataset. The Creative Commons Zero license used by the CERN, The British Library, Nature, among many others, serves this purpose (`http://wiki.creativecommons.org/CC0_use_for_data`).

For datasets that may contain sensitive or proprietary information, access to the data may be conditioned upon acceptance of a set of terms and conditions through an express agreement. This agreement can specify aspects such as duration, purpose (research, or any purpose), disclaimers of warranties, and item deletion policies (i.e., that the users of the data agree to delete partially or completely the dataset upon request).

6.7   SOFTWARE TOOLS

In this section we overview a few software tools available to support this type of research. We start by giving examples of generic graph mining software, which is widely available and fairly mature; we continue with software that can deal with action traces, which is much more rare. Finally, we outline a few efforts on visualizing viral phenomena.

6.7.1 GRAPH SOFTWARE TOOLS

Table 6.1: Summary of key capabilities of graph software

Software	License	Language (and mode)	Generate	Operate	Visualize
Gephi	GPL	Java (gui)	Yes	Yes	Yes
Pajek	Free (non-commercial use)	Windows (gui)	Yes	Yes	Yes
SNAP	GPL	C++ (cli)	Yes	Yes	No
Webgraph	GPL	Java (cli)	Yes	Yes	No
Graphviz	GPL	C++ (cli)	No	No	Yes

Tools for creating, manipulating, mining and visualizing large-scale graphs have been available for several years. We focus on a small set of well-established tools that are frequently used by researchers on this area (see Table 6.1).

Gephi (http://gephi.org) and Pajek (http://pajek.imfm.si/doku.php?id=pajek) can be regarded as *graph processing workbenches*. They implement a number of methods to generate, transform, and visualize graphs. Both provide a graphical user interface (GUI), and thus may be better suited for users without experience using command line interfaces (CLI) interfaces.

In some circumstances e.g., when involving very large graphs or batch processing, using software through a CLI may be advisable.

SNAP (http://snap.stanford.edu/snap/) is a set of tools developed to handle social networks data. These tools include many general-purpose graph algorithms including performing clustering, computing measures of centrality, etc.

Webgraph (http://webgraph.dsi.unimi.it/) and Graphviz (http://graphviz.org/) are specialized tools that focus on particular operations. Webgraph is mainly a graph compression platform to handle huge graphs –it can achieve a surprising 2.89 bits per link when dealing with web links data. Graphviz is a visualization software implementing a number of layout algorithms. Both are used through a command-line interface.

Other tools are available here: https://sites.google.com/site/ucinetsoftware/downloads.

6.7.2 PROPAGATION SOFTWARE TOOLS

Software that can deal with information/influence propagation is much more rare than generic graph-processing software.

While many authors may share their code with interested researchers upon request, only a few of them release publicly their code. Among those, we can mention Goyal et al.

[2011a] (`http://www.cs.ubc.ca/~goyal/code-release.php`), who provides software for implementing greedy seed selection as well as other algorithms and Mathioudakis et al. [2011] who provides software implementing the inference of influence on a social network among others (`http://queens.db.toronto.edu/~mathiou/spine/`).

Other software such as the Internet Network Simulator (`http://isi.edu/nsnam/ns/doc/`) can simulate propagation of information through a network (e.g., an Internet worm), but does not include any inference algorithms.

6.7.3 VISUALIZATION

In recent years some demonstrations of visualization of information propagation have emerged.

A first type are software that visualize interactions among pairs of users, e.g., phone calls (`http://senseable.mit.edu/`) or direct messages in Twitter (`http://www.youtube.com/watch?v=ECqzsom7axQ`).

A second type is software to visualize a especialized aspect of information propagation in social networks in order to analyze it. In general, these methods visualize the sub-graph induced by a single action as it propagates, as in `http://blog.socialflow.com/post/5246404319/breaking-bin-laden-visualizing-the-power-of-a-single`. Truthy (`http://truthy.indiana.edu/`) deals with detecting fake political grassroot activism (also known as "astroturfing"). The visualizations they provide allow analysts to quickly detect anomalous structures among the users using a certain term or hashtag, such as a densely connected graph or a deviation from the expected for polarizing political topics which is a graph made of two dense subgraphs separable by a small graph cut.

A third type is software that generates visualization for consumption by the general public. Mass media is becoming increasingly interested in mining social media as a way of understanding society and/or contributing to the journalistic process. The Guardian, for instance, presented a visualization of rumors as they appear, propagate, and die (`http://www.guardian.co.uk/uk/interactive/2011/dec/07/london-riots-twitter`). The New York Times' "Project Cascade" depicts the propagation of links to news using a solar system metaphor in which the original news item is the Sun (`http://nytlabs.com/projects/cascade.html`).

6.8 CONCLUSIONS

The data used by most researchers in this area tend to suffer from one of the following drawbacks: (i) it does not describe explicitly the action traces, (ii) it does not include a explicit social network, or (iii) it is proprietary.

To a large extent, researchers resort to using synthetic propagations on existing social networking data. While this may be enough for some purposes, it is clearly desirable that experimental validation is done over datasets that resemble closely real-world datasets, especially for research that claims to be significant for real-world applications. Results on proprietary data sources, which may be more realistic, are not reproducible and hence may not be a solid ground for further research.

The lack of appropriate data can seriously slow down research on influence and information propagation. The scarcity of reference implementations of well-known algorithms may hamper efforts to reproduce and compare different algorithms. Both problems can be dealt with if the research community embraces reproducibility as a fundamental value, and collectively shares the datasets and software needed to move forward.

CHAPTER 7

Conclusion and Challenges

Most of the research covered in this book is motivated by practical applications. In addition, there is an implicit thesis underlying all this work: viral phenomena can not only be modeled accurately, but they can also be engineered. For instance, in the area of marketing, there is a certain expectation that a campaign can be designed to "*go viral.*"

In general, translating theoretical results into practice is rarely straightforward, and information/influence propagation research is no exception. On one hand, we have shown empirical results that demonstrate that indeed influence is a real phenomenon and it resembles some of the abstractions that have been proposed to model it. On the other hand, some questions still remain about how industries can actually leverage the results of this research and successfully deploy the techniques in a real viral marketing setting.

In this final chapter, we first outline these questions and then present some open technical problems and our concluding remarks.

7.1 APPLICATION-SPECIFIC CHALLENGES

7.1.1 PROVE VALUE FOR ADVERTISING/MARKETING

A century-old adage in the advertising industry, attributed to marketing pioneer John Wanamaker (1838-1922), states that half of the money spent in advertising is wasted, but it is hard to know which half. Measuring the return on investment of traditional marketing campaigns has never been easy. Measuring the return on investment of viral advertising is even more difficult—we have seen that there are many confounding factors.

In general, an important open question is to prove beyond doubt "the design of viral marketing campaigns" as a business proposition. At present, there is only anecdotal evidence about successful marketing campaigns, and most of this evidence is about exceptional cases. We can not draw general conclusions from such outliers. At the very least, there is a need to develop an understanding, possibly by empirical means, of under what circumstances viral marketing is likely to work.

Indeed, some authors including Bakshy et al. [2011] have described model settings under which careful seed selection is defeated by random selection of seed nodes. This happens when the nodes that may generate the largest spread cost more to activate, which corresponds to a plausible situation in which "A-list" celebrities or public figures charge more for their endorsements than "B-list" ones. Of course, the balance depends on the specific parameters of each setting. In this setting, spread by itself may not be the right objective to optimize. As discussed in Section 4.3, (expected) profit is the right objective to optimize in this case. In that section, we gave an account of a principled approach for optimizing this objective.

There is a pressing need for thorough independent studies that compare the return on investment of viral campaigns versus traditional ones. These studies are needed before recommendations can be made to companies to shift spending from traditional marketing to viral marketing. A combination of laboratory and field studies seems a possible way of addressing this challenge.

By contrast, the advances made to evaluate these methods on a different application, contamination detection in water distribution networks, is impressive. In August 2006, the Battle of Water Sensor Networks (BWSN) [Ostfeld and Salomons, 2004, Ostfeld et al., 2006] was organized as an international challenge to find the best sensor placements for a real (but anonymized) metropolitan area water distribution network. The CELF algorithm [Leskovec et al., 2007], discussed in Chapter 3, was actually used in this competition. It would be interesting and useful to find out whether an approach similar to CELF (or any "influence maximization" approach) is actually used in any city's water distribution network.

7.1.2   LEARN TO DESIGN FOR VIRALITY

There is currently a gap between *descriptive* and *prescriptive* research outcomes. Descriptive outcome deals with questions such as how and to what extent a certain idea or virus propagates, and with the strengths of a community to influence propagation. Prescriptive outcome arises from studying questions such as how to engineer a viral phenomenon, e.g., how to make an idea or product spread virally. Clearly, domain experts and business managers care about the prescriptive outcome as much as they care about the descriptive outcomes.

There can be many elements including intrinsic characteristics of the content, as well as of the community and in general the context in which a propagation takes place (e.g., the time of the year, the geographical region, etc.) which could play a role in deciding whether an idea or product spreads virally. There is no doubt marketing agencies, political parties, and activist groups, among many others, put a significant amount of resources and effort in creating campaigns that can "go viral." But for every one that succeeds, many fizzle out, demonstrating the intrinsic challenge in answering the following questions. What makes a product or idea spread virally? Can we learn to design products and ideas that can reach a large number of people through viral diffusion, especially in the presence of competitors? Answering these questions requires a substantial amount of experimentation, which in turn requires appropriate experimentation methodologies as well as benchmarking datasets.

7.1.3   CORRECT FOR SAMPLING BIASES

There are vast amounts of data being collected today about the behavior of people online. These data allow analysts to observe and analyze the interests and opinions of millions of people about politicians, celebrities, brands, products, etc. Using some of the methods we have described, this data should allow us, for instance, to determine which people and ideas are more influential.

However, the huge datasets that are obtained from social media are often neither representative nor complete. The observations we obtain from social media have numerous biases, starting with the fact that they contain only people who have access to social media technologies. Currently, this means that the samples are likely to over-represent educated people in urban areas, that have some disposable income, and do not belong to marginalized or minority groups.

For certain applications such as viral marketing of technologies and products, this bias may not be a serious issue. However, in general, conclusions that are drawn from biased data samples, no matter how large, are of limited value. Some social media research has been criticized precisely for assuming social media communities to be representative panels of the general population. For instance, Gayo-Avello [2012] and Furnas [2012], among others, have pointed out methodological errors in a recent line of research that aims at predicting the outcome of political elections using Twitter.

Reputable pollsters are extremely careful when selecting panels for opinion polls or other studies. It is important for scientists working in this field to demonstrate that it is possible to correct for the biases in the source data when observing various online phenomena such as cascades. This is important to ensure that the conclusions drawn are of value to social science research.

7.1.4   CONTRIBUTE TO OTHER APPLICATIONS

We discussed the Battle of Water Sensor Networks (BWSN) competition, which attracted and fueled a large body of influential work. It is interesting to ask what it would take to organize a similar competition in the business world for viral marketing.

Marketing is only one application domain among many others where propagation phenomena can be observed and leveraged. We have mentioned the health domain, in which understanding how an infection propagates, how it can be contained, and how to take preventive measures (e.g., vaccination campaigns) can actually save lives. To have real impact, it is critical for computer scientists working in this area to collaborate with health scientists and medical centers.

In the humanitarian sector, creating successful education or training programmes, often requires reaching out to influential people recruited from the same communities to which these programs are addressed. In a setting in which target populations are large in comparison to the available resources, word-of-mouth diffusion may be the only way of reaching a large fraction of the population.

There are probably many other high-impact applications where these methods may have potentially huge social and commercial impact. Finding such applications and validating the usefulness of this research is another substantial open challenge.

7.2   TECHNICAL CHALLENGES

Besides the challenges from the application perspective described above, there are many technical challenges in this research area. We have discussed various open problems and possible extensions towards the end of each technical chapter, and thus focus here on discussing grand challenges facing social influence research and social network research in general.

One big technical challenge is dealing with large-scale graphs. Real-life social graphs typically have hundreds of millions to billions of nodes and edges. For a large graph with n nodes and m edges, near-linear-time algorithms, i.e., those with running time $O((m + n) \, \text{polylog}(n))$ or $O((m + n)^{1+o(1)})$, are desirable, while quadratic algorithms with running time $\Theta((m + n)^2)$ is already infeasible.

For example, for the fundamental problems of computing all-pairs shortest paths and the diameter of a graph, the best known algorithm for unweighted and undirected sparse graphs ($m \leq n \log \log n$) only achieves slightly sub-quadratic running time of $O(n^2 \log^2 \log n / \log n)$ [Chan, 2012], and thus is still infeasible for very large graphs. As for influence maximization, our Theorem 3.7 shows that the basic greedy algorithm has a very high running time of $O(\varepsilon^{-2} k^3 n^2 m \log n)$, where k is the number of seeds to be selected and ε is the additive slack in the approximation ratio. Fortunately, a recent work by Borgs et al. [2012] proposes a clever algorithm to bring down the running time, for the IC model, to the near linear time of $O(\varepsilon^{-3}(m + n)k \log n)$. It is interesting to investigate whether a similar approach can be developed for other diffusion models and for the various variants of the influence maximization problem discussed in this book.

The theoretical computer science community has developed a number of important techniques for near-linear-time graph algorithm design, including graph sparsification [Benczúr and Karger, 1996] and Laplacian linear system solver [Spielman and Teng, 2004]. These techniques have lead to a breakthrough in approximate max-flow computation, bringing down the more-than-ten-year-old running time of $\tilde{O}(mn^{1/2}\varepsilon^{-1})$ of the previous best algorithm [Goldberg and Rao, 1998] to $\tilde{O}(mn^{1/3}\varepsilon^{-11/3})$ [Christiano et al., 2011],[1] where ε is the slack for achieving $(1 - \varepsilon)$-approximation in the max-flow problem. Very recently, two independent studies following a similar approach final bring down the running time of max-flow problem to the near linear time of $\tilde{O}(m^{1+o(1)}\varepsilon^{-2})$ [Kelner et al., 2013, Sherman, 2013]. These exciting successes in near-linear-time max-flow algorithms may provide insights and inspiration for applying near-linear-time Laplacian solvers and graph sparsifiers to other graph problems.

However, certain graph problems such as graph diameter computation are likely to remain as hard problems, perhaps admitting only close to quadratic-time algorithms. This may suggest a complexity treatment of graph problems, classifying graph problems within the quadratic or low-polynomial order range into different complexity classes, and using near-linear-time reductions to compare their relative hardness. Complexity theory typically treats complexity classes such as P or NP with polynomial-time reductions, but for scalable graph algorithms, P is too coarse a class, and a refined classification based on near-linear-time reductions would be desirable. As a case in point, in computational geometry, a number of problems have been classified as 3-Sum-hard problems: these problems can be reduced from the 3-Sum problem using subquadratic-time

---

[1]The notation $\tilde{O}(f(n))$ means $O(f(n) \log^c f(n))$ for some constant c.

reductions, meaning that if any of them has a subquadratic-time solution, then 3-Sum also has a subquadratic solution [Gajentaan and Overmars, 1995]. However, we have not seen such studies in the context of graph problems, and this may be a fertile area for research given the renewed demand for scalable graph algorithms.

Therefore, social network-related problems, such as influence maximization demand scalable algorithms with near linear running time, and this generate new challenges of developing algorithmic techniques and new complexity classes for scalable graph problems. All our discussions on, and indeed the majority of algorithmic research in, influence maximization have focused on sequential algorithms. Distributed paradigms such as MapReduce [Dean and Ghemawat, 2004] and graph processing engines such as Pregel [Malewicz et al., 2010] and GraphLab [Low et al., 2012] offer promise and should be explored for developing approaches that scale to networks with billions of nodes and edges.

Besides the challenges of developing near-linear-time algorithms, another algorithmic challenge is dealing with dynamic graphs. The models and problems addressed in this book, and in most research literature, are on static social graphs. However, in the real world, social networks change dynamically because users change their relationships and users join or leave the network. Future studies need to properly incorporate network dynamics in influence diffusion models and influence maximization algorithms to achieve more realistic and more applicable results. This is another widely open area with both challenges and opportunities.

As pointed out in Chapter 4, the bulk majority of the studies in influence maximization, with or without competition, have ignored the crucial role played by the owners (hosts) of online social networking sites. Without explicit permission from them, activating specific nodes for a viral campaign may not be possible. While we discussed some initial work on the importance of fairness and fairness maximization in Section 4.2.4, many questions remain open. What is the impact of the host on competitive influence or profit maximization? What is the impact of a dynamic network on competitive marketing? What kind of protocols between competing companies and the host are necessary in order to make the campaigns effective and relevant to the real business world?

Last but not the least, all our discussion has been confined to homogeneous networks. There may be interesting marketing opportunities in heterogeneous networks. To give one example, consider a network consisting of people and products. There are relationships between people and between products. Additionally, people provide ratings or reviews on products. By analyzing their rating behavior, can we identify which people are influential over what kind of products and take advantage of that in targeted advertising and marketing?

7.3   CONCLUSIONS

We have witnessed great advances in theory, analysis, and algorithms related to viral phenomena. As mentioned in the previous section, there are many open research directions that we envision will make this a fruitful research area for years to come.

An important reminder, though, is that *engineering* viral phenomena, in order to bring to life many of the applications discussed in this book, has yet to be taken out of the laboratory and put into practice at a large societal or industrial scale. This is important at once for the society, the industry, and the scientists, as most of this research is indeed motivated by practical problems. This area can benefit from deploying the solutions developed by the research community in practical settings and observing how these solutions behave in practice and what new challenges arise there. Last but not least, closing the gap between theory and practice is fundamental for the society at large to be able to reap the benefits of this research.

APPENDIX A

Notational Conventions

We summarize the notational conventions used in this book in the following table. The table only covers important notations used throughout the book. Other notations only appear locally and should be clear from their confined contexts, and thus are not included in this table.

Notation	Terminology and description
$G = (V, E)$	social graph G, with vertex set V and arc set E
$N^{out}(u)$	out-neighbors of node u
$N^{in}(u)$	in-neighbors of node u
$\Pr(\mathcal{E})$	probability of event $\mathcal{E}$
$\mathbb{E}(X)$	expected value of random variable X
S_0	seed set, $S_0 \subseteq V$
S_t	active node set at time t
$p(u, v), p_{uv}$	influence probability on arc (u, v), in the IC model
$w(u, v), w_{uv}$	influence weight on arc (u, v), in the LT model
$\Phi(S_0)$	final active node set after diffusion ends, given seed set S_0
$\sigma(S_0)$	influence spread of S_0, i.e., expected number of nodes activated by seed set S_0, $\sigma(S_0) = \mathbb{E}(|\Phi(S_0)|)$
$R_G(S)$	set of nodes reachable from S in graph G
$R_G^t(S)$	set of nodes reachable from S within t steps in graph G
$d_G(u, v)$	distance from node u to node v in graph G
$d_G(S, v)$	distance from set of nodes S to node v in graph G
$f_v(S)$	threshold function for the general threshold model
$p_v(u, S)$	activation function for the general cascade model

Bibliography

Eytan Adar and Lada A. Adamic. Tracking Information Epidemics in Blogspace. In *Proc. of the 2005 IEEE/WIC/ACM Int. Conf. on Web Intelligence*, pages 207–214. IEEE CS Press, September 2005. DOI: 10.1109/WI.2005.151. 125

Aris Anagnostopoulos, Ravi Kumar, and Mohammad Mahdian. Influence and correlation in social networks. In *Proc. 14th ACM SIGKDD Int. Conf. on Knowledge Discovery and Data Mining*, pages 7–15. ACM, 2008. ISBN 978-1-60558-193-4. doi: 10.1145/1401890.1401897. DOI: 10.1145/1401890.1401897. 5, 127

R. M. Anderson and R. M. May. *Infectious Diseases of Humans: Dynamics and Control.* Oxford University Press, 2002. 11

Sinan Aral, Lev Muchnik, and Arun Sundararajan. Distinguishing influence-based contagion from homophily-driven diffusion in dynamic networks. In *Proc. National Academy of Sciences*, pages 21544–21549, 2009. DOI: 10.1073/pnas.0908800106. 5

Lars Backstrom, Dan Huttenlocher, Jon Kleinberg, and Xiangyang Lan. Group formation in large social networks: membership, growth, and evolution. In *Proc. 12th ACM SIGKDD Int. Conf. on Knowledge Discovery and Data Mining*, pages 44–54. ACM Press, 2006. doi: 10.1145/1150402.1150412. DOI: 10.1145/1150402.1150412. 127

Eytan Bakshy, Jake M. Hofman, Winter A. Mason, and Duncan J. Watts. Everyone's an influencer: quantifying influence on twitter. In *Proc. 4th ACM Int. Conf. Web Search and Data Mining*, pages 65–74. ACM, 2011. ISBN 978-1-4503-0493-1. doi: 10.1145/1935826.1935845. DOI: 10.1145/1935826.1935845. 135

John Barnes. Class and Committees in a Norwegian Island Parish. *Human Relations*, 7:39–58, 1954. DOI: 10.1177/001872675400700102. 1

Peter S. Bearman, James Moody, and Katherine Stovel. Chains of Affection: The Structure of Adolescent Romantic and Sexual Networks. *American J. of Sociology*, 110(1):44–91, July 2004. DOI: 10.1086/386272. 130

Oren Ben-Zwi, Danny Hermelin, Daniel Lokshtanov, and Ilan Newman. An exact almost optimal algorithm for target set selection in social networks. In *Proc. 10th ACM Conf. on Electronic Commerce*, pages 355–362, 2009. DOI: 10.1145/1566374.1566424. 23, 102

András A. Benczúr and David R. Karger.   Approximating s-t Minimum Cuts in $\tilde{O}(n^2)$ Time. In *Proc. 28th Annual ACM Symp. on Theory of Computing*, pages 47–55, 1996. DOI: 10.1145/237814.237827. 138

Smriti Bhagat, Amit Goyal, and Laks V. S. Lakshmanan. Maximizing product adoption in social networks. In *Proc. 5th ACM Int. Conf. Web Search and Data Mining*, pages 603–612. ACM, 2012.   ISBN 978-1-4503-0747-5.   doi: 10.1145/2124295.2124368. DOI: 10.1145/2124295.2124368. 95, 96, 127

Shishir Bharathi, David Kempe, and Mahyar Salek. Competitive Influence Maximization in Social Networks. In Xiaotie Deng and Fan Graham, editors, *Internet and Network Economics*, volume 4858 of *Lecture Notes in Computer Science*, pages 306–311. Springer Berlin / Heidelberg, 2007. DOI: 10.1007/978-3-540-77105-0. 71, 74

Bela Bollobás and Oliver Riordan. *Percolation*. Cambridge University Press, 2006. DOI: 10.1017/CBO9781139167383. 32

Francesco Bonchi. Influence Propagation in Social Networks: a Data Mining Perspective. In *WI-IAT*, pages 573–582, 2011. DOI: 10.1109/WI-IAT.2011.286. 120

Christian Borgs, Michael Brautbar, Jennifer T. Chayes, and Brendan Lucier. Influence Maximization in Social Networks: Towards an Optimal Algorithmic Solution. Technical Report 1212.0884, arXiv, 2012. 66, 138

A. Borodin, Y. Filmus, and J. Oren. Threshold models for competitive influence in social networks. In *Proc. 6th Workshop on Internet and Network Economic*, 2010. DOI: 10.1007/978-3-642-17572-5_48. 71, 73, 74, 77, 83, 90, 91

Linda Briesemeister, Patrick Lincoln, and Phillip A. Porras. Epidemic profiles and defense of scale-free networks. In *Proc. 2003 ACM Workshop on Rapid Malcode*, pages 67–75, 2003. DOI: 10.1145/948187.948200. 28, 29

Ceren Budak, Divyakant Agrawal, and Amr El Abbadi. Limiting the spread of misinformation in social networks. In *WWW11*, pages 665–674, 2011. DOI: 10.1145/1963405.1963499. 71, 73, 78, 84, 85

Carlos Castillo, Wei Chen, and Laks V. S. Lakshmanan. Information and Influence Spread in Social Networks, August 2012. Tutorial in the 18th ACM SIGKDD Int. Conf. on Knowledge Discovery and Data Mining (KDD'12). Slides available at http://research.microsoft.com/en-us/people/weic/kdd12tutorial_inf.aspx. 7

Damon Centola and Michael Macy. Complex contagion and the weakness of long ties. *American J. of Sociology*, 113(3):702–734, 2007. DOI: 10.1086/521848. 11, 15

Meeyoung Cha, Alan Mislove, and Krishna P. Gummadi. A measurement-driven analysis of information propagation in the flickr social network. In *Proc. 18th Int. World Wide Web Conf.*, pages 721–730. ACM, 2009. ISBN 978-1-60558-487-4. doi: 10.1145/1526709.1526806. DOI: 10.1145/1526709.1526806. 127

Deepayan Chakrabarti, Yang Wang, Chenxi Wang, Jure Leskovec, and Christos Faloutsos. Epidemic thresholds in real networks. *ACM Trans. Information System Security*, 10(4), 2008. DOI: 10.1145/1284680.1284681. 28

Timothy M. Chan. All-pairs shortest paths for unweighted undirected graphs in o(mn) time. *ACM Trans. on Algorithms*, 8(4):34:1–34:17, October 2012. doi: 10.1145/2344422.2344424. DOI: 10.1145/2344422.2344424. 138

Ning Chen. On the approximability of influence in social networks. In *Proc. 19th Annual ACM-SIAM Symp. on Discrete Algorithms*, pages 1029–1037. Society for Industrial and Applied Mathematics, 2008. DOI: 10.1137/08073617X. 23, 101, 102

Wei Chen, Yajun Wang, and Siyu Yang. Efficient influence maximization in social networks. In *Proc. 15th ACM SIGKDD Int. Conf. on Knowledge Discovery and Data Mining*, pages 199–208, 2009. DOI: 10.1145/1557019.1557047. 44, 45, 50, 51, 52

Wei Chen, Yifei Yuan, and Li Zhang. Scalable Influence Maximization in Social Networks under the Linear Threshold Model. In *Proc. 2010 IEEE Int. Conf. on Data Mining*, pages 88–97, 2010. 36, 44, 45, 50, 51, 52, 59, 66, 84

Wei Chen, Alex Collins, Rachel Cummings, Te Ke, Zhenming Liu, David Rincón, Xiaorui Sun, Yajun Wang, Wei Wei, and Yifei Yuan. Influence Maximization in Social Networks When Negative Opinions May Emerge and Propagate. In *SDM*, pages 379–390, 2011. 59, 71, 73, 86, 87, 88

Wei Chen, Wei Lu, and Ning Zhang. Time-critical influence maximization in social networks with time-delayed diffusion process. In *Proc. 27th National Conf. on Artificial Intelligence*, 2012. 15, 59, 101

Nicholas A. Christakis and James H. Fowler. *Connected: The Surprising Power of Our Social Networks and How They Shape Our Lives – How Your Friends' Friends' Friends Affect Everything You Feel, Think, and Do*. Little, Brown, 2011. ISBN 0316036137. 3

Nicholas A. A. Christakis and James H. H. Fowler. The Spread of Obesity in a Large Social Network over 32 Years. *N. Engl. J. Med.*, 357(4):370–379, July 2007. ISSN 0028-4793. doi: 10.1056/nejmsa066082. DOI: 10.1056/NEJMsa066082. 2, 123, 130

Paul Christiano, Jonathan A. Kelner, Aleksander Madry, Daniel A. Spielman, and Shang-Hua Teng. Electrical flows, laplacian systems, and faster approximation of maximum flow in undirected graphs. In *Proc. 43rd Annual ACM Symp. on Theory of Computing*, pages 273–282, 2011. DOI: 10.1145/1993636.1993674. 138

P. Clifford and A. Sudbury. A model for spatial conflict. *Biometrika*, 60(3):581–588, 1973. DOI: 10.1093/biomet/60.3.581. 29

Edith Cohen. Size-Estimation Framework with Applications to Transitive Closure and Reachability. *J. Computer and System Sciences*, 55(3):441–453, 1997. DOI: 10.1006/jcss.1997.1534. 51

R. Cohen, S. Havlin, and D. Ben Avraham. Efficient immunization strategies for computer networks and populations. *Physical Review Letters*, 91(34), 2003. DOI: 10.1103/PhysRevLett.91.247901. 28, 29

Koustuv Dasgupta, Rahul Singh, Balaji Viswanathan, Dipanjan Chakraborty, Sougata Mukherjea, Amit A. Nanavati, and Anupam Joshi. Social ties and their relevance to churn in mobile telecom networks. In *Advances in Database Technology, Proc. 11th Int. Conf. on Extending Database Technology*, pages 668–677. ACM, 2008. ISBN 978-1-59593-926-5. doi: 10.1145/1353343.1353424. DOI: 10.1145/1353343.1353424. 123, 128

A. Davis, B. B. Gardner, and M. R. Gardner. *Deep South*. The University of Chicago Press, 1941. 129

Richard Dawkins. *The Selfish Gene*. Oxford University Press, September 1990. ISBN 0192860925. 124

Jeffrey Dean and Sanjay Ghemawat. MapReduce: Simplified Data Processing on Large Clusters. In *Proc. 6th Symposium on Operating System Design and Implementation*, pages 137–150, 2004. DOI: 10.1145/1327452.1327492. 139

Neal Desai, Andre Pineda, Majken Runquist, Mark A. Fusunyan, Katy Glenn, Gabrielle K. Gould, Michelle R. Katz, Henry Lichtblau, Maggie J. Morgan, Sophia Wen, and Sandy Wong. Torture at Times: Waterboarding in the Media. Technical report, Joan Shorenstein Center on the Press, Politics, and Public Policy, April 2010. 125

Shahar Dobzinski and Michael Schapira. An improved approximation algorithm for combinatorial auctions with submodular bidders. In *Proc. 17th Annual ACM-SIAM Symp. on Discrete Algorithms*, 2006. DOI: 10.1145/1109557.1109675. 102

Pedro Domingos and Matthew Richardson. Mining the network value of customers. In *Proc. 7th ACM SIGKDD Int. Conf. on Knowledge Discovery and Data Mining*, pages 57–66, 2001. DOI: 10.1145/502512.502525. 30, 31, 35

R. Durrett. *Lecture Notes on Particle Systems and Percolation.* Wadsworth Publishing, 1988. 10

E. Even-Dar and A. Shapira. A note on maximizing the spread of influence in social networks. In *Proc. 3rd Workshop on Internet and Network Economic,* 2007. DOI: 10.1007/978-3-540-77105-0_27. 29, 30

Uriel Feige. A threshold of ln n for approximating set cover. *J. ACM,* 45(4):634–652, 1998. ISSN 0004-5411. doi: 10.1145/285055.285059. DOI: 10.1145/285055.285059. 44, 101

Uriel Feige, Vahab S. Mirrokni, and Jan Vondrák. Maximizing Non-Monotone Submodular Functions. In *Proc. 48th Annual Symp. on Foundations of Computer Science,* pages 461–471, 2007. DOI: 10.1109/FOCS.2007.40. 99

Alexander Furnas. You Can't Use Twitter to Predict Election Results. *The Atlantic,* May 2012. 137

Anka Gajentaan and Mark H. Overmars. On a Class of $O(n^2)$ Problems in Computational Geometry. *Comput. Geom.,* 5:165–185, 1995. DOI: 10.1016/0925-7721(95)00022-2. 139

Ayalvadi J. Ganesh, Laurent Massoulié, and Donald F. Towsley. The effect of network topology on the spread of epidemics. In *Proc. 24th Annual Joint Conf. of the IEEE Computer and Communication Societies,* pages 1455–1466, 2005. DOI: 10.1109/INFCOM.2005.1498374. 28

Michael R. Garey and David S. Johnson. *Computers and Intractability; A Guide to the Theory of NP-Completeness.* W. H. Freeman & Co., 1990. ISBN 0716710455. 65

Daniel Gayo-Avello. "I Wanted to Predict Elections with Twitter and all I got was this Lousy Paper": A Balanced Survey on Election Prediction using Twitter Data, April 2012. 137

S. German and D. German. Stochastic relaxation, Gibbs distributions, and the Bayesian restoration of images. *IEEE Trans. Pattern Analy. Machine Intell.,* 6:721–741, 1984. DOI: 10.1109/TPAMI.1984.4767596. 31

M. Girvan and M. E. J. Newman. Community structure in social and biological networks. *Proc. National Academy of Sciences,* 99(12):7821–7826, June 2002. ISSN 0027-8424. doi: 10.1073/pnas.122653799. DOI: 10.1073/pnas.122653799. 130

Sharad Goel, Duncan J. Watts, and Daniel G. Goldstein. The structure of online diffusion networks. In *Proc. 13th ACM Conf. on Electronic Commerce,* pages 623–638, 2012. DOI: 10.1145/2229012.2229058. 6

Andrew V. Goldberg and Satish Rao. Beyond the Flow Decomposition Barrier. *J. ACM,* 45(5): 783–797, 1998. DOI: 10.1145/290179.290181. 138

Sharon Goldberg and Zhenming Liu. The Diffusion of Networking Technologies. In *Proc. 24th Annual ACM-SIAM Symp. on Discrete Algorithms,* pages 1577–1594, 2013. 102

J. Goldenberg, B. Libai, and E. Muller. Talk of the Network: A Complex Systems Look at the Underlying Process of Word-of-Mouth. *Marketing Letters*, 12(3):211–223, 2001a. DOI: 10.1023/A:1011122126881. 11

J. Goldenberg, B. Libai, and E. Muller. Using Complex Systems Analysis to Advance Marketing Theory Development. *Acad. of Marketing Science Rev.*, 2001b. 11

Daniel Golovin and Andreas Krause. Adaptive Submodularity: Theory and Applications in Active Learning and Stochastic Optimization. *J. Artificial Intel. Res.*, 42:427–486, 2011. 102

Amit Goyal and Laks V.S. Lakshmanan. RecMax: Exploiting Recommender Systems for Fun and Profit. In *Proc. 18th ACM SIGKDD Int. Conf. on Knowledge Discovery and Data Mining*, pages 1294–1302. ACM, 2012. DOI: 10.1145/2339530.2339731. 104

Amit Goyal, Francesco Bonchi, and Laks V. S. Lakshmanan. Discovering leaders from community actions. In *Proc. 17th ACM Int. Conf. on Information and Knowledge Management*, pages 499–508. ACM, 2008. ISBN 978-1-59593-991-3. doi: 10.1145/1458082.1458149. DOI: 10.1145/1458082.1458149. 128

Amit Goyal, We Lu, and Laks V. S. Lakshmanan. CELF++: Optimizing the Greedy Algorithm for Influence Maximization in Social Networks (poster entry). In *WWW09*, 2009. 44, 45, 50, 51, 60

Amit Goyal, Francesco Bonchi, and Laks V.S. Lakshmanan. Learning influence probabilities in social networks. In *Proc. 3rd ACM Int. Conf. Web Search and Data Mining*, pages 241–250. ACM, 2010. ISBN 978-1-60558-889-6. doi: 10.1145/1718487.1718518. DOI: 10.1145/1718487.1718518. 67, 69, 109, 112, 113, 116, 119, 120

Amit Goyal, Francesco Bonchi, and Laks V. S. Lakshmanan. A Data-Based Approach to Social Influence Maximization. *PVLDB*, 5(1):73–84, 2011a. 67, 70, 71, 127, 131

Amit Goyal, Wei Lu, and Laks V. S. Lakshmanan. SIMPATH: An Efficient Algorithm for Influence Maximization under the Linear Threshold Model. In *Proc. 2011 IEEE Int. Conf. on Data Mining*, pages 211–220, 2011b. DOI: 10.1109/ICDM.2011.132. 52, 60, 61, 64, 65, 66

Amit Goyal, Francesco Bonchi, Laks V.S. Lakshmanan, and Suresh Venkatasubramanian. On minimizing budget and time in influence propagation over social networks. *Social Network Analysis and Mining*, 2(1), 2012. DOI: 10.1007/s13278-012-0062-z. 15, 101

Sanjeev Goyal and Michael Kearns. Competitive contagion in networks. In *Proc. 44th Annual ACM Symp. on Theory of Computing*, pages 759–774, 2012. DOI: 10.1145/2213977.2214046. 103

M. Granovetter. Threshold models of collective behavior. *American J. of Sociology*, 83(6):1420–1443, 1978. DOI: 10.1086/226707. 15

Geoffrey Grimmett. *Probability on Graphs*. Cambridge University Press, 2010. 25

Daniel Gruhl, R. Guha, David Liben-Nowell, and Andrew Tomkins. Information diffusion through blogspace. In *Proc. 13th Int. World Wide Web Conf.*, pages 491–501. ACM, 2004. ISBN 1-58113-844-X. doi: 10.1145/988672.988739. DOI: 10.1145/988672.988739. 6, 106, 125

Xinran He, Guojie Song, Wei Chen, and Qingye Jiang. Influence Blocking Maximization in Social Networks under the Competitive Linear Threshold Model. In *Proc. 2012 SIAM Conf. on Data Mining*, pages 463–474, 2012. 59, 71, 73, 84

Wassily Hoeffding. Probability inequalities for sums of bounded random variables. *J. American Statistical Association*, 58(301):13–30, 1963. DOI: 10.1080/01621459.1963.10500830.

T. Hogg and G. Szabó. Diversity of User Activity and Content Quality in Online Communities. In *Proc. 3rd Int'l AAAI Conf. on Weblogs and Social Media*, 2009. 90

Minqing Hu and Bing Liu. Mining and summarizing customer reviews. In *Proc. 10th ACM SIGKDD Int. Conf. on Knowledge Discovery and Data Mining*, pages 168–177. ACM, 2004. ISBN 1-58113-888-1. doi: 10.1145/1014052.1014073. DOI: 10.1145/1014052.1014073. 126

Junming Huang, Xueqi Cheng, Huawei Shen, Tao Zhou, and Xiaolong Jin. Exploring social influence via posterior effect of word-of-mouth recommendations. In *Proc. 5th ACM Int. Conf. Web Search and Data Mining*, pages 573–582, 2012. DOI: 10.1145/2124295.2124365. 6, 127

O. Hugo and E. Garnsey. The emergence of electronic messaging and the growth of four entrepreneurial entrants. In *New Technology Based Firms in the New Millennium*, , pages 97–124. Pergamon Press, Manchester, UK, 2002. 3

Dino Ienco, Francesco Bonchi, and Carlos Castillo. The Meme Ranking Problem: Maximizing Microblogging Virality. In *SIASP10*, 2010. DOI: 10.1109/ICDMW.2010.127. 101, 102

Raghuram Iyengar, Christophe Van den Bulte, and Thomas W. Valente. Opinion Leadership and Social Contagion in New Product Diffusion. *Marketing Science*, 30(2):195–212, 2011. DOI: 10.1287/mksc.1100.0566. 6

A. Java, P. Kolari, T. Finin, A. Joshi, and T. Oates. Feeds that matter: A study of bloglines subscriptions. In *Proc. 1st Int'l AAAI Conf. on Weblogs and Social Media*. Citeseer, 2007. 127

Qingye Jiang, Guojie Song, Gao Cong, Yu Wang, Wenjun Si, and Kunqing Xie. Simulated Annealing Based Influence Maximization in Social Networks. In *Proc. 26th National Conf. on Artificial Intelligence*, 2011. 66

Kyomin Jung, Wooram Heo, and Wei Chen. IRIE: Scalable and Robust Influence Maximization in Social Networks. In *Proc. 2012 IEEE Int. Conf. on Data Mining*, pages 918–923, 2012. DOI: 10.1109/ICDM.2012.79. 52, 66

Shlomo Kalish. A New Product Adoption Model with Price, Advertising, and Uncertainty. *Management Science*, 31(12):1569–1585, 1985. DOI: 10.1287/mnsc.31.12.1569. 97

G. Karakostas. A better approximation ratio for the vertex cover problem. *ACM Trans. on Algorithms*, 5(4), 2009. DOI: 10.1145/1597036.1597045. 65

Jonathan A. Kelner, Lorenzo Orecchia, Yin Tat Lee, and Aaron Sidford. An Almost-Linear-Time Algorithm for Approximate Max Flow in Undirected Graphs, and its Multicommodity Generalizations. Technical Report 1304.2338, arXiv, 2013. 138

David Kempe, Jon M. Kleinberg, and Éva Tardos. Maximizing the spread of influence through a social network. In *Proc. 9th ACM SIGKDD Int. Conf. on Knowledge Discovery and Data Mining*, pages 137–146, 2003. DOI: 10.1145/956750.956769. 10, 15, 17, 20, 23, 24, 35, 38, 40, 44, 45, 102, 105, 109

Samir Khuller, Anna Moss, , and Joseph Naor. The budgeted maximum coverage problem. *Inf. Proc. Letters*, 70(1):39–45, 1999. DOI: 10.1016/S0020-0190(99)00031-9. 40

Masahiro Kimura, Kazumi Saito, and Ryohei Nakano. Extracting Influential Nodes for Information Diffusion on a Social Network. In *Proc. 22nd National Conf. on Artificial Intelligence*, pages 1371–1376, 2007. DOI: 10.1007/s10618-009-0150-5. 51

Ross Kindermann and J. Laurie Snell. *Markov Random Fields and Their Applications*. American Mathematical Society, 1980. DOI: 10.1090/conm/001. 30

Jon Kleinberg. Bursty and hierarchical structure in streams. In *Proc. 8th ACM SIGKDD Int. Conf. on Knowledge Discovery and Data Mining*, pages 91–101. ACM, 2002. ISBN 1-58113-567-X. doi: 10.1145/775047.775061. DOI: 10.1145/775047.775061. 126

Jon M. Kleinberg and Éva Tardos. *Algorithm Design*. Addison-Wesley, 2006. 93

Robert D. Kleinberg and Frank Thomson Leighton. The Value of Knowing a Demand Curve: Bounds on Regret for Online Posted-Price Auctions. In *Proc. 44th Annual Symp. on Foundations of Computer Science*, pages 594–605, 2003. DOI: 10.1109/SFCS.2003.1238232. 98

Jan Kostka, Yvonne Anne Oswald, and Roger Wattenhofer. Word of Mouth: Rumor Dissemination in Social Networks. In *Proc. 15th Int. Colloquium on Structural Information and Communication Complexity*, pages 185–196, 2008. DOI: 10.1007/978-3-540-69355-0_16. 71

Andreas Krause and Carlos Guestrin. A note on the budgeted maximization on submodular functions. Technical Report CMU-CALD-05-103, Carnegie Mellon University, 2005. 40

Valdis Krebs. Uncloaking Terrorist Networks. *First Monday*, 7(4):Paper 1, April 2002. DOI: 10.5210/fm.v7i4.941. 130

K. Lerman. Social Information Processing in News Aggregation. *IEEE Internet Comput.*, 11(6):16–28, November 2007. ISSN 1089-7801. doi: 10.1109/mic.2007.136. DOI: 10.1109/MIC.2007.136. 127

Jure Leskovec, Andreas Krause, Carlos Guestrin, Christos Faloutsos, Jeanne M. VanBriesen, and Natalie S. Glance. Cost-effective outbreak detection in networks. In *Proc. 13th ACM SIGKDD Int. Conf. on Knowledge Discovery and Data Mining*, pages 420–429, 2007. DOI: 10.1145/1281192.1281239. 4, 48, 60, 136

Jure Leskovec, Lars Backstrom, and Jon Kleinberg. Meme-tracking and the dynamics of the news cycle. In *Proc. 15th ACM SIGKDD Int. Conf. on Knowledge Discovery and Data Mining*, pages 497–506. ACM, 2009. ISBN 978-1-60558-495-9. doi: 10.1145/1557019.1557077. DOI: 10.1145/1557019.1557077. 126

Yanhua Li, Wei Chen, Yajun Wang, and Zhi-Li Zhang. Influence diffusion dynamics and influence maximization in social networks with friend and foe relationships. In *Proc. 6th ACM Int. Conf. Web Search and Data Mining*, pages 657–666, 2013. DOI: 10.1145/2433396.2433478. 29, 30

David Liben-Nowell and Jon Kleinberg. Tracing information flow on a global scale using Internet chain-letter data. *Proc. National Academy of Sciences*, 105(12):4633–4638, March 2008. doi: 10.1073/pnas.0708471105. DOI: 10.1073/pnas.0708471105. 126

T. M. Liggett. *Interacting Particle Systems*. Springer, 1985. DOI: 10.1007/978-1-4613-8542-4. 10

Bo Liu, Gao Cong, Dong Xu, and Yifeng Zeng. Time Constrained Influence Maximization in Social Networks. In *Proc. 2012 IEEE Int. Conf. on Data Mining*, pages 439–448, 2012. DOI: 10.1109/ICDM.2012.158. 15, 101

Yucheng Low, Joseph Gonzalez, Aapo Kyrola, Danny Bickson, Carlos Guestrin, and Joseph M. Hellerstein. Distributed GraphLab: A Framework for Machine Learning and Data Mining in the Cloud. *PVLDB*, 5(8):716–727, 2012. 139

Wei Lu and Laks V.S. Lakshmanan. Profit Maximization over Social Networks. In *Proc. 2012 IEEE Int. Conf. on Data Mining*, pages 479–488. IEEE, 2012. DOI: 10.1109/ICDM.2012.145. 97, 98, 100

Wei Lu, Francesco Bonchi, Amit Goyal, and Laks V.S. Lakshmanan. The bang for the buck: fair competitive viral marketing from the host perspective. In *Proc. 19th ACM SIGKDD Int. Conf. on Knowledge Discovery and Data Mining*. ACM, 2013. 83, 89, 90, 91, 94

N. Madar, T. Kalisky, R. Cohen, D. Ben Avraham, and S. Havlin. Immunization and epidemic dynamics in complex networks. *The European Phys. J. B*, 38(2):269–276, 2004. DOI: 10.1140/epjb/e2004-00119-8. 28, 29

Grzegorz Malewicz, Matthew H. Austern, Aart J. C. Bik, James C. Dehnert, Ilan Horn, Naty Leiser, and Grzegorz Czajkowski. Pregel: a system for large-scale graph processing. In *Proc. 2010 ACM SIGMOD Int. Conf. on Management of Data*, pages 135–146, 2010. DOI: 10.1145/1807167.1807184. 139

Michael Mathioudakis and Nick Koudas. TwitterMonitor: trend detection over the twitter stream. In *Proc. 2010 ACM SIGMOD Int. Conf. on Management of Data*, pages 1155–1158. ACM, 2010. ISBN 978-1-4503-0032-2. doi: 10.1145/1807167.1807306. DOI: 10.1145/1807167.1807306. 126

Michael Mathioudakis, Francesco Bonchi, Carlos Castillo, Aristides Gionis, and Antti Ukkonen. Sparsification of influence networks. In *Proc. 17th ACM SIGKDD Int. Conf. on Knowledge Discovery and Data Mining*, pages 529–537. ACM, 2011. ISBN 978-1-4503-0813-7. doi: 10.1145/2020408.2020492. DOI: 10.1145/2020408.2020492. 109, 132

Yutaka Matsuo and Hikaru Yamamoto. Community gravity: measuring bidirectional effects by trust and rating on online social networks. In *Proc. 18th Int. World Wide Web Conf.*, pages 751–760. ACM, 2009. ISBN 978-1-60558-487-4. doi: 10.1145/1526709.1526810. DOI: 10.1145/1526709.1526810. 127

Michel Minoux. Accelerated greedy algorithms for maximizing submodular set functions. In *Proc. 8th IFIP Conf. on Optimization Techniques*, pages 234–243, 1978. DOI: 10.1007/BFb0006528. 48

Michael Mitzenmacher and Eli Upfal. *Probability and Computing: Randomized Algorithms and Probabilistic Analysis*. Cambridge University Press, 2005. ISBN 978-0-521-83540-4. 43

Elchanan Mossel and Sebastien Roch. On the submodularity of influence in social networks. In *Proc. 39th Annual ACM Symp. on Theory of Computing*, pages 128–134. ACM, 2007. ISBN 978-1-59593-631-8. doi: 10.1145/1250790.1250811. DOI: 10.1145/1250790.1250811. 24

G. Nemhauser, L. Wolsey, and M. Fisher. An analysis of the approximations for maximizing submodular set functions. *Math. Prog.*, 14:265–294, 1978. DOI: 10.1007/BF01588971. 39

M. E. J. Newman. Spread of epidemic disease on networks. *Physics Review E*, 66(1), 2002. DOI: 10.1103/PhysRevE.66.016128. 28

M. E. J. Newman. Threshold effects for two pathogens spreading on a network. *Physics Review Letters*, 95(10), 2005. DOI: 10.1103/PhysRevLett.95.108701. 28

M. E. J. Newman. *Networks*. Oxford University Press, 2010. DOI: 10.1093/acprof:oso/9780199206650.001.0001. 26, 28

A. Ostfeld and E. Salomons. Optimal layout of early warning detection stations for water distribution systems security. *J. Water Resources Planning and Management*, 130(5):377–385, 2004. DOI: 10.1061/(ASCE)0733-9496(2004)130:5(377). 4, 136

A. Ostfeld, J. G. Uber, and E. Salomons. Battle of water sensor networks (BWSN): A design challenge for engineers and algorithms. In *8th Annual Water Distribution System Analysis Symposium*, 2006. DOI: 10.1061/(ASCE)0733-9496(2008)134:6(556). 4, 136

Nishith Pathak, Arindam Banerjee, and Jaideep Srivastava. A Generalized Linear Threshold Model for Multiple Cascades. In *Proc. 2010 IEEE Int. Conf. on Data Mining*, 2010. DOI: 10.1109/ICDM.2010.153. 29, 30, 71

G. Peng and J. Mu. Technology Adoption in Online Social Networks. *J. of Product Innovation Management*, 28(s1):133–145, 2011. DOI: 10.1111/j.1540-5885.2011.00866.x. 90

B. Aditya Prakash, Deepayan Chakrabarti, Michalis Faloutsos, Nicholas Valler, and Christos Faloutsos. Threshold Conditions for Arbitrary Cascade Models on Arbitrary Networks. In *Proc. 2011 IEEE Int. Conf. on Data Mining*, pages 537–546, 2011. DOI: 10.1109/ICDM.2011.145. 28

Foster J. Provost, Tom Fawcett, and Ron Kohavi. The Case against Accuracy Estimation for Comparing Induction Algorithms. In *Proc. 15th Int. Conf. on Machine Learning*, 1998. DOI: 10.1023/A:1007442505281. 119

Alfred Radcliffe-Brown. On Joking Relationships. *Africa: Journal of the International African Institute*, 13(3):195–210, 1940. doi: 10.2307/1156093. DOI: 10.2307/1156093. 1

Francesco Ricci, Lior Rokach, Bracha Shapira, and Paul B. Kantor. *Recommender Systems Handbook*. Springer, 2011. ISBN 978-0-387-85820-3. DOI: 10.1007/978-0-387-85820-3. 104

Matthew Richardson and Pedro Domingos. Mining knowledge-sharing sites for viral marketing. In *Proc. 8th ACM SIGKDD Int. Conf. on Knowledge Discovery and Data Mining*, pages 61–70, 2002. DOI: 10.1145/775047.775057. 30, 31

P. Rosin and E.B. Royzman. Negativity bias, negativity dominance, and contagion. *Personality and Social Psychololgy Review*, 5(4):296–320, 2001. 87

Eldar Sadikov, Montserrat Medina, Jure Leskovec, and Hector Garcia-Molina. Correcting for missing data in information cascades. In *Proc. 4th ACM Int. Conf. Web Search and Data Mining*, pages 55–64. ACM Press, February 2011. ISBN 978-1-4503-0493-1. doi: 10.1145/1935826.1935844. DOI: 10.1145/1935826.1935844. 125

Kazumi Saito, Ryohei Nakano, and Masahiro Kimura. Prediction of Information Diffusion Probabilities for Independent Cascade Model. In *Proc. 12th Int. Conf. on Knowledge-Based Intelligent Information and Engineering Systems*, pages 67–75. Springer-Verlag, 2008. ISBN 978-3-540-85566-8. doi: 10.1007/978-3-540-85567-5_9. DOI: 10.1007/978-3-540-85567-5_9. 67, 106, 108, 109

T. Schelling. *Micromotives and Macrobehavior*. Norton, 1978. 15

Jonah Sherman. Nearly Maximum Flows in Nearly Linear Time. Technical Report 1304.2077, arXiv, 2013. 138

Yoav Shoham and Kevin Leyton-Brown. *Multiagent Systems - Algorithmic, Game-Theoretic, and Logical Foundations*. Cambridge University Press, 2009. ISBN 978-0-521-89943-7. 98

Parag Singla and Matthew Richardson. Yes, there is a correlation: - from social networks to personal behavior on the web. In *Proc. 17th Int. World Wide Web Conf.*, pages 655–664. ACM, 2008. ISBN 978-1-60558-085-2. doi: 10.1145/1367497.1367586. DOI: 10.1145/1367497.1367586. 128

Daniel A. Spielman and Shang-Hua Teng. Nearly-linear time algorithms for graph partitioning, graph sparsification, and solving linear systems. In *Proc. 36th Annual ACM Symp. on Theory of Computing*, pages 81–90, 2004. DOI: 10.1145/1007352.1007372. 138

Tao Sun, Wei Chen, Zhenming Liu, Yajun Wang, Xiaorui Sun, Ming Zhang, and Chin-Yew Lin. Participation Maximization based on Social Influence In Online Discussion Forums. In *Proc. 5th Int'l AAAI Conf. on Weblogs and Social Media*, 2011. 101

Maxim Sviridenko. A note on maximizing a submodular set function subject to a knapsack constraint. *Oper. Res. Letters*, 32(1):41–43, 2004. DOI: 10.1016/S0167-6377(03)00062-2. 40

Chenhao Tan, Jie Tang, Jimeng Sun, Quan Lin, and Fengjiao Wang. Social action tracking via noise tolerant time-varying factor graphs. In *Proc. 16th ACM SIGKDD Int. Conf. on Knowledge Discovery and Data Mining*, pages 1049–1058. ACM, 2010. ISBN 978-1-4503-0055-1. doi: 10.1145/1835804.1835936. DOI: 10.1145/1835804.1835936. 127

Daniel Trpevski, Wallace K. S. Tang, and Ljupco Kocarev. Model for rumor spreading over networks. *Physics Review E*, 81:056102, May 2010. DOI: 10.1103/PhysRevE.81.056102. 71

Jason Tsai, Thanh H. Nguyen, and Milind Tambe. Security Games for Controlling Contagion. In *Proc. 27th National Conf. on Artificial Intelligence*, 2012. 103

L. G. Valiant. The complexity of enumeration and reliability problems. *SIAM J. on Comput.*, 8(3):410–421, 1979. DOI: 10.1137/0208032. 36, 60

Jan Vondrák. Optimal approximation for the submodular welfare problem in the value oracle model. In *Proc. 40th Annual ACM Symp. on Theory of Computing*, 2008. DOI: 10.1145/1374376.1374389. 102

Chi Wang, Wei Chen, and Yajun Wang. Scalable influence maximization for independent cascade model in large-scale social networks. *Data Mining and Knowledge Discovery*, 25(3):545–576, 2012. A preliminary version appears as W. Chen, C. Wang and Y. Wang, Scalable influence maximization for prevalent viral marketing in large-scale social networks, KDD, 2010. DOI: 10.1007/s10618-012-0262-1. 36, 44, 45, 50, 51, 52, 53, 54, 57, 58, 88, 103

Yu Wang, Gao Cong, Guojie Song, and Kunqing Xie. Community-based greedy algorithm for mining top-K influential nodes in mobile social networks. In *Proc. 17th ACM SIGKDD Int. Conf. on Knowledge Discovery and Data Mining*, pages 1039–1048, 2010. DOI: 10.1145/1835804.1835935. 66

Stanley Wasserman and Katherine Faust. *Social network analysis: Methods and applications*, volume 8. Cambridge University Press, 1994. DOI: 10.1017/CBO9780511815478. 1

Duncan J. Watts and Jonah Peretti. Viral Marketing for the Real World. *Harvard Business Review*, pages 22–23, 2007. 6

Shaomei Wu, Chenhao Tan, Jon M. Kleinberg, and Michael W. Macy. Does Bad News Go Away Faster? In *Proc. 5th Int'l AAAI Conf. on Weblogs and Social Media*, 2011. 126

De-Nian Yang, Hui-Ju Hung, Wang-Chien Lee, and Wei Chen. Maximizing acceptance probability for active friending in online social networks. In *Proc. 19th ACM SIGKDD Int. Conf. on Knowledge Discovery and Data Mining*, 2013. 103

Wayne W. Zachary. An Information Flow Model for Conflict and Fission in Small Groups. *J. of Anthropological Research*, 33(4):452–473, 1977. ISSN 00917710. doi: 10.2307/3629752. 129

Aylin Zafar. Whatever Happened to Ted Williams, the 'Golden-Voiced' Homeless Man? http://newsfeed.time.com/2012/01/13/whatever-happened-to-ted-williams-the-golden-voiced-homeless-man/, January 2012. 3

S. Zhao, R. Meyer, and J. Han. The Enhancement Bias in Consumer Decisions to Adopt and Utilize Product Innovations. *Research Collection Lee Kong Chian School of Business*, 2003. 90

Wayne X. Zhao, Jing Jiang, Jianshu Weng, Jing He, Ee P. Lim, Hongfei Yan, and Xiaoming Li. Comparing twitter and traditional media using topic models. In *Proc. 33rd European Conf. on IR Research*, pages 338–349. Springer-Verlag, 2011. ISBN 978-3-642-20160-8. DOI: 10.1007/978-3-642-20161-5_34. 126

Authors' Biographies

WEI CHEN

Wei Chen is a Senior Researcher in Microsoft Research Asia, Beijing, China. He is also an Adjunct Professor at Tsinghua University. He received Bachelor and Master of Engineering degrees from Tsinghua University, and a Ph.D. Degree from Cornell University. His research interests include computational and game theoretic aspects of social networks, algorithmic game theory, distributed computing, and fault tolerance. He won the William C. Carter Award in 2000 in the area of dependable computing for his dissertation research on failure detection, and his co-authored paper on game-theoretic community detection won

the best student paper award in ECML PKDD 2009. He has done a series of research work on social influence dynamics, and social influence maximization, which appeared in recent KDD, ICDM, SDM, WSDM, ICWSM, ICML and AAAI conferences. He is also active in the social network research community, including organizing an international workshop, guest-editing ACM TKDD special issue on computational aspects of social networks, and participating in program committees of KDD, WWW, WSDM, etc. He is a member of Task Force on Big Data of Chinese Computer Federation.

LAKS V.S. LAKSHMANAN

Laks V. S. Lakshmanan is a professor in the Department of Computer Science and an associate member of the Department of Statistics at UBC. He received his Bachelors degree in Electronics and Communications Engineering from the A.C. College of Engineering and Technology, Karaikudi, India, and his Masters and Ph.D. in Computer Science from the Indian Institute of Science, Bangalore, India. He was awarded the Witold Lipski Memorial Best Student Paper Prize at the International Conference on Database Theory, Rome, Italy, in September

1986, and the Gold Medal for the Best Doctoral Dissertation in Electrical Science Division at the Indian Institute of Science, Bangalore (1990). He was a postdoctoral fellow in the Department of Computer Science and Computer Systems Research Institute at the University of Toronto. Laks has published extensively in data management and mining and has served on the PC of all major database and data mining conferences including SIGMOD, PODS, VLDB, ICDE, KDD, ICDM, and WSDM as member or Area Chair. He has served as an Associate Editor of IEEE TKDE in the past and is currently an Associate Editor of the *VLDB Journal*. He has served as a reviewer for NSF, NSERC (Canada), other granting councils across the world, as well as for various top-tier journals. His research interests span a wide spectrum of topics in Data Management and Mining and related areas, including: relational and object-oriented databases, advanced data models for novel applications, OLAP and data warehousing, database mining, data integration, semi-structured data and XML, directory-enabled networks, querying the WWW, information and social networks and social media, recommender systems, and personalization. A common theme underlying his research is to model problems not traditionally viewed as standard data management problems and bring the technology of efficient data management and mining to bear on them, thus pushing the frontiers of technology. He collaborates widely worldwide with both industry and academia. He has been a consultant to H.P. Labs, Palo Alto, CA, and AT&T Labs Research, Florham Park, NJ, Oracle Corp., and Yahoo! Research, and has held visiting positions at several universities and research centers across the world. His research is funded by the Natural Sciences and Engineering Research Council of Canada (NSERC), Mathematics of Information Technology and Complex Systems (MITACS), and an NSERC strategic grant on Business Intelligence. He is a Research Fellow of the BC Advanced Systems Institute.

CARLOS CASTILLO

Carlos Castillo is a Senior Scientist at the Qatar Computing Research Institute in Doha. He received his Ph.D. from the University of Chile (2004), and was a visiting scientist at Universitat Pompeu Fabra (2005) and Sapienza Universitá di Roma (2006) before working as a research scientist at Yahoo! Research (2006-2012). He has been influential in the areas of adversarial web search and web content quality and credibility. He has served in the PC or SPC of all major conferences in his area (WWW, WSDM, SIGIR, KDD, CIKM, etc.), and co-organized the Adversarial Information Retrieval Workshop and Web Spam  Challenge in 2007 and 2008, the ECML/PKDD Discovery Challenge in 2010 and the Web Quality Workshop from 2011–2013. His current research focuses in the application of web mining methods to problems in the domain of on-line news and humanitarian crises.

Index

Printed in the United States
by Baker & Taylor Publisher Services